THE ENGLISH PARLIAMENT IN THE MIDDLE AGES

PROFESSOR J. S. ROSKELL

R. G. DAVIES
J. H. DENTON
editors

The English
Parliament
in the
Middle Ages

MANCHESTER
UNIVERSITY PRESS

First published by Manchester University Press 1981
Special edition for Sandpiper Books Ltd, 1999

Published by Manchester University Press
Oxford Road, Manchester M13 9NR
http://www.man.ac.uk/mup

British Library Cataloguing-in-Publication Data
A catalogue record for this book is available from the British Library

05 04 03 02 01 00 99   7 6 5 4 3 2

ISBN 0 7190 0833 6

Printed in Great Britain by
Bookcraft (Bath) Ltd, Midsomer Norton

Contents

Preface

A SUCCINCT PHRASE in John Roskell's 'Perspectives in English parliamentary history' provides the theme of every chapter of our tribute: 'participation in government at the sovereign's command'. We have aimed, within a framework which is essentially but not exclusively chronological, to survey some of the results of the study, during the last fifty years or so, of the medieval English parliament, and, in doing so, to open up some new lines of enquiry. Our intention has been to provide more a review than a comprehensive account; and, although the contributors have worked in concert to produce a connected whole, each chapter has been written independently, so that differences of emphasis and some repetitions have been unavoidable. It is a work of co-operation, for a colleague and friend who as researcher and as teacher has selflessly shared with others his skills and his energies in the interests of scholarship. Throughout the planning and preparation of this book we have had before us the inspiration of his example: a meticulous attention to detail combined with an eagerness to view in the broad the main lines of the development of the medieval parliament.

Those few who have had the opportunity to contribute directly to the book are aware that they represent many more colleagues and former pupils who would wish to share in a tribute to John Roskell, especially those who worked with him and under him in the Universities of Nottingham and Manchester during the course of his distinguished teaching and professional career. In publishing this book Manchester University Press joins in this presentation to its former chairman, and the editors and contributors are especially grateful to Martin Spencer and John Banks of the Press for their keen interest and expert advice. To John and Evelyn Roskell we offer our warmest good wishes for their future.

R.G.D.
J.H.D.

Abbreviations

ALL WORKS CITED by more than one contributor are abbreviated in the foot-
notes and listed below. Works cited by only one contributor do not appear
in this list but are given in full where they first appear and thereafter in
abbreviated form, with the initials of the author or editor retained.

Recent bibliographies of the history of parliament in the middle ages can
be found in Fryde and Miller, I, pp. 374–81, II, pp. 331–8, *A Bibliography
of English History to 1485*, ed. E. B. Graves (Oxford, 1975), pp. 503–24, and
*Conference on British Studies Bibliographical Handbooks: The High Middle
Ages in England 1154–1377*, ed. B. Wilkinson (Cambridge, 1978), pp. 8–27,
and *Late-Medieval England 1377–1485*, ed. D. J. Guth (1976), pp. 8–29. For
subsequent work see the Royal Historical Society's *Annual Bibliography of
British and Irish History*, ed. G. R. Elton, and the *International Medieval
Bibliography*, directed by P. H. Sawyer (University of Leeds).

Anonimalle. The Anonimalle Chronicle, ed. V. H. Galbraith (Manchester,
    1927, reprinted 1970).
Bellamy, *Treason*. J. G. Bellamy, *The Law of Treason in England in the
    Later Middle Ages* (Cambridge, 1970).
BIHR. Bulletin of the Institute of Historical Research.
BJRUL. Bulletin of the John Rylands University Library of Manchester
    [formerly (to 1972) *Bulletin of the John Rylands Library*].
Cam, *Liberties and Communities*. H. M. Cam, *Liberties and Communities
    in Medieval England* (Cambridge, 1933, reprinted London, 1963).
CCR. Calendar of the Close Rolls (HMSO, 1892–1954).
Chrimes, *Eng. Const. Ideas*. S. B. Chrimes, *English Constitutional Ideas in
    the Fifteenth Century* (Cambridge, 1936).
Chron. Angliae. T. Walsingham, *Chronicon Angliae*, ed. E. M. Thompson
    (RS, 1874).

Clementi, 'Statute of York of 1322'. D. Clementi, 'That the Statute of York of 1322 is no longer ambiguous', in *Album Helen Maud Cam*, II (Studies presented to the International Commission for the History of Representative and Parliamentary Institutions, Louvain, Paris, 1960).

CS. Camden Society.

CYS. Canterbury and York Society.

Dignity of a Peer. Reports from the Lords' Committees . . . touching the Dignity of a Peer (5 vols., London, 1820–9).

Edwards, *Commons*. J. G. Edwards, *The Commons in Medieval English Parliaments* (The Creighton Lecture for 1957, London, 1958).

Edwards, ' "Justice" '. J. G. Edwards, ' "Justice" in early English parliaments' (first printed in *BIHR*, XXVII (1954), pp. 35–53), in Fryde and Miller, I, pp. 279–97.

Edwards, 'Personnel of the commons'. J. G. Edwards, 'The personnel of the commons in parliament under Edward I and Edward II' (first printed in *Essays in Medieval History presented to T. F. Tout*, ed. A. G. Little and F. M. Powicke (Manchester, 1925), pp. 197–214), in Fryde and Miller, I, pp. 150–67.

Edwards, '*Plena potestas*'. J. G. Edwards, 'The *plena potestas* of English parliamentary representatives' (first printed in *Oxford Essays in Medieval History presented to H. E. Salter* (1934), pp. 141–54), in Fryde and Miller, I, pp. 136–49.

Edwards, *Second Century of Parliament*. J. G. Edwards, *The Second Century of the English Parliament* (Oxford, 1979).

EHD. English Historical Documents: IV, 1327–1485, ed. A. R. Myers (London, 1969).

EHR. English Historical Review.

English Government at Work. The English Government at Work, 1327–1336, ed. J. F. Willard *et al.* (3 vols., Cambridge, Mass., 1940–50).

Faction and Parliament, ed. Sharpe. *Faction and Parliament: Essays in Early Stuart History*, ed. K. Sharpe (Oxford, 1978).

Foedera. T. Rymer, *Foedera* (RC, 1816–30).

Fryde and Miller. *Historical Studies of the English Parliament: I, Origins to 1399, II, 1399–1603*, ed. E. B. Fryde and E. Miller (Cambridge, 1970).

Gray, *Influence of the Commons*. H. L. Gray, *The Influence of the Commons on Early Legislation* (Cambridge, Mass., 1932).

Harriss, *King, Parliament and Public Finance*. G. L. Harriss, *King, Parliament and Public Finance in Medieval England to 1369* (Oxford, 1975).

Haskins, 'Petitions of representatives'. G. L. Haskins, 'The petitions of representatives in the parliaments of Edward I', *EHR*, LIII (1938), pp. 1–20.

HBC. Handbook of British Chronology, ed. F. M. Powicke and E. B. Fryde (2nd edn., London, 1961).

HMC. Historical Manuscripts Commission (London).

HMSO. Her (His) Majesty's Stationery Office.

Holmes, *Good Parliament*. G. A. Holmes, *The Good Parliament* (Oxford, 1975).

JEccH. Journal of Ecclesiastical History.

Lapsley, *Crown, Community and Parliament.* G. T. Lapsley, *Crown, Community and Parliament in the Later Middle Ages.*

Lunt, 'Consent of lower clergy to taxation'. W. E. Lunt, 'The consent of the English lower clergy to taxation during the reign of Henry III', in *Persecution and Liberty: Essays in Honor of G. L. Burr* (New York, 1931), pp. 117–69.

McFarlane, *Nobility.* K. B. McFarlane, *The Nobility of Later Medieval England* (Oxford, 1973).

McKisack, *Borough Representation.* M. McKisack, *The Parliamentary Representation of the English Boroughs during the Middle Ages* (London, 1932).

Maddicott, 'County community'. J. R. Maddicott, 'The county community and the making of public opinion in fourteenth-century England', *TRHS,* 5th ser., XXVIII (1978), pp. 27–43.

Maddicott, *English Peasantry.* J. R. Maddicott, *The English Peasantry and the Demands of the Crown, 1294–1341 (Past and Present* Supplement, I, 1975).

Memo de Parl. Memoranda de Parliamento, 1305, ed. F. W. Maitland (RS, 1893). Introduction reprinted in part in Fryde and Miller, I, pp. 91–135.

Modus. Modus tenendi parliamentum, ed. M. V. Clarke, in *Medieval Representation and Consent* (London, 1936), pp. 374–84, and see now *Parliamentary Texts of the Later Middle Ages,* ed. N. Pronay and J. Taylor (Oxford, 1980).

Myers, 'Parliamentary petitions'. A. R. Myers, 'Parliamentary petitions in the fifteenth century', *EHR,* LII (1937), pp. 385–404, 590–613.

Parl. Writs. Parliamentary Writs and Writs of Military Summons, ed. F. Palgrave (2 vols. in 4, London, 1827–34).

Pike, *House of Lords.* L. O. Pike, *A Constitutional History of the House of Lords* (London, 1894).

Plucknett, 'Parliament'. T. F. T. Plucknett, 'Parliament', in *English Government at Work,* I, pp. 82–128 (also printed in Fryde and Miller, I, pp. 195–241).

Pollard, *Evolution of Parliament.* A. F. Pollard, *The Evolution of Parliament* (2nd edn., London, 1926).

Powell and Wallis, *House of Lords.* J. E. Powell and K. E. Wallis, *The House of Lords in the Middle Ages* (London, 1968).

PRO. Public Record Office.

Proc. P.C. Proceedings and Ordinances of the Privy Council of England, ed. N. H. Nicolas (7 vols., RC, 1834–7).

Putnam, 'Transformation of keepers of the peace'. B. H. Putnam, 'The transformation of the keepers of the peace into the justices of the peace, 1327–1380', *TRHS,* 4th ser., XII (1929), pp. 19–48.

Rayner, ' "Commune petition" '. D. Rayner, 'The forms and machinery of the "commune petition" in the fourteenth century', *EHR,* LVI (1941), pp. 198–233, 549–70.

RC. Record Commission.

Return of Members. Return of the Name of every Member of the Lower House of the Parliaments of England, Scotland and Ireland . . . 1213–1874 (London, 1878).

Richardson and Sayles, 'King's ministers in parliament'. H. G. Richardson and G. O. Sayles, 'The king's ministers in parliament, 1272–1377', *EHR*, XLVI (1931), pp. 529–50, XLVII (1932), pp. 194–203, 377–97.

Richardson and Sayles, 'Early statutes'. H. G. Richardson and G. O. Sayles, 'The early statutes', *Law Quarterly Review*, L (1934), pp. 201–24, 540–71.

Roskell, 'Attendance of the lords'. J. S. Roskell, 'The problem of the attendance of the lords in medieval parliaments', *BIHR*, XXIX (1956), pp. 153–204.

Roskell, *Commons in 1422*. J. S. Roskell, *The Commons in the Parliament of 1422* (Manchester, 1954).

Roskell, 'Perspectives'. J. S. Roskell, 'Perspectives in English parliamentary history' (first printed in *BJRUL*, XLVI (1964), pp. 448–75), in Fryde and Miller, II, pp. 296–323.

Roskell, *Speakers*. J. S. Roskell, *The Commons and their Speakers in English Parliaments, 1376–1523* (Manchester, 1965).

Rot. Parl. Rotuli Parliamentorum (6 vols., London, 1767–77).

Rot. Parl. Hactenus Ined. Rotuli Parliamentorum Anglie Hactenus Inediti, 1279–1373, ed. H. G. Richardson and G. O. Sayles (CS, 3rd ser., LI, 1935).

Sayles, *King's Parliament*. G. O. Sayles, *The King's Parliament of England* (London, 1975).

Statutes. Statutes of the Realm (1101–1713), ed. A. Luders *et al.* (11 vols., RC, 1810–28).

Stubbs, *Const. Hist*. W. Stubbs, *The Constitutional History of England*, I (5th edn., Oxford, 1896), II (3rd edn., 1886), III (5th edn., 1898).

Stubbs, *Select Charters. Select Charters and other Illustrations of English Constitutional History from the Earliest Times to the Reign of Edward I*, ed. W. Stubbs (9th edn., Oxford, 1913).

Tout, *Chapters*. T. F. Tout, *Chapters in the Administrative History of Medieval England* (6 vols., Manchester, 1920–33).

Treharne, *Baronial Plan of Reform*. R. F. Treharne, *The Baronial Plan of Reform, 1258–63* (Manchester, 1932).

TRHS. Transactions of the Royal Historical Society.

YB. Year Book.

J. C. HOLT

1

The Prehistory
of Parliament

THE PREHISTORY OF WHAT? 'Parliament', after all, has proved to be a contentious word. How soon the occasion became an institution; what the essential features of that institution were; whether the sessions were regular or occasional and the business 'judicial' or, in addition, political, legislative and financial: all these questions have been examined, re-examined and debated *non sine pulvere* in what has become one of the major controversies of medieval English constitutional history. This essay is not intended as a direct contribution to that controversy. Its aim is to investigate the origins of certain features of the medieval English parliament which distinguish it from many of the estates of continental Europe. It would be misleading to claim that the argument carries no implications for the more general controversy. None the less these have not been the starting point.

A *coup d'oeil* of the estates of medieval Europe, say in the third quarter of the fourteenth century, would reveal many local variants. Among these the English parliament would seem unusual in at least two obvious respects. First, it was becoming bi-cameral. The first estate, the clergy, had begun to sit separately as the convocations of Canterbury and York, leaving a remnant, if the bishops and the abbots of the greater monasteries can be so described, sitting with the second estate as the lords; and part of the second estate, the lesser nobility, the knights of the shire, had come to be represented along with the third estate, the burgesses, as the commons. This arangement was unique. Secondly, parliament had absorbed to itself a wide variety of business: judicial, political and financial. It dealt with matters which in France, for example, were the concern of two separate sets of institutions: the *parlements* and similar bodies like the Norman exchequer, on the one hand, and, on the other, the provincial estates and the estates general.

In both these matters by this time the English parliament had moved beyond the first experimental, adventitious shifts. The representatives of the lower clergy, though still summoned, had been allowed to enjoy in their separate conclave the theory rather than the practice of the independence claimed by their order. A separate estate of merchants had been conjured up by royal taxation of, and intervention in, the wool trade, but that had proved a mere expedient and was now defunct, leaving parliament as the sole body with which the crown negotiated the critical levies on wool. Judicial business embodied in individual petitions, after threatening to swamp parliamentary sessions at the turn of the century, had been siphoned off to chancery and other courts, leaving a residue, the common petitions, which were beginning on occasion to lead to some kind of legislative or executive response. Parliament, in short, had taken shape as an institution, and one markedly different from its neighbouring counterparts on the continent and recognisable as the natural antecedent to the parliament of the sixteenth century. Indeed, it is plain that its many-sided function and the increasing weight acquired and exercised by the commons as a result of the association there of both knights of the shire and burgesses had much to do with the enduring part which parliament played between the sixteenth and eighteenth centuries.

Perhaps because of this it is sometimes assumed too readily that what happened had to happen. At any point in its long history a survey of the organisation and function of parliament would inevitably reveal the seeds of the future to those looking for them, and the transition from seed to fruit seems natural, something requiring little or no explanation. In fact the changes sketched above were neither inevitable nor easy. At the end of the third quarter of the fourteenth century they were not even complete: knights and burgesses, for example, might sit together as the commons but they were by no means equal in status,[1] and it took another half-century to achieve a real amalgamation of

---

[1] Sayles, *King's Parliament*, pp. 120–1.

county and borough representation.[2] Yet somehow they have acquired an aura of inevitability, and one reason is that the knights and burgesses who attended these assemblies shared a number of characteristics: as distinct from the lords, they were representatives, of shire, city or borough; from 1275 their election was almost invariably initiated by a single writ directed to the sheriff;[3] and as a result the sheriff was the returning officer for county and borough alike. There need be little wonder, therefore, that historians have grouped them together as 'the commons' long before they sat together as such.[4] It is with the origins and expanding function of this system of representation that this chapter is concerned.

To start with a simple question: how did a medieval king know what to do? Not how did a king decide what to do, for that leads to the long-standing interest of constitutional historians in 'counsel and consent', but how did he obtain the information on which to found his policies, such as they were? What fact-finding facilities, what sensors of public opinion, such as it was, did he have at his disposal?

Broadly speaking, there were three. First, the king could travel, like King Edgar, 'who winter and spring went everywhere within the realm through all the provinces of the English, diligently seeking out how the rules of the law and the provisions of his decrees were kept by the chief men and whether the poor suffered the oppressions of the mighty'. That idealised picture painted by Florence of Worcester[5] was still pertinent to the functions of monarchy centuries later. The itineration of the Norman and Angevin kings is well known and understood;[6] and long ago, in a note on the charter roll of 1252–3, Maitland commented on the effects of Henry III's travels on the witness lists to royal charters.[7] This remained the most primitive, the most arduous but the most accurate method of finding out what to do: no one intervened between the king and the facts.

Secondly, the king could delegate the task to others. He could use

---

[2] Roskell, *Commons in 1422*, p. 133.

[3] Exceptions occurred in 1265 and September 1283 when writs summoning burgesses were sent separately to the mayors and bailiffs of cities and towns.

[4] Most notably perhaps by J. G. Edwards in 'Personnel of the commons'.

[5] *Florensis Wigornensis Chronica*, ed. B. Thorpe, I (English Hist. Soc., 1848), p. 144. For further discussion see *Select Cases of Procedure without Writ under Henry III*, ed. H. G. Richardson and G. O. Sayles (Selden Soc., LX, 1941), p. xxi.

[6] See J. le Patourel, *The Norman Empire* (Oxford, 1976), pp. 121–32; J. E. A. Jolliffe, *Angevin Kingship* (London, 1955), pp. 139–65.

[7] 'History from the charter roll', *EHR*, VIII (1893), pp. 726–33.

spies and special agents; of these, necessarily, little is known.[8] He could also send out commissioners or justices, and of these a great deal is known. The advantage was that the Domesday *legati* of 1086, for example, or the justices conducting the hundred roll enquiries in 1274, could amass a far greater body of information than a king could hope to encompass in the whole of his lifetime. This was the best method of finding out what to do where action was to be based on predetermined questions which could be asked and answered throughout the land.

Thirdly, instead of, or in addition to, sending his agents out to investigate specific situations or ask particular questions, the king could call the local community in, to himself or his itinerant agents, in the persons of the responsible administrative officer or of an elected or nominated body of men, or of both. Those who gave sworn testimony to the Domesday *legati* include the priest, reeve and six villeins of every vill. Not only that, it is clear that the evidence of the 'whole hundred' was taken, not in a full assembly of the hundred court, but from juries of the hundred in the shire court;[9] for Cambridgeshire the names of the jurors, eight for each hundred, are recorded in the *Inquisitio Comitatus Cantabrigiensis* and *Inquisitio Eliensis*.[10] The *Leges Henrici Primi* of 1116–18 record that in the absence of the lord and his steward, the reeve, the priest and four of the better men of the vill could attend both shire and hundred on behalf of all those who had not been summoned by name to the pleadings.[11] The procedure laid down in the Assize of Clarendon involved not only the indictment of reputed criminals by juries of twelve lawful men of the hundred and six lawful men of the vill but also the presentation of cases to the royal justices by two lawful men who carried the record of shire and hundred.[12] Similar procedures were used in civil actions. 'Glanville' devoted the latter part of Book VIII of the *De Legibus* to the transfer of recorded judgements from lower to higher courts.[13] The appropriate writ, the *recordari facias loquelam*, was already standardised:

[8] But see M. C. Hill, *The King's Messengers, 1199–1377* (London, 1961), especially pp. 95–8.
[9] V. H. Galbraith, *The Making of Domesday Book* (Oxford, 1961), pp. 123–45; id., *Domesday Book: its Place in Administrative History* (Oxford, 1974), pp. 40–5.
[10] Ed. N. E. S. A. Hamilton (London, 1876), *passim*.
[11] *Leges Henrici Primi*, ed. L. J. Downer (Oxford, 1972), caps. 7, 7; 7, 8 (pp. 100, 316).
[12] Caps. 1, 4 (Stubbs, *Select Charters*, p. 170).
[13] R. de Glanvill, *Tractatus de Legibus*, ed. G. D. G. Hall (London, 1965), VIII, 5–11 (pp. 98–103).

The king to the sheriff, greeting. I command you to cause the plea between this party and that, concerning so much land in such-and-such a vill, to be recorded in your county, and to have the record of that plea before me or my justices at a certain term by four lawful knights who were present at the making of that record . . .[14]

Well before the end of the twelfth century, therefore, this method of collecting information was put to many different ends and was part of the ordinary routine of government.

As Helen Cam was never tired of emphasising, it was in this third method of collecting information that representation first took root in England. In origin it was administrative, centred not on voluntary association, as in the continental communes, but on the ancient communities of vill, hundred and shire.[15] This primitive 'representation' was not fully analogous to that of corporate bodies, still less to the fully developed plenipotentiaries of the thirteenth century. The representative character of the Domesday jurors was not defined; they probably comprised those men in the local communities who were 'in the know'. The representatives of the vill in the *Leges Henrici Primi* acted not for the whole vill but simply for those who happened to be absent from court; it is easy to read too much into the single word *pro*, which denoted their relationship with those whom they represented. Those who bore the record of the shire spoke for the county court, or rather, as Maitland put it, the county spoke through them; but if the record was challenged it was not necessarily one of them, but a free man of the court, probably a professional champion, who would take up the wager of battle.[16] Hence the finer shades of the theory lacked definition. But if theory was as yet unfashioned practice was strongly rooted. Indeed, the apparent lack of concern with theory may well have left practice less confined. It seems simply to have been the appreciation of an emergency rather than any new insight into representation that led King John, first, in August 1212, to issue general writs to all counties summoning representatives to meet him as soon as possible, and secondly, in October 1213, to issue a similar summons requiring representatives to meet him at one and the same time and place. This last

[14] *Ibid.*, p. 102.
[15] 'The theory and practice of representation in medieval England', in *Law-finders and Law-makers*, pp. 159–75. See also R. S. Hoyt, 'Representation in the administrative practice of Anglo-Norman England', in *Album Helen Maud Cam*, II (Louvain, 1961), pp. 15–26.
[16] Pollock and Maitland, I, pp. 536–7, II, pp. 667–9.

meeting is the first well recorded occasion of a national assembly of knights of the shire and certainly the first for which the writ of summons has survived. It was called twenty years before the first appearance of the word 'parliament' in official records; it therefore finds no place in the Royal Historical Society's list of parliaments and related assemblies, although it was treated as the starting point in the House of Commons' *Return of Members*.[17] Stubbs paid no attention to it in chapter 15 of the *Constitutional History*, where he treated 1215 as the major starting point of his discussion, although in his account of John's reign he mentioned it along with Roger of Wendover's garbled account of an assembly at St Albans in August 1213.[18] Powicke, in a much neglected chapter in the *Cambridge Medieval History*, mentioned both writs and commented aptly on their importance.[19]

It would be hazardous to guess how these measures were conceived. There was an easy progression from requiring representatives of the shires to appear *ad hoc* in the king's court as legal process demanded, to requiring them to appear all at one and the same time in the face of some great emergency. It was equally possible to imagine that if juries could be assembled before the justices in the counties to answer the articles of the eyre, for example, then, with some extra effort and in-convenience, they could be mustered before the king to answer other questions. Either route led to the same conclusion. Moreover once representatives were summoned they could be put to purposes other than that of providing information. They could be required to convey information from the king to the community just as much as from the community to the king. They could be instructed to act. This further step, if such it was, and if the words of the writ can be read literally, was taken in the first general summons of all, that of August 1212, for the sheriffs were instructed to appear before the king bringing from their bailiwicks 'six of the more lawful and discreet knights who are to do what we shall tell them'.[20]

---

[17] *HBC*, pp. 492–544. This list commences with 1242, since it was compiled before the earliest official reference to 'parliament' was advanced to 1236. For the earlier date see P. Spufford, *Origins of the English Parliament* (London, 1967), p. 28, and H. G. Richardson and G. O. Sayles, 'The earliest known official use of the term "parliament"', *EHR*, LXXXII (1967), pp. 747–50.

[18] *Const. Hist.* I, pp. 565–7.

[19] VI, ch. 7, 'England: Richard I and John', p. 230.

[20] 'Et tu ipse sis coram nobis sub quanta poteris festinacione et adducas tecum sex de legalioribus et discrecioribus militibus ballie tue ad faciendum hoc quod eis dicemus' (*Rotuli Litterarum Clausarum*, I (RC, 1833), p. 132).

What the king told them is a matter of conjecture. On 16 August 1212, as he lay at Nottingham, John received news of the baronial plot against his life.[21] On 17 August he authorised general letters to all sheriffs promising concessions to all those who owed debts of the Jews; the summons of the sheriffs and the six knights formed the concluding section of these letters. In all likelihood, therefore, the summons was part of the king's immediate reaction to the sudden crisis which had beset him. He knew the identity of two men who were a party to the plot, Robert fitz Walter and Eustace de Vesci, and he suspected others.[22] But he cannot have known, county by county, of all those involved, and he may well have seen a need to test feeling and initiate action. Something like this must have underlain the one process of which any detail has survived, that against Robert fitz Walter in Essex, for, despite John's urgency, the first appeal against Robert was not made until the October session of the shire court, and when it was finally made it included nine other men, among whom were Roger fitz Walter, archdeacon of Hereford, and Gervase of Heybridge, chancellor of St Paul's. Against Robert the charge was laid in a royal writ which was later included in the county's record of the case. The writ made no reference to the others charged. The king must have derived their names from local sources before he ordered that they should be sought, and that must have taken some time, thus possibly explaining why the process was not begun before the October session. The evidence, such as it is, is entirely consistent with the hypothesis that John used the six knights of the shire summoned on 17 August to discover something of the true extent of complicity in the plot in the county of Essex.[23]

The summons of November 1213 is more difficult. It is easy enough to set it in a political context: on 1 November John met the northerners

---

[21] The chronology here depends on the king's letters of 16 August dismissing the feudal host which was mustering at Chester and announcing that the king could not come 'propter quaedam agenda nostra quae nos revocaverunt' (*Rotuli Litterarum Patentium*, I (RC, 1835), p. 94).

[22] J. C. Holt, *The Northerners* (Oxford, 1961), pp. 82–3.

[23] The argument here assumes that all the monthly sessions of the shire court were held in the last months of 1212 and that the accused were appealed in successive sessions. Since the accused were outlawed in full session on 2 January 1213 it would follow from this that the process began in October. The record enumerated all ten of the accused 'qui demandati fuerunt per preceptum domini regis et per breve suum super eundem Robertum' (*Rot. Litt. Claus.*, I, p. 165). The case made out above is supported not only by the absence of the nine from the writ but also by the distinction implied between the king's *preceptum* and *breve*.

at Wallingford, and, through the mediation of the archbishop and the papal legate, reached some form of settlement of their incipient rebellion against his demand for service in Poitou: and on 4 November at Woodstock he took steps to placate two leading figures in the East Anglian baronage, Robert fitz Walter and Geoffrey de Mandeville.[24] On 7 November at Witney he authorised general writs to all sheriffs conveying multiple instructions: they were to ensure that the knights already summoned to Oxford for the 15th were now to come armed; the barons, in contrast, were to come unarmed; in addition, the sheriffs were to arrange that four discreet knights would attend on the same day 'to speak with us concerning the affairs of our realm'.[25]

The writ presents a number of problems. The phrase *corpora baronum* is odd and unusual; it suggests prisoners, but could perhaps simply have been intended to indicate that the barons were to appear in person;[26] it may be that the draft or the enrolment was not fully explicit at this point. Moreover it allowed a mere eight days between the date of the summons and the proposed meeting. Stubbs commented warily that 'we do not even know that the assembly was ever held',[27] and Professor Sayles, more vigorously, that the writ 'seems merely derisory. We can but wonder whose folly inspired such an absurdity.'[28] In later times members of parliament from the most distant counties, Cornwall and Cumberland, were allowed eight days' expenses each way for a meeting in London.[29] Oxford was more accessible. Nevertheless the interval allowed in 1213 was quite inadequate for the despatch and receipt of the writ, the nomination of the four knights and their subsequent journey to the meeting; still more time would have been needed for the knights to be elected in the shire courts. It may have been envisaged that the representatives would be chosen from the knights already summoned to muster at Oxford, but the instruction was sent not to them but to the sheriffs, and many of the sheriffs must have received it long after the knights had departed; the same applies to the order that the knights were now to come armed. On the face of it, therefore,

[24] J. C. Holt, *op. cit.*, pp. 95–6.
[25] Stubbs, *Select Charters*, p. 282.
[26] See the undertaking of the *mainpernours* in Gloucestershire in 1297 'de habendo corpus eius prout in breve precipitur' (*Parl. Writs*, I, p. 58).
[27] *Const. Hist.* I, p. 567.
[28] *King's Parliament*, p. 24.
[29] Cam, *Liberties and Communities*, pp. 237–8.

the writ embodies something of the classic recipe for confusion : order, counter-order, disorder. But despite the infeasibility which John's urgency at a time of crisis had created, there can be no doubt what he intended. Moreover he was certainly at Oxford from 15 to 17 November. He must have made do with an assembly of those representatives who could be mustered by that time. In any case he is unlikely to have expected much support from the northern counties.

One later instance of the summoning of representatives does something to reduce, but not resolve, the difficulty. In the summer of 1258 four knights were nominated in each county to investigate local grievances under the terms of the Provisions of Oxford; they were summoned to meet the council in parliament after Michaelmas. The enrolled writ addressed to the knights of Dorset and the accompanying mandate to the sheriff were dated 4 August. They are followed in the usual manner by a note that similar instructions were sent to the other counties, and the names of the knights are given for each.[30] However, the writ to the knights of Hertfordshire, enrolled incorrectly as Herefordshire, was dated not 4 August but 28 July, for that is the date on the copy in the *Liber Additamentorum* of Matthew Paris, who must surely have obtained it locally.[31] Now it may be possible to imagine reasons why two identical letters bearing different dates were sent to the knights of Hertfordshire, but it is much more likely that the circumstances in which the letters were authorised led to some variation in the date on the outgoing copies.[32] Be that as it may, the Hertfordshire letters make it impossible to place absolute reliance on the enrolled date of 4 August as applicable to all copies, and the doubt must extend to other similar general letters. In short, the letters of 1258 create just a little elbow room around the summons of 7 November 1213. On that occasion likewise some of the writs could have gone out a few days earlier than the date on the enrolled copy. Even so, it is unlikely that

[30] *CPR*, 1247–58, pp. 645–9; *Documents of the Baronial Movement of Reform and Rebellion, 1258–67*, selected by R. F. Treharne, ed. I. J. Sanders (Oxford, 1973), pp. 112–15.

[31] *Chronica Majora*, ed. H. R. Luard, VI (RS, 1882), pp. 396–400.

[32] For possible reasons for the discrepancy see H. C. Maxwell-Lyte, *Historical Notes on the Use of the Great Seal of England* (London, 1926), pp. 241–61, and P. Chaplais, *English Royal Documents* (Oxford, 1971), pp. 17–19. It should be noted that the drafts of such letters were undated; G. O. Sayles, 'Representation of cities and boroughs in 1268', *EHR*, XL (1925), pp. 580–5.

the instruction was authorised before 1 November, when King John met the northerners at Wallingford.[33]

A little elbow room, but not enough. True, the summons did not specify how the knights were to be selected, but even if the period of notice were stretched to a fortnight there would still have been no time even for the most summary procedure in the more distant countries. The assembly which met at Oxford on 15 November 1213 cannot have been complete.

Now this difficulty also arises in other instances. In 1261 the leaders of the baronial party summoned three knights from every shire to a meeting at St Albans on 21 September. The date of the original summons is not known, but on 11 September the king authorised writs directing that the knights were to come to him at Windsor instead.[34] Much of the apparent muddle of 1213 was here repeated. True, in this case the king's intervention was concerned with a change of venue rather than the choice of representatives from scratch, and to that extent compliance was more practicable, but as in 1213 the writ was directed to the sheriffs, not to the knights, and by the time the sheriffs received them the knights who had complied with the summons to St Albans must have been well on their way and beyond call. One of them was discovered en route by the justiciar, who informed the chancellor, suggesting that the king should write to the representative direct in order to divert him from St Albans.[35] Historians have doubted whether either assembly met.[36] It was not simply that the king's instruction was unworkable: the two summonses were contradictory. In 1264 also the summons required rapid compliance. After the battle of Lewes the king had to summon four knights from every shire to meet at London

[33] It is worth noting that the date of the enrolled copy is not in doubt. As it is entered in PRO, C57/7 m. 7d, the words *die Novembr'* are placed above the line in order to avoid a smudge which overlies a few illegible strokes of the pen, but there is little ground in this for doubting that the date as enrolled is correct.

[34] Stubbs, *Select Charters*, pp. 394–5; *Documents of the Baronial Movement*, pp. 246–9.

[35] Sayles, *King's Parliament*, p. 62.

[36] Treharne surmised that the knights 'probably stayed at home' (*Baronial Plan of Reform*, p. 267). Sanders noted 'presumably because of this order no meeting took place at St Albans and there is no evidence of an assembly at Windsor' (*Documents of the Baronial Movement*, p. 249 n). The editors in *HBC*, p. 503, concluded that 'probably no assembly of knights took place at either Windsor or St Albans'. F. M. Powicke did not comment in *King Henry III and the Lord Edward* (Oxford, 1947), II, p. 424. The king was in fact at Windsor on 21 September.

on 22 June 'at the latest'.[37] The summons was dated 4 June. It was part of a more general instruction to the keepers of the peace appointed after the baronial victory, and they may have been in a better position than the sheriffs in the other cases to ensure rapid compliance with the instruction. Nevertheless the writ laid down that the knights were to be elected by the county and were to come *pro toto comitatu*. On the face of it this summons gave ten days' more notice than that of 1213 and eight days' more than the king's writ of 1261. Yet the requirement that the knights should be elected in the shire courts must have made it just as impracticable. Even so, in this case, unlike those of 1213 and 1261, historians have not doubted that the assembly met.

There is finally the most famous of all Montfortian assemblies, that of 20 January 1265. For this, the first writs of summons addressed to the bishop of Durham and other churchmen were dated 14 December at Worcester. A further batch was sent out to abbots, priors, earls and barons, dated 24 December at Woodstock. If the form *mandatum est . . . in forma supradicta* is taken literally, as the sequence of the enrolment inescapably implies, the letters summoning representatives from shires and boroughs must have carried this later date. That allowed twenty-seven days' notice as against the eighteen provided the previous June. If imagination can be stretched to allow that that could be managed in the depth of winter, there can be no doubt that something went awry with the summons to those staunch Montfortian allies, the men of the Cinque Ports. The list of outgoing writs ends with a note that summonses were sent to them. The enrolled copy of the letter to the barons and bailiffs of Sandwich which follows was witnessed by the king at Westminster on 20 January, the very day of the assembly.[38]

Just what was reasonable notice? An earlier generation, thinking of different circumstances and other purposes, defined it in cap. 14 of Magna Carta, 1215, as forty days. Later, part of the answer depended on how knights or other representatives were chosen. If they were elected in the county courts, then something depended on whether a special session was called for the election; if so, the size, and difficulty of communication within each county must have caused delays of

---

[37] Stubbs, *Select Charters*, pp. 399–400; *Documents of the Baronial Movement*, pp. 290–3.
[38] Stubbs, *Select Charters*, pp. 403–4; *Documents of the Baronial Movement*, pp. 300–5. Sanders takes the date on the writ to the men of Sandwich as 'an indication of the disorganized state of the realm' (*ibid.*, p. 52).

varying length. In the later middle ages the sheriffs usually held the elections at the next regular session of the county courts, which met every four weeks in all counties except Lancashire, Lincolnshire, Northumberland and Yorkshire, where the interval between sessions was six weeks.[39] This procedure, too, required an interval, varying from county to county. Writs for an election which arrived just in time for the monthly or six-weekly session in one county must have just missed it in another; in a few instances emergency sessions called to hold elections became the starting point of new four-weekly cycles.[40] If, therefore, a travelling time of eight days each way is added to the six-weekly interval between the sessions of the shire court of Northumberland, the maximum notice necessary was eight weeks and a day. That assumes that the writ arrived the day after the court's ordinary session, that the sheriff waited for the next six-weekly meeting, and that neither the writ nor the elected members were delayed by storm, flood or other impediment.

That is a theoretical maximum. Practice was markedly different in at least two respects. First, it took considerably longer than eight days for the writs to reach the more distant counties, and secondly, sheriffs seem to have accepted much less notice than the maximum interval before the next session of the court before they recorded their unease. The representatives to Stubbs's 'model' parliament of 1295 were first summoned on 3 October for 13 November. Subsequently writs of 2 November prorogued the meeting to the 27th. These last writs were received by the sheriff, in Nottinghamshire and Derbyshire on the 11th, in Gloucestershire, Hampshire, Warwickshire and Leicestershire on the 12th, in Herefordshire and Wiltshire on the 13th, in Devon on the 21st, and in Shropshire and Staffordshire on the 22nd. In short, the maximum time for the delivery of the order was not eight but twenty days. These dates of receipt were recorded in memoranda which the sheriffs added to their returns of members.[41] It is probable that they were all seeking to explain why they could not comply with the new instruction. A few were more explicit. The sheriff of Warwickshire and Leicestershire stated that he had returned the names of members in reply to the original writ of summons on the very day on which the

---

[39] J. J. Alexander, 'The dates of early county elections', *EHR*, XL (1925), pp. 1–12; 'The dates of county days', *BIHR* III (1926), pp. 89–95.

[40] J. J. Alexander, 'The dates of early county elections', pp. 4–7.

[41] *Parl. Writs*, I, pp. 35–45.

writ of prorogation arrived. The sheriff of Hampshire had done even better and answered the first instruction before the second arrived. The sheriff of Nottinghamshire and Derbyshire, less explicably, received the new instruction on Friday 11 November but answered the old one on Sunday the 13th. The sheriff of Devon, among the last to receive the second writ, noted the date of receipt on the 22nd and added that he could not put the prorogation into effect throughout his bailiwick. Since the original summons was for the 13th, that is scarcely surprising.

In 1295 the eleven-day notice of prorogation was plainly insufficient. In 1290 the writs for the parliament of 15 July were dated 14 June. On this occasion none of the sheriffs' surviving returns contains a note of the date of receipt.[42] None, in short, chose to record inadequate notice. Four weeks seem to have been sufficient. Only one other Edwardian assembly was called at shorter notice than this, that of 1297, which was summoned by Edward of Caernarvon, in the king's absence, on 15 September for 6 October. On this occasion only the sheriff of Northumberland chose to record the date of receipt: he got his writ on the afternoon of 28 September.[43] This evidence therefore suggests that difficulties were experienced once the notice was reduced from four to three weeks.

But this is not the whole story. Under pressure something had to give. The sheriff had to nominate the knights, or use some other in-formal procedure, rather than have them formally elected; or he had to call a special session of the shire court; or he waited on the regular session, thereby incurring a delay so that the knights would turn up late.

This logic is inescapable, but it is only occasionally that it is under-pinned by exact evidence. Designation was the least likely way out of difficulty. True, the earliest writs of 1212 and 1213 do not specify election; nor do the summons of burgesses in 1268 or the writs for Edward I's first parliament of April 1275. In this last instance election is not mentioned in any of the surviving returns;[44] but the mainpernours who guaranteed the members' attendance can scarcely have been pro-vided other than in the county courts. The writ of summons to Edward's second parliament of October 1275 commands the sheriffs to have the

[42] *Ibid.*, I, pp. 21–4.
[43] *Ibid.*, I. p. 60.
[44] C. Hilary Jenkinson, 'The first parliament of Edward I', *EHR*, XXV (1910), pp. 231–42; G. O. Sayles, 'Representation of cities and boroughs', pp. 580–5.

knights elected in full county.[45] The well known return from the sheriff of Gloucestershire for the parliament of 1283 states that the knights were elected in full county.[46] Election was not merely usual but essential, and sheriffs went out of their way to emphasise that it had taken place. For the parliament of 1297, called at three weeks' notice, they reported that the election was made in full county (Oxfordshire) or with the assent of the whole county (Lancashire).[47] The knights of Sussex refused to proceed to an election in the absence of the archbishop of Canterbury and of the bishops, earls, barons and knights who were overseas with the king.[48] The knights of Surrey elected John d'Abernon, who was in Hampshire on the king's service, 'and refused to elect any other in his place'.[49] In neither case did the sheriff nominate. Indeed, nomination was more likely to occur where the electors were held to be politically unreliable. In 1268 the chancellor noted that Roger Leyburn was to nominate the representatives of the Cinque Ports.[50] Roger was deputy warden and had the task of bringing these stalwart Montfortian supporters to heel.[51] Otherwise there are few instances where the sheriff may have nominated or resorted to informal consultation. In 1290 each of the three representatives of Cumberland was simply returned as *attachiatus*; no reference was made to election.[52] In the same year the return from Yorkshire simply gave the names of the representatives with their mainpernours, with no indication of the method of choice.[53] In 1297 the sheriff of Cumberland reported that before the arrival of the writ of summons the knights returned had been assigned with others to the defence of the March, where it was essential for them to remain;[54] hence it seems likely that attendance at the court must at the very least have been reduced. The sheriff of Northumberland, too, who noted the date of receipt of the writ, was somewhat imprecise in his return, *feci eligere pro tota comitate (sic)*,[55]

[45] Stubbs, *Const. Hist.*, II, p. 235 n.
[46] PRO, C219, Parl. Writs and Returns, 1/2, illustrated in *The Seventh Century of Simon de Montfort's Parliament*, ed. M. F. Bond (London, 1965), plate 17.
[47] *Parl. Writs*, I, pp. 58, 60.
[48] *Ibid.*, I, p. 60.
[49] *Ibid.*, I, p. 61.
[50] *EHR*, XL, p. 584.
[51] F. M. Powicke, *King Henry III and the Lord Edward*, II, pp. 521–2; A. Lewis, 'Roger Leyburn and the pacification of England', *EHR*, LIX (1939), pp. 193–214.
[52] *Parl. Writs*, I, p. 21.
[53] *Ibid.*, I, p. 21.
[54] *Ibid.*, I, p. 57.
[55] *Ibid.*, I, p. 60.

which leaves a less certain impression than the usual formulae, *electi sunt per totam communitatem comitatus* or *electi sunt in pleno comitatu*. It may be significant that all these instances come from more distant counties, two of which, Northumberland and Yorkshire, had six-weekly courts. Nevertheless such hints are both ambiguous and rare. The overwhelming impression is that the sheriffs did their utmost to hold elections in the county courts.

Whether they held special sessions to answer an urgent summons is even more difficult to determine. There is no certain indication that this was done in any of the surviving returns of 1290 or 1297, except possibly in Lincolnshire, where in 1297 the sheriff reported, 'Accepto brevi isto sine dilatione eligi feci . . . de probioribus et legalioribus militibus comitatus Lincolniensis ex assensu predicti comitatus'.[56] In times of crisis it may well have been possible to assemble a shire court at very short notice. In 1264 and 1265, especially, the county suitors were in turmoil and presumably ready to respond to immediate demands for representatives. It may also be that each county had standing arrangements for calling emergency sessions. But, if so, it cannot have been easy for the sheriffs to maintain and use such arrangements against local insistence on the letter of cap. 35 of Magna Carta, 1217, which laid down minimum intervals of a month.[57]

Finally, elected representatives could simply turn up late. In 1297 the sheriff of Northumberland received the summons of 15 September only on the 28th. The representatives of the county can scarcely have been in London by 6 October, whatever procedures he followed. Indeed, dilatory attendance must have been common. In 1295 the writs of prorogation took nine days to reach Nottinghamshire and Derbyshire, ten days to reach Gloucestershire, Hampshire, Warwickshire and Leicestershire, eleven to reach Herefordshire and Wiltshire, nineteen to reach Devon and twenty days to reach Shropshire and Staffordshire. There is no reason to think that representatives going up for the session would travel any faster. It is difficult to avoid the conclusion that a session held at a month's notice would at first be sparsely attended and a session held at three weeks' notice would be limited at first to the representatives of the more accessible counties where the writ of summons happened to arrive at a conveniently short interval

[56] *Ibid.*, I, p. 58.
[57] For comment see J .C. Holt, *Magna Carta* (Cambridge, 1965), pp. 279–84; F. M. Powicke, *King Henry III and the Lord Edward*, I, pp. 147–8.

before the next meeting of the county court. It is significant that under Edward I eight weeks' notice or more was usually given. On three occasions it was as short as six weeks,[58] in 1290 and 1294 little more than a month,[59] and in 1297 three weeks.

There is no doubt that the procedures apparent under Edward were followed at a very early date. One of the curiosities of the history of the earliest assemblies is that in the *Select Charters* Stubbs included the writ of summons of 1226 of four knights from each of eight counties, but failed to note that this was cancelled and was followed in 1227 by a similar summons sent out to thirty-five counties.[60] Both writs were quite precise: the sheriffs were to instruct the knights and honest men of their bailiwicks in full county court that they were to elect four of the more lawful and discreet knights among their number. On each occasion the notice was more than adequate. The writs for the full assembly of 1227 were dated 13 August and the meeting was due on 19 October. In 1254, when two knights were summoned from every county to answer for aid to the king, similar notice was allowed, from 11 February to 26 April, and on that occasion too the sheriffs were instructed to have the knights elected in the county courts.[61] But these are the only early occasions when the notice was entirely adequate. In 1213 and 1261 (as regards the king's summons) it was plainly insufficient. In June 1264 it was little better. In December 1264 it was still barely enough, and for the Cinque Ports, on the face of it, utterly derisory.

One of these early assemblies is in a category of its own and is of special interest. The Provisions of Oxford of June 1258 provided for the election of four knights of the shire to investigate and receive complaints against the sheriffs and other local officials. There is no other evidence that the knights to whom the writs of summons were sent at the end of July and the beginning of August were in fact elected. Powicke assumed that they were, and certainly there would probably

[58] 1 September 1275 for 13 October; 30 September–3 October 1295 for 13 November (prorogued to 27 November); 10–13 April 1298 for 25 May.
[59] 13–14 June 1290 for 15 July; 8–9 October 1294 for 12 November.
[60] Stubbs, *Select Charters*, p. 353; *Rot. Litt. Claus.*, II, pp. 154, 212–13. In 1227 Cornwall and Westmorland were inexplicably omitted from the list of counties. In his only comment Stubbs attached no particular significance to this summons (*Const. Hist.*, II, pp. 222–3). On the whole question see A. B. White, 'Some early instances of concentration of representatives in England', *American Historical Review*, XIX (1914), pp. 735–50, especially pp. 736–40.
[61] Stubbs, *Select Charters*, pp. 365–6.

have been sufficient time if instructions were sent out very soon after the first meeting of the Oxford parliament on 9 June.[62] Treharne and Sanders, on the other hand, considered that the knights were appointed by the council as part of the final agreement on the Provisions which Henry proclaimed on oath on 4 August.[63] They were commissioners, not representatives. This second view seems much the more likely. Quite apart from the lack of any evidence of election in the counties, three of the named knights for Shropshire were found to be unfit; they were replaced by others of whom the sheriff, Peter de Montfort, sent word. From Devon also the sheriff wrote with news that two of that county's four knights were sick; he was commanded to send others in their place.[64] There is evidence, in short, that originally men were named in ignorance of their true state of health, and that points to nomination before or by the council rather than to election in the county courts. Finally, the writs of 28 July and 4 August are best read as initiating rather than further defining the investigations embodied in the Provisions.[65] These writs summoned the knights to Westminster in the octave of Michaelmas to present the results of their enquiries in person and under seal to the council. The articles of enquiry were very detailed.[66] There were a mere two months in which to complete the task, and the council recognised the need for haste if it was to be done in time; the knights and sheriffs were instructed that their oath should be taken in full county, or before the sheriff and the coroners if there was no county session in the immediate future. In the event the interval between early August and 6 October seems to have been inadequate. Writs of expenses of 4 November ordered payments to the knights of ten counties who had come before the king at Westminster not a week but a month after Michaelmas. These are followed on the roll by further undated writs of expenses which ordered payment to the knights of at least seven counties who had come before the council at

[62] *King Henry III and the Lord Edward*, I, p. 395. The Provisions, contrary to Powicke's summary, do not refer to election *in the shire*, nor are the letters of 4 August addressed to *elected* knights.

[63] Treharne, *Baronial Plan of Reform*, pp. 108–9; I. J. Sanders in *Documents of the Baronial Movement*, p. 12.

[64] *CPR 1247–58*, pp. 647–8.

[65] The writ, after reviewing the decision taken at Oxford, instructs the commissioners to take an oath to execute their task faithfully and then to proceed with the enquiry. They cannot therefore have taken the oath previously and the enquiry cannot yet have begun. Powicke introduced the notion of 'defining' (*op. cit.*, I, p. 395).

[66] *Chronica Majora*, VI (RS), pp. 397–400.

Westminster at some unspecified date after Michaelmas.[67] Of the important parliament of October 1258, the first to meet under the Provisions of Oxford, this, then, can be said: the knights who attended were nominated, not elected; some of them certainly attended three weeks after the original date of summons; that fact and the existence of two forms of writ of expenses suggest that they did not all attend at one and the same time.

It is from such improvisation that the attitude of King John and Henry III, of their officers and counsellors, of baronially dominated parliaments and councils, and of the knights themselves, towards the summoning of knights of the shire and their attendance at general assemblies or before the king's council or parliament has to be pieced together. There was no theory. But there were assumptions and understandings expressed in the manner in which the machinery of government was brought into play. It is obvious that the arrangements could be makeshift, even hit-or-miss. If in the view of the government the circumstances allowed for lengthy notice, well and good. Then, as in 1227, when the meeting was postponed from the previous year, the writs could lay down that the elections should take place in the next full meeting of the county courts. But if there was no such elbow room, if at the other extreme time and need were pressing, then the sheriffs could be left to get the county knights returned as best they could, or the knights could be told to come to the king wherever he might be and as soon as possible, or the king might put up, as John presumably did in 1213 and Henry III in 1261, with incomplete assemblies. And it cannot be emphasised too strongly that these apparent inadequacies were inseparable from the measures taken. They were not accidental. In 1213 John must have known that he would get an incomplete response to his summons. In 1261 Henry III must have known that he would be unlikely to divert many knights from St Albans to Windsor. In June and again in December 1264 Simon de Montfort must have known that he was calling knights in at inadequate notice. Yet they all did it. Indeed, they persisted. There is no way of telling how many of the knights summoned on 24 December 1264 assembled in London on 20 January 1265. On 15 February writs of expenses which recorded that the knights had spent more time in London than they had expected

---

[67] H. M. Cam, 'The parliamentary writs "de expensis" of 1258', *EHR*, XLVI (1931), pp. 630–2; *CCR 1256–9*, pp. 332–3.

were made out on behalf of the knights of Yorkshire.[68] They presumably had done their duty and were on their way home. Eight days later, on 23 February, royal letters were sent to the sheriff of Shropshire and Staffordshire expressing surprise and anger that no knights had yet arrived from those two counties; they were now to come on 8 March, 'wherever we may then be in England'.[69] It may be that deepening troubles in the Welsh Marches prevented elections in Shropshire;[70] it is also possible that the politically volatile Hamo l'Estrange, who was replaced as sheriff on 5 February, was an immediate cause of the delay;[71] but there can be no doubt that over a month after the date fixed for the original meeting the Monfortian royal council still wanted to see the representatives of these two counties, who would arrive at best long after the rest of the knights had gone home.

These assemblies were summoned for purposes which would now be described as administrative and political. There was only one exception, in 1254. All the rest, as far as is known, were concerned with receiving information, or sensing the political condition of the country, or ensuring that the government's intentions were conveyed to the localities and, within the localities, to the centres where government policies were customarily proclaimed, the county courts. King John's purposes in 1212 and 1213 have already been discussed above.[72] In 1227 the knights were summoned to present any complaints they might have against the sheriffs over some of the articles of the Great Charter; arguments had arisen, particularly in Lincolnshire, around the sessions of the shire court as laid down in cap. 35 of the 1217 reissue.[73] In 1258 they were summoned to report on the investigation of local *querelae* in the county courts under the terms of the Provisions of Oxford; those conducting the investigation and those summoned were one and the same.[74] The twin assemblies of 1261, like that of 1213, were the product of a political crisis; both the barons and the king turned to the knights for support as the rift between them over the execution of the

---

[68] *Documents of the Baronial Movement*, pp. 305–7.

[69] *Ibid.*, pp. 307–9.

[70] So suggests Sanders (*ibid.*, p. 309 n). The case seems stronger for Shropshire than for Staffordshire.

[71] *List of Sheriffs* (PRO, *Lists and Indexes*, IX, 1898), p. 117.

[72] See above, pp. 5–10.

[73] J. C. Holt, *Magna Carta*, pp. 279–80, 283–4.

[74] See above, pp. 9, 16–17.

reforming Provisions widened.[75] The summons of June 1264 was part of the settlement of the country after the baronial victory at Lewes; the summons was included as part of the general writ of pacification. The summons of December 1264 was for an assembly in which Simon de Montfort hoped to turn the uneasy armistice which had followed Lewes into a final peace. According to the London chronicler, when the assembly met, King Henry swore that neither he nor the Lord Edward would bear malice against the earls of Leicester and Gloucester and that he would observe both the charter of liberties and the charter of the forest and adhere to the form of peace agreed in 1264; other assurances were also given both by him and by the Lord Edward and Henry of Almain.[76] Knights reporting these ceremonies and commitments to the shire courts could be expected to provide valuable reinforcement for the Montfortian cause.

If such were the purposes and objectives in summoning these men it is easy to understand why lack of notice, late attendance and other impediments were tolerated, and not simply tolerated but accepted as integral features of the methods of communication between central government and local communities. Completeness and coincidence in the muster made an impressive show and perhaps made for some effective communication, but they could both be sacrificed to urgency. More often than not they were. Administrative and political necessities were the determinant.

The role allotted to these assemblies in the writs of summons was variously defined. In 1212 they were to come 'to do what we shall tell them'; in 1213 'to speak with us concerning the affairs of our realm'; in 1227 'to present any complaint they have' against the sheriffs; in 1258 'to present their sealed enquiries in person to our council'; in 1261 to 'treat on the common affairs of the realm' with the magnates and 'to talk with us on these matters' with the king; in 1264 'to treat with us on the aforesaid matters' (the settlement after Lewes); and in 1265 'to treat with us and with the magnates of our realm and to give your

---

[75] Such is the usual interpretation of an incident for which the evidence is far from complete. See Treharne, *Baronial Plan of Reform*, pp. 353–4; Powicke, *King Henry and the Lord Edward*, II, pp. 424–5; Sanders, in *Documents of the Baronial Movement*, pp. 38–9.

[76] *Liber de Antiquis Legibus*, ed. T. Stapleton (CS, old ser., XXXIV, 1846), p. 71.

counsel on these matters'.[77] The writs convey what is obvious from other evidence: after 1258 the knights came to pull more weight; both king and magnates paid more attention to their desires and responses. But it was only at the height of the Montfortian revolution in 1265 that knights and burgesses were admitted in formal terms to 'giving counsel'. That apart, they contributed not so much to the discussion of policy as to the information on which others founded it. At most they were summoned 'to treat', and that conventional translation of 'tractare' or 'tractaturi' may well convey too emphatic an impression of sharply defined negotiation. The knights had no *locus standi* from which to negotiate. Government sought to 'treat' with them because willy-nilly the views and responses of the knights had become part of the information on which sound policy had to be founded. The knights had no legislative role. Except in 1254 they had nothing to do with finance.

The summoning of knights of the shire has come to be treated as part of the history of popular representation. It was so only in a strictly limited sense. The knights represented the shire and the shire court. They came *pro toto comitatu* or *ex parte communitatum comitatum*.[78] There was no difference in this from bearing witness of the shire before the king's court. They did not come as representatives of the community of the realm. Inadequate notice would have made a mockery of that. It was only in the exceptional summons of 1254 that they were instructed that they would be required to act with the knights of other shires. On that occasion they had ten weeks' notice. But even then they were viewed as representatives of the parts, acting concurrently, not as representatives of the whole. They came 'on behalf of each and every man' of the county 'to provide, along with the knights of other counties whom we shall cause to be called for the same day'. Indeed, it is difficult to see that contemporaries—ministers, counsellors or clerks of chancery—drew any distinction between summoning representatives from the counties and summoning them from other groups and organisations. Representatives were called from the Cinque Ports in 1204, 1225 and 1235, and from the Jewish communities of the towns in 1231

---

[77] This is the wording of the writ to the Cinque Ports. The form of writ to the counties does not survive. The subsequent writ to Shropshire and Staffordshire recapitulates the earlier summons 'to treat with us and with the magnates, on behalf of the communities of those counties, concerning these affairs and to give their counsel' (*Documents of the Baronial Movement*, pp. 304–5, 307–8).

[78] These are the phrases of 1227, 1264 and 1265.

and 1241.[79] The men of the Cinque Ports in 1225, like the knights in 1258, brought information under seal. In 1235, like the knights in 1213, they came 'to speak with us about our affairs'. The Jews in 1231 came 'to hear the precept of the king', like the knights in 1212, who were 'to do what we shall tell them'. In 1241, on the face of it, they did better; they were then 'to treat with us concerning both our interest and theirs'. On both occasions the Jews, like the knights, were summoned through the sheriffs.

These arguments suggest that in the general debate about parliamentary origins the summoning of knights of the shire has been placed on the wrong side. The dominating figure of Stubbs has persuaded his successors on both sides of the argument that the presence of county representatives tells in favour of a broad definition of parliamentary functions standing in sharp contrast to the view which insists on its official, conciliar and judicial structure and role. Yet on every occasion, except apparently one, in 1254, it is possible to embody the summoning of knights, and for that matter of other representatives, within the ordinary functioning of government. And that holds good at all points in the reigns of John and Henry III. It is equally true both before and after the establishment of those combined sessions of the royal council and the courts which by 1236 were officially described as parliaments. It is as true for King John, seeking information on the conspirators of 1212, as for Simon de Montfort, making his final attempt in 1265 to impose the settlement of Lewes on an unwilling king and on the shires. Whether government was dominated by a headstrong king or a visionary earl did not matter. Representation was an extension of, not an antithesis to, royal and conciliar government. It had much to do with communication. It had something to do with counsel, for there was no sharp division between the provision of factual information and the assertion of interested opinion; facts, in any case, could be slanted and selected, as, for example, the history of the bounds of the royal forest in the thirteenth century repeatedly reveals. As yet, it had nothing at all to do with consent.

Two obvious considerations lend support to such a revision. First, between the bearing of the witness of the shire on the one hand and attendance at a national assembly on the other there were many intermediate roles for representatives to play. Two were particularly im-

[79] For all these examples and others not involving representation see A. B. White, *American Hist. Rev.*, XIX (1914), pp. 742–50.

portant: the acquisition and defence of privilege and the investigation or presentation of complaints against officials. They are párticularly well illustrated in the relationship of the sheriff to the county court. In 1204 the knights of Devon acquired a charter of privileges which, among other provisos, restricted the sheriff's tourn to one occasion in the year.[80] In 1214 six knights of the county along with the prior of Kerswell had to defend their privilege in the king's bench against the sheriff, Eudo de Beauchamp, who, in the local view, had exceeded his functions as defined in the charter granted ten years earlier and was seeking pretexts to mulct those who stood by the limited sessions and attendance for which the charter had provided.[81] In 1217 an attempt was made to deal with the problem nationally; cap. 35 of Magna Carta confirmed the customary sessions of the county courts and laid down that the sheriffs were not to hold their tourns in the hundreds more than twice a year; it did not mention other sessions of the hundred courts. In 1226 the knights of Lincolnshire conducted an epic legal struggle against the attempts of the sheriff to hold the county court, as they alleged, at less than the customary forty-day interval and to transfer unfinished cases from the county to the combined session of the wapentakes of Kesteven. The sheriff and four knights reported on the case, but two knights who led the resistance also stated the case for the county at the preliminary hearing in the bench.[82] Just as the knights of Devon relied in 1214 on their charter of 1204, so the knights of Lincolnshire in 1226 relied on the Great Charter of liberties. In June 1226, after the case had gone through the courts and finally been dismissed by the king, four knights were summoned from eight counties, including Lincolnshire, to settle disputes which had arisen between the sheriffs and the men of the shires about some of the articles of the Great Charter.[83] That meeting was never held, but it was followed in 1227 by a meeting of representatives from thirty-five counties with identical terms of reference.[84] Finally, in 1234, the king issued two instructions on the matter. The second, sent out after cap. 35 of the Charter had been read before archbishops, bishops, earls and barons, was enrolled under the heading 'Concerning the interpretation of a

[80] *Foedera*, I, part 1, p. 89.
[81] *Curia Regis Rolls*, VII (HMSO, 1935), pp. 158–9.
[82] *Ibid.*, XII (HMSO, 1957), no. 2142.
[83] Stubbs, *Select Charters*, p. 353.
[84] See above, p. 16.

clause in the liberties, how it ought to be understood'.[85] This at last made clear that in addition to the biennial tourns mentioned in cap. 35 of the Charter the courts of hundred and wapentake were also to meet every three weeks for the maintenance of the peace.

In this well known story representation appears in many forms, but always to a single end: the preservation and defence of liberties. The source of these liberties might lie in a local charter or in the Great Charter of liberties itself. The representatives might be acting for one county, or eight, or virtually all. They might present their case in the bench as the knights of Devon did in 1214 or they might be summoned before the king as in 1227. But throughout their role remained unchanged. The scope and definition of privilege was one with which later parliamentary sessions were much concerned. These men were defining their liberties in the bench or before the king very much as individuals and communities later sought to protect them by parliamentary petition. In short, it is very difficult to distinguish these actions from many of the matters which the king and his ministers and advisers might determine in parliament in the years after 1236. That is to look forward. Looking backwards, it seems likely that such representative functions had a long history. It is difficult to see how the men of Surrey could have purchased the partial disafforestation of their county in 1190 without some use of representation.[86] It is impossible to imagine that all the Londoners importuned Henry I *en masse* to secure their first charter of 1130–3. Even the judges and jurors of the county court of Yorkshire may have been too numerous personally to negotiate the settlement of £100, recorded in the pipe roll of 1130, whereby they secured their release from further service.[87] The antecedent to the common petition was the communal fine.

In this matter of the sessions of the local courts the knights provided feedback. They gave the government information on how a liberty or privilege, once conceded, was working. The interests of the knights themselves were part of that information. Sometimes it was freely sought by the king. Sometimes it was pressed on him by the knights. But the business could not have been concluded efficiently without it. None the less, the knights were not among those whose counsel was

---

[85] *CCR 1231–4*, pp. 551, 588–9, 592–3. The enrolment runs: 'De interpretatione clausule contente in libertatibus qualiter debeat intelligi.'

[86] *Pipe Roll 2 Richard I* (Pipe Roll Soc., new ser. 1, 1925), p. 67.

[87] *Magnus Rotulus Scaccarii de anno 31° Henrici I*, ed. J. Hunter (RC, 1833; facsimile reprint, with corrections by C. Johnson, HMSO, 1929), p. 34.

enlisted by the king in making his final ruling in 1234, and this leads to the second consideration.

No one in the early thirteenth century pretended that an assembly of knights of the shire represented the community as a whole. This was not simply because of the obvious objection that the knights could not represent other orders, the townsfolk or the clergy, but because there was another more ancient view, namely that the magnates could speak for the community. At rock bottom this notion was feudal; the magnates participated as suitors in the decisions of the king's court; the 'common counsel of the realm' in the assessing of aids and scutages was provided by archbishops, bishops, abbots, earls and greater barons summoned individually and by all other tenants-in-chief summoned through the sheriffs. The obvious impracticality of these provisions of cap. 14 of Magna Carta, 1215, should not obscure the fact that they expressed the commonly accepted assumption about how the realm could be brought to collective decision and action. And the assumption persisted. The reissue of Magna Carta of 1225 was agreed in such a feudal assembly. In return a fifteenth was granted by 'archbishops, bishops, abbots, priors, earls, barons, knights and free tenants'. The names of some of those present are known from the attestation of the charter. They were practically all of baronial standing. None was a simple free-tenant. Free-tenants were included among those participating in the grant because they participated in the *quid pro quo*—the benefits conferred in the Great Charter.[88] Any lingering doubt is removed by the phrases of the next writ of assessment of the fortieth of 1232. Here the enumeration of the participants ends with the statement that '. . . knights, freemen and villeins of our realm have conceded to us in aid . . .'[89] Five years later that literal absurdity was corrected. The writ of assessment of the thirtieth of 1237 announced that '. . . knights and freemen, on their own behalf and on behalf of their villeins, have conceded to us in aid . . .'[90] In none of these cases is there any indication that the grants were made by other than an assembly

[88] The link is explicitly established in letters sent to the justices in Kent: 'Make it quite clear to them that so many as withhold this gift, and their heirs, will have no share in the liberty granted to our worthy men by our charters.' See *CPR 1216–25*, pp. 572–3, quoted Powicke, *King Henry III and the Lord Edward*, I, p. 37, whose translation I have followed.

[89] Stubbs, *Select Charters*, p. 356.

[90] *Ibid.*, pp. 358–9.

of magnates.[91] The assumption made in these phrases is plain. The magnates could give consent on behalf of the whole community, and they could do so because they spoke for the tenants-in-chief, whose consent embodied that of their tenants and therefore that of the whole realm. It embraced the first attempts at legislation as well as grants in aid. The Provisions of Merton were conceded by the advice of such an assembly.[92] Since the assembled magnates constituted a feudal court it too, like the shire court, could be represented. Hence there was no theoretical impediment in 1258 to arranging in the Provisions of Oxford for twelve honest men to be elected by 'le commun' to treat with the king and his council in parliament. Professor Sayles is surely right to insist that 'le commun' were the baronage,[93] if only because, within these feudal assumptions, the assembled baronage represented the community as a whole.

In this there was one major snag. Men accepted the representative capacity of the tenants-in-chief or magnates, only to encounter the fact that much the strongest administrative link between the crown and the magnates' vassals was forged in the shires, through the sheriffs and in the shire courts. True, juries of knights brought the record of their lord's feudal court before the king or his justices, just as they did for the shire. Again, knights consulted in the shire court might hesitate to act in the absence of, or without consultation with, the magnates of the shire.[94] But throughout the twelfth and thirteenth centuries there was only one occasion when the feudal was preferred to the county organisation in the execution of a major measure. That was the enquiry into feudal service in 1166.

This difficulty in part explains the peculiarities of the one summons of knights in the early thirteenth century in which, at first sight, they seem to encroach on the magnates' capacity to act for the community. Stubbs described the 'summons for two knights of the shire to grant an aid' in 1254 as 'an important landmark in the parliamentary history of England'.[95] The suggestion that here there was some great leap forward

---

[91] A. B. White did, however, argue that some form of real consent from representatives was sought in 1237 (American Hist. Rev., XIX, pp. 745–7). The evidence for this, drawn from the Tewkesbury annals, is frail.

[92] CCR 1234–7, p. 337.

[93] King's Parliament, pp. 55–6.

[94] See the objections of the knights of Yorkshire to the assessment of the carucage of 1220 (Rot. Litt. Claus., I, p. 427; Royal and other Historical Letters illustrative of the Reign of Henry III, I, ed. W. W. Shirley (RS, 1862), pp. 151–2).

[95] Stubbs, Select Charters, pp. 365–6.

has remained, in diminished form perhaps, ever since. In reality there was simply a muddle. Henry III sent home from Gascony seeking assistance against a threatened invasion of the duchy by Alfonso of Castile which never in fact materialised. The prelates promised an aid in the event of such an invasion, but would not commit the lower clergy without their consent.[96] It is sometimes assumed that this example was copied by the magnates,[97] but there is no direct evidence to that effect. All the magnates did was to promise to come 'with their full power' if the Castilian invasion took place. That left those who would not take part in the expedition, and it was from these that the queen and Richard of Cornwall planned to seek aid, to establish which they summoned two knights from each county to come before the council at Westminster.[98] The intended 'aid', in short, was not on a par with the levies of 1225, 1232 and 1237. It was a bid to develop and amalgamate the fine *pro non transfretando* and the payment of scutage by rear-vassals. It perpetuated the confusion of scutage and aid which had sprouted from the seed sown in 1215 in Magna Carta.[99] The magnates on this occasion had not abandoned their traditional capacity to grant a feudal aid. This was not a feudal aid; it was not a general tax at all. It was sharp practice. None the less it reflected a home truth. The only satisfactory method of obtaining the compliance of the rear-vassals was through the shire courts. Moreover sharp practice did not preclude—indeed, it encouraged—administrative innovation. This was the first occasion on which the knights were summoned for financial purposes, and, because the business was financial, the writ laid down that they were to come *vice omnium et singulorum*. The first hint of 'full powers' was inspired by expediency.

In thirteenth-century England there were two distinct notions of representation. One was rooted in administrative practice. The other stemmed from feudal preconceptions. In retrospect they seem mutually inconsistent. At the time they were combined in different functions. In 1258 the Provisions of Oxford provided for the representation of the community by twelve honest men, perhaps the most extreme of all expressions of the feudal point of view, and at the same time arranged

---

[96] Lunt, 'Consent of lower clergy to taxation', pp. 139–44.

[97] Powicke, *King Henry III and the Lord Edward*, I, p. 344 n; Clementi, 'Statute of York of 1322', p. 97.

[98] *Royal Letters of Henry III*, ed. W. W. Shirley, I, pp. 101–2; Stubbs, *Select Charters*, pp. 365–6.

[99] J. C. Holt, *Magna Carta*, pp. 204–5, 218–21, 286–7.

that knights of the shire should investigate and subsequently report the *querelae* of the counties. The twelve honest men met the council to constitute a parliament; the knights reported to the king and council in parliament. But time told in favour of the knights of the shire. In the end they, along with the burgesses, came to speak for 'le commun', indeed to constitute the commons. They earned their new role. In the supervision of local government, in the collection and presentation of local complaints, in the assessment and collection of taxation, in the ordinary processes of the law both in the local courts and before the king and his justices, above all perhaps in preserving the liberties won in 1215 and sustained in 1225 and the subsequent recurrent crises of Henry III's reign, they were the work-horses of thirteenth-century government. Their work was largely determined by the county and the county court. The county court also provided the framework of their representation. This was what administrative convenience required. Magna Carta cap. 14 and the Provisions of Oxford provided an alternative solution. In time, administrative convenience won.

G. L. HARRISS

2

The Formation of Parliament, 1272–1377

THE CENTURY OF THE FIRST three Edwards saw the formation of parliament as a political institution. By 1377 its membership was settled and had divided into two houses, its business procedures were established, its acts were officially recorded by its own clerk, and it had acquired some acknowledged powers and privileges. Most significant was the fact that its proceedings commanded the attention not merely of those who directed the political life of the realm but of the realm itself. Parliament came into existence by royal will and as an instrument of royal government, but by the end of Edward III's reign it could authoritatively voice the interests of the whole political community. Nearly all these developments came to fruition under Edward III, and the year 1327, in which parliament participated in the deposition of a king, divides as accurately an any single date can the phase when parliament was still essentially a royal tool from that when it developed a political momentum of its own. But throughout the middle ages parliament could develop only within the context of monarchical rule, and our first approach to its evolution must be through the personality and purpose of each king.

King and parliament

The fact that Edward I inherited the concept of parliament from the baronial reformers of 1258–65 made him the more determined that it should be the instrument of the crown. His parliament did indeed, in the words of the Provisions of Oxford, 'review the state of the realm and treat of the common business of king and kingdom', but under royal direction and, of course, solely upon the royal summons. For twenty years after his return to England in 1274 he summoned parliaments with deliberate regularity at Michaelmas and Easter whenever he was in the realm. The great majority were meetings with his ministers, magnates and prelates. In them Edward took counsel on matters touching the realm and crown, received complaints, provided remedies for abuses by judgement and legislation, and discussed external relations. The invitation to present grievances, with the promise of redress, had won wide support for the baronial reformers in 1258, but Edward was resolved to have no justiciar other than the king, and, though petitions continued to be presented at the eyre, the regularity of parliaments and the opportunity they gave to review all aspects of administration and justice made them the place where petitions could most conveniently be presented and answered. Adjudication of complaints against royal officials or disputes between the crown and its subjects gave this work a judicial imprint, and the first two decades of the reign were one of those exceptional periods when adjustments in the relationship of the crown and its subjects and in landed and mercantile society were given considered legal formulation. In this sense the character of the early parliaments bore the imprint of the English Justinian, but they could hardly have functioned so regularly and effectively had not the king established in these years a harmony of purpose with his magnates and a body of able, devoted and trusted ministers. As the political scene changed in the 1290s so did the role of parliament. Edward's deteriorating relations with his magnates and churchmen, his distrust of his ministers, his obsessive pursuit of a military solution in Scotland, and the burdens this imposed on his subjects, were all mirrored in the later parliaments. After 1294 the regularity of the biannual meetings could not be maintained, petitions continued unabated but were increasingly seen as an impediment to more pressing royal business, taxation was sought more frequently and urgently, legislation dwindled to a trickle, and the only statutes of significance were those which embodied concessions wrung from the king as safeguards against royal demands and deceptions. Parliament began to wear the aspect of a place of confrontation between king and subjects, where the common profit of the realm and the dignity of the crown were no longer defined and provided for by the king but were invoked by subjects in opposition to royal government. By the end of the reign there were signs that Edward was no longer eager for its assembly.

The reign of Edward II accentuated rather than reversed this trend. Compelled by the continuing demands of an unwinnable war to seek financial and military support from his magnates and the communities, Edward compounded the difficulties of the crown by his military incompetence and dependence on favourites. In the Ordinances of 1311 parliament is seen as the instrument through which the magnates could force their counsel on the king, control his exercise of government, and compel him to conserve the rights and dignity of the crown for the common profit of the realm. As the second decade wore on, parliaments became the setting for the manoeuvres of baronial factions which justified opposition to the king by adducing the ills of the realm and the complaints of the people. By the time the king was given the opportunity to reassert royal control over parliament in 1322 he found it expedient to define by statute not only the invalidity of restraints imposed by subjects upon the crown's authority and executive powers but also the validity accorded by parliamentary assent to measures which touched the good of king and kingdom.[1] Yet because Edward remained distrustful of parliament he never gave it an effective role, and the events of 1327 reaffirmed the baronial use of it to criticise, judge and reform royal government. Parliament's assent was secured for the deposition of the king on the ground that he had broken his coronation oath, denuded the realm and derogated from the rights of the crown.[2]

It was left to Edward III to re-establish royal direction of parliament, and the key to this lay, as in the early years of Edward I, in the king's relations with his magnates. Edward III succeeded, as Edward II had not, in forging the sense of a common enterprise among magnates of his own age and outlook. The ambitious scope of Edward's war plans, which made demands on all ranks of society, gave prominence to parliament's functions of giving counsel, granting taxation and recording grievances. Frequent meetings, the formal recording of its acts, and its repeated

---

[1] For interpretations of the Statute of York see Lapsley, *Crown, Community and Parliament*, pp. 153–230; Clementi, 'Statute of York of 1322'.

[2] *Vita Edwardi Secundi*, ed. N. Denholm-Young (London, 1957), p. 136. The doubts about whether the assembly of 1327 was legally a parliament are analysed by B. Wilkinson, 'The deposition of Richard II and the accession of Henry IV', *EHR*, LIV (1939), pp. 223–30 (and in Fryde and Miller, I, pp. 337–44).

authorisation of levies of national taxation all served to transform parliament from an occasion into a body with its own political will and traditions. Henceforth it comprised a prescribed representative element which was essential for certain acts of government that touched the common profit of the community. Although the commons increasingly saw themselves as spokesmen for the communities of the shires, the king was never very ready to accept parliament as a critic of royal government and was careful never to let criticism provoke a confrontation with the royal prerogative. Only in 1340–1 and in the last years of his decline did he lose control over it as a result of factional splits within the royal circle and genuine grievances over ineptitude and corruption in government. For the greater part he was able to impose his consistent view of parliament as the place where the support of the realm could be authoritatively secured for the policies of the crown and nobility, these being essentially the furtherance of their military ambitions.

Parliament in the framework of government

Parliament's formation, while undoubtedly moulded by the will of the king, took place within the context of a phenomenal enlargement of the administrative organs of government and their consolidation into a system the framework of which survived into the seventeenth century. The reign of Edward I began the effective separation of the chancery from the household and its establishment as the largest and most prestigious of the administrative offices.[3] Through its wide though well defined autonomy in the issue of *de cursu* writs for both administrative and judicial processes, and its authorisation of mandates from the king and council, it was the agent for a mass of business in which the interests of king and subjects intermingled—the redress of wrongs, the grant of favours, the control of local officials, the conduct of foreign relations, the management of royal resources, and much else. In most of the matters raised in parliament the chancery was at some stage involved, and it was the chancery clerks who serviced parliament when it met. The chancellor was the crown's leading minister and

[3] B. Wilkinson, *The Chancery under Edward III* (Manchester, 1929), chs. II, III; *id.*, 'The chancery', in *English Government at Work*, I, pp. 162–205; G. O. Sayles, *Select Cases in the Court of King's Bench*, V (Selden Soc., 1958), pp. lxxi–xcvii.

principal councillor; frequently it fell to him to present the business of parliament, and in the course of the fourteenth century he developed a remedial jurisdiction by delegation from that of the council, drawing away from parliament some of the complaints hitherto presented there.

In fiscal administration the years 1290–1327 likewise saw a considerable enlargement of business and definition of routine. In part this reflected the increase of taxation and the demands of war. Before 1290 Edward I had levied only two taxes on property; in the rest of the reign there were seven. During the years 1294–7 the wool tax of 6s 8d per sack was raised to 40s, and a new custom was levied from 1303 to 1311 and after 1322. War expenditure was principally channelled through the wardrobe, and the latter part of the reign saw an almost unlimited expansion of wardrobe credit. Although ultimately this brought financial chaos, it proved a forcing house for administrative experiment and for making the crown's financial policies a political issue.[4] The wardrobe was brought under exchequer control first by the baronial Ordinances of 1311 and then more systematically in the exchequer ordinances of 1319 and 1323–6. The exchequer's responsibility for all expenditure and all accounts was reflected in the enlargement and definitive recasting of its records. Testimony to the scope of its business was the enlargement of its records: by 1325 the pipe rolls were declared to be four times and the memoranda rolls five times their size under Edward I.[5] It became the unchallenged agency of national finance, mirroring in its daily business not merely the needs of the crown but the interests of the political community.

The increasing business of these central departments was reflected in the emergence of the council as the co-ordinating agent of government, acting with, but also at times apart from, the king. Its nucleus was a small body of professional ministers—the chancellor, treasurer, justices and household officers, whose almost daily meetings produced a wide variety of warrants comprising administrative orders, appointments of officials, expenditure, or the endorsement of petitions. To it the departments of state and courts of law referred difficulties and conflicts for judicial and administrative review and resolution. Perhaps it was busiest at meetings of parliament for which it prepared the

---

[4] M. Prestwich, *War, Politics and Finance under Edward I* (London, 1972), pp. 157–76.
[5] *The Red Book of the Exchequer*, ed. H. Hall, III (RS, 1896), pp. 884–5, 860–1; J. F. Willard, 'The memoranda rolls and the remembrancers, 1282–1350', in *Tout Essays*, p. 216, notes a tenfold increase between 1282 and 1336.

agenda, and where, reinforced with leading nobility and churchmen, it dealt with the more pressing and weighty business deferred to that occasion, as well as receiving further business from petitions.[6] The connection between parliament and council had also a political dimension. Misgovernment was more readily ascribed to evil councillors than to the king, and the remedy for it was seen to lie in naming magnates as a continual council to oversee the great matters of state. This had already occurred in c. 1244 and in 1258, and parliament's development as the channel for complaint made it natural for the magnates to seek parliamentary endorsement for similar demands under Edward II. By the reign of Edward III a baronial council was emerging as parliament's own remedy against arbitrary and unpopular acts of the crown and its officers. Although such specific afforcements of the council were occasional and transient, they betokened the magnates' increasing political influence as the king's principal councillors in parliament, which, as the status of the judges and officials declined, turned them into a house of lords.[7]

The formalisation of the judicial machinery had been largely achieved under Henry III. The courts of king's bench and common pleas became distinct bodies with different series of rolls and a rough division of business, and the latter ceased to itinerate with the king. The increasing volume of judicial work led to the devolution of crown pleas to justices of assize and gaol delivery, each with their own series of records, and the emergence of a highly trained and organised legal profession. Above all, the century 1190–1290 was the great age of the eyre, the very success of which in drawing in complaints from the communities, in revealing local misgovernment by royal officials, in investigating and checking infringements of royal rights, and in bringing justice and retribution in disordered areas, led to its collapse under the weight of demands upon it. By the end of the thirteenth century clamour for the redress of wrongs by people of all classes was even more vociferous, and, whether this reflected a decline in law and order or a greater ex-

---

[6] J. F. Baldwin, 'The king's council', in English Government at Work, I, pp. 129–61; S. B. Chrimes, An Introduction to the Administrative History of Mediaeval England (Oxford, 1952), pp. 160–4. The 'array' or agenda for the parliaments of 1275 and 1322 are discussed by Sayles, King's Parliament, pp. 68–9, Edwards, ' "Justice" ', in Fryde and Miller, I, p. 288, and J. C. Davies, The Baronial Opposition to Edward II (Cambridge, 1918), pp. 582–3. For a council discussion during parliament see The War of Saint-Sardos, ed. P. Chaplais (CS, 3rd ser., LXXXVII, 1954), p. 89.
[7] Sayles, King's Parliament, pp. 97–101; Baldwin, 'The king's council', pp. 131–2.

pectation of it, it made itself felt upon the organs of central government: chancery, courts of law, council and parliament. Under this pressure the crown expanded its responsibilities for law enforcement through the agencies of king's bench, commissions of trailbaston, gaol delivery, and oyer and terminer, and the semi-professional commissions of the peace. While this decreased parliament's role as a court of instant redress, it made the problem of law enforcement the direct concern of its members and the subject of their complaint in session after session.[8]

In administration, finance and justice these years tell the same story, of a dramatic increase in the scope of government which impinged on the interests of a substantially wider sector of the community but at the same time provided facilities for subjects to assert and defend their rights. This is the context in which parliament came to fulfill its unique function as both an instrument of royal government and the voice of the community. In parliament's judicial aspect this duality was featured in its role as a high court—for resolving judicial difficulties, hearing appeals from lesser courts, settling the conflicts between the rights of the king and his greater subjects, and conducting state trials—and in its capacity for dealing with the petitions of individuals and communities. Financially it was the place where the king's demand for taxation for the common needs of the realm received the approval and assent of the whole community, but also where relief might be secured from the burdens placed on individuals and communities by the crown's fiscal dues, such as purveyance. Less definable was parliament's role as a forum for discussion of matters on which the king wished either to test the opinions or secure the formal support of the great body of magnates. In many of these functions it differed little if at all from the council of which it was, in a sense, an enlarged and more solemn session. Like the council it met at the king's will, was not a court of record, and possessed no elaborate staff, though it was more public and formal in its attendance, business and decisions. In contrast to the departments of state and the courts its role was unspecialised, that of a clearing house and talking shop. It reviewed, co-ordinated and decided matters which had often originated elsewhere. If its meet-

[8] A. Harding, *The Law Courts of Medieval England* (London, 1973), pp. 75–92; Sayles, *Select Cases of King's Bench*, IV, V; B. H. Putnam, *The Place in Legal History of Sir William Shareshull* (Cambridge, 1950); T. A. Green, 'The jury and the English law of homicide, 1200–1600', *Michigan Law Review*, LXXIV (1976), pp. 460–1.

ings were occasional and not prolonged, this added to their solemnity, while the number and importance of those who attended imparted an authority based not merely on the royal will but on the consensus of the political nation.

Although the formation of parliament can be comprehended only in relation to these institutional developments, it was also fashioned by political factors and changes in society. Reference has already been made to conflicts between the crown and its magnates. Of equal or greater importance was the commitment to a testing if intermittent war with France and Scotland.[9] The levying of taxes, troops and supplies on the basis of communities, not lordships, enforced the common obligation to share the burden of defence for the common safety. Frequent parliaments served to cultivate this sense of unity and common purpose, and to secure agreement for and impart authority to such levies. But the burdens of war weighed most heavily on those classes whose lack was greatest. Seizures of victuals and beasts for war—it has been argued—could precipitate starvation among the peasantry and bred fears of a popular rising.[10] The idea that parliament was a place where such ills could be redressed probably made headway among the lesser orders of society but it fell to the land-holding class beneath the baronage to voice the discontents of the shire, to safeguard its welfare, and to sanction or resist the crown's demands on it. It was these 'buzones', possessing land worth £20 a year or more, who formed an elite within the shire and came as its elected representatives to parliament.[11] At the top of the social scale the late thirteenth and early fourteenth centuries saw the nobility changing from an undifferentiated mass of landholders worth more than £20 a year, headed by a dozen earls, into a structured class of earls and barons constituting the peerage, which excluded the knights and lesser landholders.[12] This was reflected in the emergence of an upper house of parliament based on summons by writ. That parliament within its own framework had begun to mirror social divisions, the importance which the nobility attached to

[9] G. L. Harriss, 'War and the emergence of the English parliament, 1297–1360', *Journal of Medieval History*, II (1976), pp. 35–56.

[10] Maddicott, *English Peasantry*; E. Miller, 'War, taxation and the English Economic Development, ed. J. M. Winter (Cambridge, 1975), pp. 11–33. economy in the late thirteenth and early fourteenth centuries', in *War and*

[11] Lapsley, *Crown, Community and Parliament*, pp. 63–110; N. Denholm-Young, *The Country Gentry in the Fourteenth Century* (Oxford, 1969), ch. 2.

[12] McFarlane, *Nobility*, ch. 8.

birth and rank, and the idea that representation gave the authority to speak for the communities of the shires and boroughs, are indications of how naturally parliament had grown out of and reflected the life of the whole political nation.

If we see the emergence of parliament as part of this vigorous and violent but also extraordinarily creative period of political and institutional growth, we shall not be tempted to isolate any one political factor or any one aspect of its activity as determining its evolution.[13] It flourished because, as its name implies, it was an occasion when the concerns of the king, his magnates and the realm could be reviewed, provided for and remedied, and all concerned could have their say. By 1327 it was beginning to have the look of a permanent institution and in the reign of Edward III we can examine more closely its mechanism and functions.

The mechanism of parliament

Parliament usually met in the Palace of Westminster, its full sessions being held at times in the Hall but probably more often in the Painted Chamber, from which the lords withdrew for their deliberations to the White Chamber, and the commons in the later fourteenth century to the chapter house. Under Edward I and II royal campaigns in the north had led to its meeting at Berwick (1292), Carlisle (1307), York (1298, 1314, 1320, 1322, 1332–5), Lincoln (1301, 1316, 1327) and Stamford (1309), but the French war restored the centre of political gravity to the south, and between 1338 and 1377 it always met at Westminster. It was expected to meet frequently, the pattern of Easter and Michaelmas parliaments established by Edward I being in some degree maintained into the 1330s but thereafter becoming more usually annual.[14] This frequency of assembly meant that, with rare exceptions, each parliament had only a single session, although its length could vary considerably. Some parliaments lasted less than a week, though ten days to two weeks was more typical; but the parliament that was in session during the deposition of Edward II lasted two months, that of

[13] Sayles, *King's Parliament*, gives a clear and erudite account of this formative period but should be read alongside other schools of thought represented in Fryde and Miller, I.

[14] Edwards, *Second Century of Parliament*, pp. 4–7. The first statute prescribing annual parliaments was made in 1330, following a petition from the citizens of London in 1327; see Edwards, ' "Justice" ', in Fryde and Miller, I, pp. 290–1.

March 1340 six weeks, and the Good Parliament of 1376 eleven weeks: all these were crisis parliaments.

Writs of summons had to be sent out at least forty days in advance. Under Edward I individual writs were sent to prelates, earls, *barones* and councillors on an *ad hoc* basis and numbers varied between the thirties and eighties.[15] By early in Edward III's reign the idea of a parliamentary peerage which excluded the judges and officials emerged, and the numbers summoned were in consequence smaller.[16] How many came is another matter, for although attendance was obligatory there were occasions on which so many lords were negligent or dilatory that business had to be deferred or parliament even prorogued.[17] The writ to the sheriff summoning two representatives from each of the thirty-seven shires allowed no such backsliding; he was firmly ordered to make them come and took pledges to ensure that they did. There was less consistency about borough representation: the sheriffs chose the boroughs to which they sent writs, and our knowledge of who attended is in any case incomplete. The highest recorded attendance under Edward III was of 174 burgesses in the parliament of 1362, although the *Anonimalle Chronicle* claims that there were 280 knights and burgesses in 1376. The importance of the proctors of the lower clergy, present in earlier parliaments in large numbers, declined as a result of the firm separation of convocation from parliament after 1340.

Parliament assembled in plenary session to hear a sermon followed by the declaration of the causes of summons and was 'charged' by the chancellor (or other royal emissary) to discuss certain matters. A day was appointed for individual petitions to be presented, and panels of receivers and auditors were named to deal with them. For the work of deliberation parliament divided into groups, barons, clergy, knights and burgesses sometimes meeting separately or in changing combinations in the earlier parliaments but gradually consolidating into two houses during the 1330s.[18] On particular matters delegations from one house would visit the other and policy was sometimes decided in a small joint committee meeting in a separate room, often the chamber-

---

[15] Powell and Wallis, *Lords*, chs. 13, 18.

[16] To the parliament of 1305 were summoned ninety-five prelates, nine earls and ninety-four barons; to that of 1341, fifty-one prelates, eight earls and forty-five barons; to that of 1377, forty-six prelates, thirteen earls and forty-seven barons.

[17] Roskell, 'Attendance of the lords'.

[18] In the parliament of 1332–3 magnates and prelates are recorded as deliberating separately from the knights, and in 1339 the two houses were 'charged' separately, deliberated apart, and gave different replies; *Rot. Parl.*, II. pp. 67, 103–4.

lain's chamber, but how normal a procedure this was is difficult to say.[19] The commons usually delivered their replies on the matters referred to them through a small deputation—possibly a dozen in number—which came before the lords. The commons might also wish to communicate direct with the king or council, and did so usually through a royal officer or household knight nominated for this purpose.[20] The only record of how the commons proceeded in their own assembly comes in an unofficial report of the proceedings in the Good Parliament of 1376. There we see how the chancellor's charge to parliament—to grant a tax and consider the ills of the realm—became the theme of a succession of speakers in the chapter house who delivered their views from the central lectern.[21] We are not told how different opinions were reconciled or, if unreconciled, how the view of the majority was established. The house was probably led by a few members whose oratory, experience, personality and connections invested them with a natural authority.

In 1376 the capable summing-up by one knight, Sir Peter de la Mare, served to consolidate opinion for a reply to the lords. The choice of de la Mare to speak for the commons before the lords in 1376 formalised an office which thenceforward had a continuous history. The speaker needed the capacity to present accurately and diplomatically the commons' replies and to maintain their position under pressure.[22]

While the commons were deliberating on the king's business the auditors of petitions were dealing with the 'singular' petitions and the council (among its other business) with the 'common' petition.[23] The work of answering the former might not infrequently continue after the commons had departed—though this was an inconvenience much complained of—but the answers to the common petition were usually delivered in the final session when their tax grant was also formally presented and accepted by the king, both being entered on the roll of parliament. The first clerk of the council to compile a roll of proceedings was Gilbert de Rothbury, for the Easter Parliament of 1290, and from that date rolls of pleadings before the council, responses to

---

[19] Edwards, *Commons*, and *Second Century of Parliament*, p. 11; W. N. Bryant, 'Some earlier examples of intercommuning in parliament', *EHR*, LXXXV (1970), pp. 54–8.
[20] Roskell, *Speakers*, p. 8.
[21] *Anonimalle*, p. 80.
[22] Roskell, *Speakers*, pp. 11–13.
[23] Edwards, *Second Century of Parliament*, pp. 44–55.

petitions, memoranda of *acta*, and in 1316–18 and 1330–3 narratives of proceedings (the work of particular clerks, William Ayrmine and Henry Edinstowe) bear witness to the emergence of parliament as a continuing institution. From 1339 a parliament roll was made up as a matter of routine and from 1341 it records the appointment, each session, of a clerk of parliament.[24]

The business of parliament

The *Modus Tenendi Parliamentum*, a technical if partisan treatise on procedure (*c.* 1321), classifies the business of parliament in order of importance: first, war and whatever touched the king and royal family; second, such common business of the realm as judgements and legislation; and third, the business of private members.

(a) *The king's business: war, the rights of the crown, taxation.* The Ordinances of 1311 had prescribed parliament as the place where the king was to secure the assent of the baronage for war and where the chief officers of state, household and judiciary were to be appointed. These requirements were designed to trammel the king and were so used by Thomas of Lancaster in the following decade. But in the thirty years 1330–60 when crown and nobility bent their energies to the prosecution of a largely successful war, co-operation and consultation became normal and were perforce soon extended to the commons, who were financing and participating in the enterprise.[25] If in his first parliaments Edward III sought advice solely from the magnates about his French claims, the affairs of Ireland and the question of a crusade, in the parliament of 1332–3 the problem of what response should be made to Balliol's assumption of the Scottish crown was discussed by each estate of parliament separately, although a common answer was given.[26] Undoubtedly Edward secured the assent of lords and commons for war in 1337 and specifically asked for the voice of the commons on peace negotiations in 1343, 1348 and 1354 and subsequently for the

[24] Sayles, *King's Parliament*, p. 82; Plucknett, 'Parliament', pp. 91–2; Richardson and Sayles, 'King's ministers in parliament', *EHR*, XLVII (1932), pp. 194–5, 377–8.
[25] M. R. Powicke, *Military Obligation in Medieval England* (Oxford, 1962), pp. 232–41.
[26] *Rot. Parl.*, II, 60–1, 64–7. Edward II sought advice from the magnates about performing homage to the king of France in 1324; *Vita Edwardi Secundi*, ed. N. Denholm-Young, pp. 138–9.

renewal of the war, while their support was fostered by reports on military operations and negotiations which were read out in parliament.[27] Moreover, although the commons might protest their simplicity in military matters in 1348, during the king's absence parliament could itself assume authority for organising arrays to defend the border, for the guard of the sea, and even for expeditions to France.[28] If in these ways Edward sought to associate the realm through parliament with his military aims, for advice concerning the rights of the crown—as in negotiations for a treaty with Scotland in 1360—he turned to the lords alone.[29] But parliament could usefully attest the support of the realm in resistance to papal claims: in 1275 Edward I had referred the papal demand for tribute 'to the careful deliberation of the magnates in parliament', while in 1365 Edward III repudiated it with the support of the commons.[30] In domestic policy the voice of both lords and commons was sought for the establishment of the staple at Calais in 1362, on sumptuary legislation in 1363, on the money supply frequently between 1340 and 1351, on the position of alien merchants in 1343, and in practically every parliament from 1339 to 1362 on the problem of law and order.[31]

The business most commonly brought to parliament by the king and which most directly involved the commons was taxation.[32] Taxation was demanded by the crown in terms of the Romano-canonical doctrine of *necessitas*, by which all subjects were obliged to contribute when the welfare or existence of the realm was endangered. Such occasions of dire need were envisaged as exceptional and it was the ruler's duty to identify and proclaim them, although the community as a whole had to recognise and assent to his plea, since 'what touched all should be approved by all'. These principles were reflected in the procedures of parliament, where the chancellor's speech detailed, often graphically, the danger to the realm which the commons were then charged to consider and provide for.

Under Henry III the *magnum consilium* of the magnates had with-

[27] E. B. Fryde, 'Parliament and the French war, 1336–40', in Fryde and Miller, I, pp. 242–3; *Rot. Parl.*, II, pp. 118, 136, 147, 158, 200, 262, 265.
[28] *Rot. Parl.*, II, pp. 105, 108–10, 115, 119, 158–9, 165.
[29] *Ibid.*, pp. 269, 295.
[30] W. A. Pantin, *The English Church in the Fourteenth Century* (Cambridge, 1955), pp. 81–7.
[31] *Rot. Parl.*, II, pp. 269 (staple); 280 (sumptuary); 113, 137, 158, 225 (money); 137–8 (aliens); 103, 117, 136, 158, 165, 200, 225, 237 (law and order).
[32] For the following section see my *King, Parliament and Public Finance*.

held taxation, claiming to adjudicate the king's plea of necessity on behalf of the community of the realm. To diminish their power, and because the lay subsidy was levied on a national and not a feudal basis, Edward I insisted that it should also be granted by representatives invested by their communities with full powers to bind them to pay. Taxation now became a recurrent feature of parliament, fourteen grants being made for the Scottish war between 1297 and 1337, so that when Edward III opened the war with France he could rely on regular taxation for as long as the common danger endured. Although this was an undoubted strength to the crown it did involve it more deeply in political dialogue with its subjects. The requirement that taxation should be for the common profit made it the natural vehicle for criticism of oppressive or unjust government, particularly fiscal or military impositions. Complaint about these was recurrent in the common petitions of the middle decades of the fourteenth century, and the fact that the king had to justify his demand for taxation on each occasion induced him to heed such grievances. This did not mean that the commons were able to impose conditions or require redress as the price of a tax, for they were obliged to grant the tax to meet the emergency, whereas the king did right to his subjects as a matter of grace. It did enable the commons to resist extensions of the king's fiscal prerogatives and in practice they bargained not unsuccessfully for their rights. But only in exceptional crises did the commons use consent to taxation to force political concessions from the crown, and then always with some backing from the magnates. Moreover such concessions could be (and for the most part were) revoked by the king as contrary to the estate of the crown. The commons' right of assent to taxation was not, therefore, an effective weapon in a power struggle with the crown. Neither by intention nor by capacity were the commons or parliament as a whole fitted for such a struggle. Indeed, the story of taxation under Edward III is rather one of king and lords uniting to press the commons to grant supply for a war on which they were united, and of the commons' attempts to safeguard their rights and limit their commitments.

There was, however, one area of prolonged dispute between the crown and the commons, that of indirect or mercantile taxation.[33]

[33] The following paragraph summarises ch. 18 of my book, but see too the most recent discussion of Edward III's exploitation of the wool trade by T. H. Lloyd, *The English Wool Trade in the Middle Ages* (Cambridge, 1977), ch. 5.

Temporary increases in the customs had at times been granted by assemblies of merchants to meet emergencies before 1337, but in that year Edward III initiated an elaborate scheme to exploit the wool trade on a potentially more profitable and more permanent basis. Having placed an embargo on the export of wool, he contracted with certain merchants to invest them with a monopoly of its purchase and export in return for massive loans which would be repaid by raising the custom to 40s per sack (the *maltolt*) and by an anticipated rise in the price to purchasers in the Low Countries. Financially the scheme disappointed expectations and politically it provoked jealousy and distrust against the narrow group of major financiers upon whom the king was increasingly forced to rely. In 1340, as part of their attack on these merchants, the commons voiced their opposition to the king's continued levy of the *maltolt* while agreeing to renew the grant of it for a period limited to the present emergency. As, over the following decade, the crown pursued other schemes with various groups of merchants, large or narrow, so the commons repeatedly challenged the grant of the *maltolt* by merchants while asserting their own exclusive right to grant it for an acknowledged emergency of the realm. Divisions between the greater and lesser merchants and the tendency for any monopoly to depress prices to the wool growers strengthened the claim of parliament to speak for the common profit against the 'singular profit' which the 'king's merchants' derived from their monopoly. By the 1350s, as the war effort slackened and a succession of 'companies' of 'king's merchants' proved unable to sustain the royal demands, Edward accepted that the wool trade could best be exploited if it was free from royal intervention and charged with a high permanent tax authorised by parliament. Thus the wool subsidy came to be repeatedly renewed by parliament for the maintenance of defence and safeguard of trade, leaving direct taxation to be sought only for particular emergencies. It was a pattern of taxation that remained basically unchanged for the following 250 years.

(b) *The common business of the realm: justice, legislation.* Although it was for 'diverse great matters touching the government and safety of the realm'[34] that the king summoned parliament, it was also the place where his relations with the nobility and lesser subjects might

[34] *Rot. Parl.*, II, p. 146.

fittingly be regulated. Such work was largely judicial in character, though with a strong political flavour. Under Edward I and II disputes between the crown and magnates had been settled in parliament and sealed by the solemn confirmation of the charters, and not surprisingly the author of the *Modus* saw this as one of parliament's main functions. It was to this tradition that Archbishop Stratford was to appeal in his quarrel with Edward III. A parallel development made it the place for state trials. David ap Gruffyd in 1283 and Nicholas de Segrave in 1305 were adjudged by the king on the advice of the lords, and the king's record read before the lords in parliament convicted Roger Mortimer in 1330 and Chief Justice Thorpe in 1351. In 1321 parliament was used by the baronage to exile the Despensers convicted of accroaching the royal power, and some held that it should therefore have approved their recall. But in 1341 Edward III agreed that no peer should be put to judgement at the suit of the king except before his peers in parliament, and in 1352 the statute of treasons invalidated judgement on the king's record alone.[35] Parliament became the proper place for state trials of any kind and correspondingly the place where the heirs of those convicted sought reversal of judgement.[36] Disputes between lords which threatened the peace were also, as the author of the *Modus* noted, appropriately judged in parliament, and even at the height of the Despensers' power their victims hopefully brought their quarrels to parliament. Armed attendance at parliament was forbidden, but in 1331 one such quarrel between lords Zouche and Grey erupted into fighting within parliament itself.[37]

The Ordinances of 1311 gave currency to the view that parliament was the place where complaints against royal officials could be presented, since they could not be sued at common law for their official acts. Edward I had afforded some statutory protection against the illegal acts of sheriffs, escheators, bailiffs and purveyors, and petitions against these and the greater ministers of the crown, like the chancellor and treasurer, were delivered into the parliaments of the early fourteenth

---

[35] Bellamy, *Treason*, pp. 25, 55, 89; Plucknett, 'Parliament', p. 109; *Rot. Parl.*, II, pp. 52, 227; N. M. Fryde, *The Tyranny and Fall of Edward II* (Cambridge, 1979), pp. 52, 58.

[36] For the petitions of Richard, earl of Arundel between 1330 and 1354 see *Rot. Parl.*, II, pp. 33, 55, 224–7, 256–7; of Roger Mortimer in 1354, *ibid.*, pp. 255–6, 267; of Sir John Maltravers in 1352, *ibid.*, p. 173.

[37] *Modus*, cap XVII; N. M. Fryde, *Edward II*, pp. 44–5, 110; Powell and Wallis, *Lords*, pp. 319–21; and for other private disputes arbitrated in parliament, see *Rot. Parl.*, II, pp. 62, 267, 290.

century.[38] Following a petition in 1327, proclamation was made in 1330 that all who wished to complain of wrongs done by royal officials, councillors and other magnates should come to the next parliament.[39] The tradition of the Ordinances was reaffirmed in 1340 when, on the commons' petition, the council was empowered to judge and convict any minister of the crown at the suit of either the king or the subject. After the crisis Edward reasserted his right to judge and punish his officers, but parliament remained the place where complaint and, sometimes, judgement were delivered.[40] But in general parliament's judicial function declined from the days of *Fleta* and the Ordinances. The correction of error and the adjudication of difficult cases referred from lower courts which had then been prominent features of its work grew less common as parliaments became less frequent, as the magnate overshadowed the official element, and as the departments of state developed their own judicial expertise. It was to the council, meeting in or out of parliament, that other courts referred a wide range of cases in which the king's rights were involved, whether as supreme feudal lord, or through a point of law, or through the action of his officials.

A contrast is frequently drawn between the character of legislation under Edward I and Edward III. The former encompassed fundamental reforms in land, family, commercial and ecclesiastical law, and introduced the concept that law was embodied in written statutes. These were expertly drafted by the council, and owed their authority to their promulgation by the king, their use by the judges and their incorporation into the statute roll. By 1377, in contrast, all statutes required the assent of full parliament and most legislation was based on petitions from the commons and was the answer to immediate complaint, whether transient or recurrent. It was liable to be ill framed and diffuse, and was intended less to make permanent changes or reshape legal principles than to head off discontent; there may even have been no intention to enforce it. Such a comparison may be overdrawn. The great statutes of Edward I's reign were not a conscious programme of social engineering or tenurial reform so much as the answer to problems

---

[38] Ehrlich, *Proceedings against the Crown*, pp. 111, 153, 186. And see below, pp. 64–7.

[39] *Rot. Parl. Hactenus Ined.*, p. 134; *Rot. Parl.*, II, p. 443 (no. 93).

[40] Harriss, *King, Parliament and Public Finance*, pp. 262, 300–1.

revealed in difficult cases in council and the voluminous complaints before the justices in eyre.[41]

The change, in fact, began in the last decade of Edward I's reign, when legislation, annexed to the charters of liberties, was the response to abuses of government demonstrated by the magnates on behalf of the community of the realm. If the mistrust engendered by Edward I's duplicity over his concessions begot the promise required from his son—'Sire, do you grant to be held and safeguarded the laws and rightful customs which the community of the realm shall have chosen?'[42] —the reign of Edward II marked little advance in legislative practice. In 1309 a petition of eleven articles for the first time formed the basis of a statute—that of Stamford, which reaffirmed *Articuli super Cartas* and regulated the taking of purveyance—but thereafter the baronial dominance of parliament was largely unproductive of legislation. The recovery of the royal initiative in legislation in 1322 is demonstrated by the chance survival of the 'agenda' for parliament which the king submitted to the council. Measures for the preservation of the peace, sumptuary legislation, control of weights and measures, the repeal of the obnoxious Ordinances, and the regulation of the staple were envisaged, and many of them were given effect in a long and comprehensive statute.[43] In the following decades there emerged the common petition which sought redress and reform for a variety of abuses, many of which sprang from the strains of war. But it was not until the less tense and urgent atmosphere of the 1350s that such petitions began to have a direct impact on legislation. It has been shown that in 1352 a common petition containing forty-two articles gave rise to twenty-three articles of a statute, that in 1354 a petition of forty-one articles resulted in a statute of fifteen articles and that in 1362 a petition of twenty-four articles produced thirteen articles of a statute.[44] The common petition could thus exercise a powerful influence on law-making, and at its most direct the simple affirmative answer could be enough to transmute the petition almost verbatim into statute. But for the most part petition

[41] Cam, *Law-finders and Law-makers*, pp. 143–5, and in general T. F. T. Plucknett, *Statutes and their Interpretation in the First Half of the Fourteenth Century* (Cambridge, 1922) and Richardson and Sayles, 'Early statutes'.

[42] For a review of the interpretations of this oath see Wilkinson, *Constitutional History*, II, pp. 86–107.

[43] J. C. Davies, *Baronial Opposition to Edward II*, pp. 492–3, 582–3; Tout, *Chapters*, II, pp. 210–11.

[44] Rayner, ' "Commune petition" '; Gray, *Influence of the Commons*, p. 226.

and answer merely identified and acknowledged the abuse; the council with its professional judges, as under Edward I, drafted the statute and had wide discretion in amending the petition. Furthermore much legislation arose, as in the past, from difficult cases in the courts, administrative anomalies and royal initiatives in domestic and foreign policy.

It is instructive to examine the making of four of the major statutes of Edward III enacted in 1351–3.[45] The Statute of Labourers originated in an ordinance issued by the council in 1349. When parliament met in 1351 the commons petitioned for its enforcement, alleging that it had been ineffective. There followed long discussions between lords and commons in joint committee, and the resultant statute was carefully and expertly drafted probably under the guidance of Chief Justice Shareshull. The Statute of Provisors purported to meet the protests against papal provisions which had recurred in common petitions from 1327 to 1347, but the king had already taken effective measures to prohibit whatever provisions he disliked and the statute was simply a means of bringing pressure on Rome for an immediate diplomatic issue. The statute which abolished the Bruges staple in favour of home staples in 1354 originated in an ordinance of the previous year issued by the great council after consultation with the merchants. Representatives of the shires had been present at the council and had given their assent, since it was a policy they had long favoured and which coincided with the present interests of king, merchants and wool growers. In parliament they specifically asked for it to be enacted 'to endure for ever as a statute'. Finally, in 1348 and 1352 the commons complained that the judges were adjudging as treason or accroachment of the royal power crimes which had never been held as such before: that these mainly concerned cases of riot or resistance to royal authority suggests that this was in part a drive against lawlessness but was also linked to fiscal exploitation of prerogative and judicial rights. A strict definition of treason was also of importance to lords not merely because they stood to lose escheats but because uncertainty still persisted about the crown's ability to convict by record. The statute, essentially made by the king, lords and judges, carefully distinguished between high and petty treason, restricting the former to crimes against the

---

[45] Cam, *Law-finders and Law-makers*, pp. 138–42; T. H. Lloyd, *Wool Trade*, pp. 205–7; W. A. Pantin, *English Church in the Fourteenth Century*, pp. 65–6; C. Davies, 'The Statute of Provisors of 1351', *History*, XXXVIII (1953), pp. 116–33; Bellamy, *Treason*, ch. 4.

king's person and regality and providing for doubtful cases to be resolved in parliament by the king and lords. All these statutes were expertly drafted and dealt with critical problems in which the interests of all estates converged. Two of the four (Treason and Provisors) were in some sense the fruit of petitions, while Labourers and the Staple originated as council ordinances. Yet it was the latter that more immediately touched the interests of the commons, and in the framing of these two they were apparently more directly involved.

It has been claimed that the statutes of the early 1350s comprised 'a more vital and more far reaching code than any in the past since Edward I or any in the future until the sixteenth century',[46] but the legislation of the whole reign is impressive in its diversity, continuity and growing authority. In every decade statutes defined the duties of local royal officers, reformed legal abuses and procedures, regulated trade in wool, wine and fish, dealt with the status of alien mechants, prescribed weights and measures and monetary policy, and intervened on a variety of ecclesiastical matters.[47] While the repetitive character of some of this legislation (and the petitions it answered) suggests that the statutes were imperfectly enforced, this hardly detracts from its significance for the growth of parliament. By dealing with the everyday concerns of trade, property, family, law and order parliament established itself as the meeting place of the interests of crown and community, and reference to it implied an acceptance of its authority. Already in 1318 the council replied to a plaintiff that to change the laws of the realm required the greatest deliberation, and that in full parliament, and by the middle of the century the authority of statute to change the law was formally acknowledged. In 1377 the king agreed that statutes made in parliament should not be annulled except in parliament and by common assent.[48] By that date, too, the assent of the commons had become an integral part of the making of statutes, and Chief Justice Thorpe could claim that an act of parliament was binding on everyone immediately it had been made, without the necessity of proclamation, 'because parliament represents the body of all the realm'. Thus the legislative supremacy of parliament was being

---

[46] B. H. Putnam, *Sir William Shareshull*, p. 52.

[47] For an analysis of the legislation of the first decade of the reign see Plucknett, 'Parliament', pp. 117–23.

[48] Cam, *Law-finders and Law-makers*, p. 135; *Rot. Parl.*, II, pp. 203, 311 (no. 2), 368 (no. xxvii).

fashioned from a recognition of statute as the supreme form of law-making and recognition of the unique authority of parliament to render the assent of the community of the realm.[49]

The business of the king and realm, which took pre-eminence in parliament, was this of a diverse and fluctuating kind. Decisions about war or diplomacy, the granting of taxation and the organisation of war, the maintenance of order, political trials, the answerability of ministers, conflicts between the rights of crown and subjects, legislation covering many fields, all these involved the interests of the crown, but very little did not also involve those of the political community. Indeed, while much was brought to parliament by the king and his ministers, much was also referred to it by subjects. Although ranked by the *Modus* as private or individual business, petitioning was soon to emerge as the foremost means by which the political community made its voice heard on matters of common concern.

(c) *Private business: petitions.* The mass of petitions presented in the parliaments of Edward I—there were some 500 in that of 1305—were for the satisfaction of private grievances and favours, not for legislation. They came from a wide range of persons, and concerned very diverse matters; while the work of the auditors who answered them or referred them to other courts or the council can properly be regarded as judicial, it gave parliament the character of 'a court of first instance for a lot of petty administrative questions'.[50] Parliament long continued to be the venue for such petitions. In the middle decades of the fourteenth century it was used by members of the higher nobility to press claims to lands, franchises and money; by shire and borough communities to challenge the exchequer's fiscal claims upon them; by members of the gentry to seek redress from intimidation, maintenance or other mis-carriage of justice; even by free-tenants and villeins against the exercise of lordship. But this aspect of parliament's work declined, partly as a result of opportunities for presenting such petitions elsewhere—to the chancellor or in the king's bench—but mainly in consequence of the changing character of parliament itself. As in the 1330s parliaments became less frequent, more preoccupied with war, finance and politics,

---

[49] For the commons as assentors see *Rot. Parl.*, II, 368 (no. xxix); Chrimes, *Eng. Const. Ideas*, pp. 101, 157, and for Thorpe's statement, *ibid.*, p. 352.

[50] Maitland, 'Memoranda de Parliamento', in Fryde and Miller, I, pp. 107–24; Sayles, *King's Parliament*, pp. 78–82.

and as the commons acquired a corporate identity and purpose, such private or 'singular' petitions began to appear peripheral to these activities. They found no place on the emerging parliament roll and after 1349 their numbers speedily declined.

Correspondingly there emerged, in the early fourteenth century, the community or common petition—*commune petition*—composed of a series of itemised complaints in the form of an indented bill attested by the commons. These, as we have seen, formed the basis of the remedies provided by legislation. The models for the common petition were the articles of grievances presented by the magnates and clergy under Edward I and II. Those from the magnates claimed to be on behalf of the whole community and were designed to secure redress and retribution for royal misrule. There can be little doubt that such had the active backing of the commons, for those of 1301 were presented by a knight, Henry Keighley, and those of 1300, 1301 and 1309 were linked to grants of taxation made under strict conditions. Moreover some grievances of particular concern to the commons were included in the petitions of 1309 and 1325. The longer and more political list of complaints in 1327 was paralleled by petitions from the clergy and the citizens of London. By 1330 the responsibility of the knights of the shires for presenting the grievances of their communities is recognised in the writs ordering their election, and the petitions of the following decade, in 1333, 1334, and 1339, predominantly reflect the concerns of the non-baronial classes and seek redress from administrative abuses and royal levies not by restraints on royal power but simply as a matter of grace. At the same time the common petition was achieving its definitive form, and after 1340 the petitions and answers were enrolled as a matter of course.[51]

We may glance briefly at three of the commons' main concerns: their protest against war burdens, their interest in local government, especially law and order, and their reaction to the regulation of trade. Complaint against purveyance was directed mainly against the widespread levies of war supplies and against failure to pay for what had been taken. Non-payment was seen as a form of taxation, and the commons tried to assert the principle of assent for other than domestic purveyance. This the king would never agree to, though he conceded severe penalties against abuses, which were eventually consolidated

[51] Rayner, ' "Commune petition" '; Gray, *Influence of the Commons*, ch. 8; Harriss, *King, Parliament and Public Finance*, ch. 5.

into the statute of 1362. Equally prolonged contention followed the crown's attempt to extend the military obligations of communities for local defence to the borders of the realm or even to service overseas. On this the crown had by 1344 compromised with the offer of wages, but attempts to levy a composition for military service on middling landowners encountered strong resistance under each of the Edwards as being a form of taxation, and were abandoned after 1348. In respect of these war burdens the commons' success had been to define them as extensions of the prerogative and force the crown to abandon such levies or make them acceptable by payment.[52]

The settlement of such issues after 1350 reflected the easing of the war effort and the solidarity among the land-owning classes induced by the Black Death. The leading families of the shire now came to be invested with greater control of local government. For two decades before 1350 complaint had been made of abuses in law enforcement: of maintenance by lords and their retaining of royal justices; of the partiality of *oyer* and *terminer* commissions; and of the ready issue of pardons to criminals and outlaws. The commons had urged that local gentry be given judicial powers to enforce the keeping of the peace, 'since those who live in the shires are better and more often able to punish felons and trespassers with greater advantage and less grievance to the people than outside justices'. Effectively after 1350 and formally by 1361 the gentry began their role as justices of the peace. The commons' concern with law and order was met by stringent royal proclamations and the introduction of the power to arrest malefactors on suspicion. Whether such legislation and the inclusion of the gentry in the peace commission brought any improvement in the shires awaits investigation.[53]

In commercial matters the wool producers, the middle and great merchants, the crown, and the foreign merchant-bankers were all involved in the net of royal finance and war policy, and merchant assemblies as well as parliament were the forum for these interests. But

[52] Harriss, *King, Parliament and Public Finance*, pp. 376–400.

[53] *Rot. Parl.*, II, pp. 131, 136, 165, 174, 202; Putnam, 'Transformation of keepers of the peace', pp. 19–48; J. G. Bellamy, *Crime and Public Order in England in the later Middle Ages* (London, 1973), pp. 94–5; J. R. Maddicott, *Law and Lordship: Royal Justices as Retainers* (*Past and Present* supplement, IV, 1978), pp. 42–3; R. W. Kaeuper, 'Law and order in fourteenth-century England', *Speculum*, LIV (1979), pp. 734–84. The prevalence of banditry in 1290–1340 appears to have declined during the middle years of the century, although the French wars and plague may have contributed more than government action.

parliament's unique authority to speak for the whole community made the common petition an appropriate means for lesser merchants and growers to influence or protest against royal policy. Thus when the export of silver for war subsidies or through trade embargoes and wool monopolies produced a critical shortage of coin in the decade after 1338 it provoked petitions for bullion legislation, even if this restricted trade and the ability to export.[54] Conflicting interests were also reflected in a series of expedients from 1313 to 1353 for settling the staple in England, or abroad at Bruges, Saint-Omer or Antwerp, and in vacillations between free trade, narrow monopolies and broad-based companies. That there finally emerged in 1362–3 a stable solution regulating the wool trade on the basis of a Company of the Staple at Calais, established by parliamentary statute, was in some measure a recognition that parliament was the proper place for reconciling diverse interests in the national wealth.[55]

Wide-ranging as was the substance of the common petitions and the legislation upon them, they never attempted to prescribe royal policy and had no means of persuading the king to a course of action against his will. Yet by presenting a perpetual critique of royal policy they defined the limits beyond which it would go at its peril, just as they fortified royal government by their assent. Repeated protest by the commons and reiterated remedies from the crown were a ritual designed to deflect a confrontation between royal prerogative and the welfare of the community. No English king in the thirteenth and fourteenth centuries entirely avoided such a confrontation, whether from over-government or misgovernment; but Edward III was the first for whom it centred on parliament and embraced the whole land-owning class.

Parliament in political crises

The role of parliament in political conflicts has been variously interpreted. 'Whig' historians have identified opposition to the crown with the cause of liberty and parliamentary democracy and have seen the commons as challenging the prerogative in the name of the representa-

[54] *Rot. Parl.*, II, pp. 105, 196, 202; Lloyd, *Wool Trade*, pp. 183–5, 196–8, and his article 'Overseas trade and English money supply in the fourteenth century' in *Edwardian Monetary Affairs*, ed. N. J. Mayhew (British Arch. Reps., XXXVI, 1977), pp. 109 ff.
[55] Lloyd, *Wool Trade*, ch. 6; E. Power, *The Medieval English Wool Trade* (Oxford, 1941), ch. 5.

tive principle. At the opposite pole are those who have stressed the curial nature of the medieval parliament, seen it as peripheral to the main current of politics, and allowed little political significance to the representative character of the commons, many of whom were dependents of the lords. More recently historians have argued that parliament's survival depended upon its becoming a participant in royal government, and have viewed its opposition to the crown as sterile and obstructive. The promise held out for it by Edward I's initiative was frustrated when the magnates made parliament the instrument of opposition to his son and set it upon a course not reversed until late in the fifteenth century. The late medieval parliament, it has been claimed, 'was in no condition to be any such participant, because it was treated as a restraint, a check, fundamentally an opposition to the crown'.[56] Thus, whereas for Stubbs the political conflicts of the middle ages were milestones in the march of the constitution, they are now taken to mark the points where parliament was diverted from its true purpose and its development stultified. Yet if we set aside our views of what parliament ought to have been or done, we can perceive that the responsiveness of an emergent institution to diverse and often contradictory political currents was the measure of its political vitality and the condition of its growth. Nor should we assume that parliament's opposition was necessarily negative, aimed at frustrating the purposes of the crown and limiting its powers.

From the early years of its growth parliament had the dual charcter of an organ of royal government and the instrument through which the magnates might place constraints upon the king. These apparently conflicting roles were in fact complementary aspects of its essential purpose, to further the business and common good of the realm. The Ordainers of 1311, looking back to the tradition of 1258, prescribed certain business which was to be performed only in parliament. There the king was to secure the assent of the baronage for war (cap. 9), the chief ministers of state, household, and judiciary were to be appointed (cap. 14), grants of royal lands were to be adjudicated (cap. 7), and cases delayed at law or in dispute between judges were to be settled and bills of complaint could be brought against royal officials (caps. 29, 40).

---

[56] G. R. Elton, ' "The body of the whole realm" : parliament and representation in medieval and Tudor England', in *Studies in Tudor and Stuart Politics and Government*, II (Cambridge, 1974), pp. 30–2, although this verdict may be thought to be considerably modified by his remarks on parliament as a working institution on pp. 48–50.

Of these functions, war was to become a matter of habitual consultation, while legal review became less common; the remainder featured in every major dispute with the crown during the following century and were often subsumed in the demand for the appointment in parliament of a magnate council with certain powers of government. What gave this political role to parliament, rather than the council, was its large membership, its solemnity and its authority to judge and pronounce upon the common good. For the theme or pretext of opposition was that royal government had become oppressive or corrupt, and that retribution and redress should be exacted from royal ministers and safeguards established for honest and economical administration. These were not the only motives for baronial restraints upon the crown, for attacks upon the king's 'evil counsellors' were necessarily factional and self-interested; but neither was the appeal to the common good and the wider political community mere window-dressing. Historically, and in virtue of their political influence, the magnates held the responsibility and power to bridle the king, but their sole justification for doing so was patent misgovernment, to which the commons attested in their historic role of petitioners and complainers. And the complaints of the commons could be real enough. Parliamentary opposition was not merely baronial, nor was it designed to secure long-term changes in the balance of power. It was occasional and corrective, the intention being to restore royal government, not to abrogate it.

The myth of the baronial council as a cure for misgovernment figured briefly in the revolutions of 1327 and 1330, to be allayed by Edward III's promise to rule with wise counsel, but the larger programme of the Ordainers was resurrected in 1340 and echoes of it were still present in 1376. The crisis of 1340–1 had two aspects: it was a widespread protest against the burdens of war taxation and the privileges which the king's merchants were thought to be exploiting for their own profit, and at the same time it was a factional struggle between the magnates and churchmen grouped around Archbishop Stratford in England, and the king's councillors and companions in Brabant. Although, as the crisis grew, the commons' interests became subordinated to those of the magnates, at the outset, by making their own offer of taxation dependent on reforms detailed in their common petition, they revealed an unprecedented unity, initiative and political vision. They demanded a permanent council of magnates, to be chosen in parliament and answerable to it, which should manage all the great business of the

kingdom, ensure that taxation was wisely spent, appoint officials, investigate and punish official misdemeanours—notably those relating to
royal finances—and act as a court of review for difficult and delayed
cases. Parliament itself was to conduct a resumption and adjudication
of royal grants.[57] This updated version of the programme of 1311 shows
that for the commons, if not for the magnates, the Lancastrian tradition
still held a powerful appeal. It was a spectre to alarm the king, and
the financial and political pressure brought to bear on Edward in this
parliament forced him to invest Stratford and the home council with
vice-regal powers to govern the realm in the king's absence. When, at
the end of the year, Edward returned to attack the archbishop, dismiss
the council and imprison ministers, it was upon the authority vested in
him by the 1340 settlement that Stratford based his defence and to a
hearing in full parliament that he appealed against the 'evil counsellors'
surrounding the king. In the parliament of 1341 it was the lords who
took the initiative in ensuring Stratford's presence and in securing the
king's assent to the principle of trial by peers. But it is clear that the
statute which Edward conceded reaffirming the liberties procured in
1340, the renewed order to bring the king's merchants to account, and
the demand for the council to be chosen by the magnates, were the
joint work of lords and commons. Only the last did the king resist; for
the rest it was a humiliating settlement which revealed how deeply
the conflicts of the first quarter of the century still guided the responses
of the magnates and the ever-widening circle of knights and landowners
who looked to them for guidance and centred their political interests
on parliament. For, in contrast to the crisis of 1311, the parliamentary
setting and the active engagement of the commons gave a new political
dimension to that of 1340–1. Nevertheless Edward's speedy emancipa-
tion from the restraints imposed upon him showed that neither the
magnates nor, ultimately, the commons desired to fetter the power of
the king if, as he now promised, 'it was not his intention to grieve or
oppress his subjects but to rule them by lenience and gentleness'.[58]
  For thirty years effective co-operation between the king and his lords

---

[57] See my article 'The commons' petitions of 1340', *EHR*, LXXXVIII (1963), pp.
635–54, where the case for the commons' authorship of the petition is stated, and
King, Parliament and Public Finance, chs. 10–13, for a discussion of the whole
crisis.
[58] *Rot. Parl.*, II, p. 140 (no. 32); *Statutes*, I, p. 297.

in war left the commons to defend their communities from the burdens of royal levies while themselves serving the crown in the responsibilities of war and local government, thereby gradually acquiring political experience and standing. But from 1369 there ensued a period of twenty years in which the strains of an inescapable but unsuccessful war, the lack of effective royal authority, divisions among the nobility, resentment against the court, and social and economic ills, again made parliament the setting for debate and conflict. By the end of 1373 the French offensive had robbed Edward III of nearly all his empire. This was not for want of fiscal and military efforts by the English. Parliament had granted more than four lay subsidies, renewed the wool tax at a higher rate, and introduced tunnage and poundage for defence, but the expeditions had been either ineffectual or disastrous. Frustration with inept clerical ministers and demands that the church should bear a heavier burden of taxation erupted in 1371 and were not resisted by Edward, for such anti-clericalism attuned with his own resentments against the papacy. In the years following, as the king became enfeebled, the Black Prince an invalid, and John of Gaunt for much of the time an absentee, the court no longer gave political or chivalric leadership. Its principal officers, the chamberlain, Lord Latimer, and the steward, Lord Neville, acquired considerable influence, not so much over wider policy as over the distribution of favours and the authorisation of fiscal and commercial concessions. Their clientage spread beyond the household to embrace members of the London aldermanry (notably Richard Lyons), Italian merchants, and even the oligarchy of Great Yarmouth. Where these benefited others suffered, such as the merchants of the staple, who saw their trade through Calais decline, and the frustrated and outraged military nobility like the earl of March, Henry Percy and Sir Richard Scrope. Such men were linked by social, personal and professional ties with the knightly class, the leaders of the shire gentry, whose ear was attuned to the grievances of taxpayers, the difficulties of landlords and the forebodings of peasant unrest. In the shires there built up a reaction against the sale of offices, the perversion of justice and the spread of violence, all of which could be attributed to lack of authoritative government from the centre.

What precipitated the crisis was less any overt action by the court itself than the inept reversal of policy by which John of Gaunt attempted to extricate the crown from a losing war and secure a peace or long truce.[59] To obtain papal mediation for this meant complying with papal demands to tax the English church and relaxing the traditional hostility to papal provisions. To palliate the peace negotiations and strengthen the English position an expedition was sent to relieve the remaining fortresses of Bécherel and Saint-Sauveur (the absentee captain of which was Lord Latimer). Long delays robbed it of any value and set its commanders (notably the earl of March) at cross-purposes with Gaunt's negotiators at Bruges, who in the event obtained merely a year-long truce in return for the surrender of Saint-Sauveur. Thus the peace initiative was bungled, leaving military dishonour and subservience to the papacy as its only fruit. Further, with the expiry of the truce in 1376, England would face invasion from the reinforced French navy. Parliament therefore had to be summoned to provide a subsidy for defence, but when it met in April 1376 a further extension of the truce had removed the last restraint upon the search for scapegoats for the *débâcle* of the last five years.

That these became the courtiers was less because they were identified with these policies than because evidence of malfeasances had been collected against them and because they epitomised the court as a centre of intrigue, merchandising and self-enrichment rather than a companionship of chivalry and honour. The charge that they had 'accroached' the royal power for their own particular gains could well have been brought by the peers; it was in fact made by the commons because it was intrinsically linked with the crown's demand for taxation and the commons' refusal of it.[60] By their responsibility for granting taxation for the common profit the commons were uniquely placed to accuse the courtiers of impoverishing the kingdom by appropriating revenue to their own profit. Indeed, their denial of supply, tantamount to a vote of no confidence, depended on substantiating their allegation that if the courtiers had not misused royal revenue taxation would not have been needed. Here the testimony of the former treasurer, Sir Richard Scrope, was decisive and was greeted by a great clamour for the arrest of Latimer and Lyons. The commons could now resist royal pressure to proceed with the business of parliament until the king took action against his ministers and appointed a new council.[61] What

---

[59] For a full discussion of the policies of these years see Holmes, *The Good Parliament*.
[60] *Rot. Parl.*, II, p. 323.
[61] *Ibid.*; *Anonimalle*, pp. 80–4, 90–1.

finally secured this over the critical days 24–6 May was probably the pressure of other nobles on Gaunt and the laying of an appeal of treason for the surrender of Saint-Sauveur against Latimer's deputy, Thomas Catterton, with the possibility that it could be transferred to Latimer or even Gaunt himself.[62]

Indications of co-operation between a group of sympathetic lords and the commons had already been manifested when the commons requested certain lords to 'intercommune' with them at the beginning of parliament, and some of these lords now formed the new council. Latimer was formally arraigned, and his trial took place before the lords and in full parliament, with the king's permission but on the common accusation of the commons acting on behalf of the crown. The elements of the process of impeachment—complaint by the commons and judgement by the peers—had already been envisaged in 1340–1 as a means of bringing ministers to account, but it was the first occasion on which the commons as a body had preferred charges in parliament and seems to have been improvised when it appeared that neither the king nor the lords would prosecute.[63]

Two questions have commonly been asked about the Good Parliament: how independent were the actions of the commons, and how should we assess its results and significance? Undoubtedly the knights who presented the accusations depended on certain lords for political support and upon them and the merchants for evidence to substantiate their charges of corruption. But it is clear that in framing, presenting and persisting with the accusations the commons took the lead, and that but for them the attack on the court could hardly have been mounted, let alone have succeeded. Constitutionally their refusal of taxation was crucial, for it could only be justified and sustained by a formal verdict of misgovernment. In political terms the dissident nobility were by themselves no match for Gaunt and the court, while both bishops and merchants were incapable of leadership; by contrast the knights presented a steadfastly united front, and were not an isolated group with particular grievances but linked through personal and political ties with the nobility, shared a common membership of the lower house with the burgesses and, as representatives, responded

[62] J. G. Bellamy, 'Appeal and impeachment in the Good Parliament', *BIHR*, XXXIX (1966), pp. 35–46.
[63] T. F. T. Plucknett, 'The impeachment of 1376', *TRHS*, 5th ser., I (1951), pp. 153–64.

to the prejudices and concerns of the shires.[64] The last was important, for although at one level the impeachments were an attack on a curial clique by their disadvantaged rivals, at another they encapsulated the pent-up and puritanical reaction of shire gentry against vacillatory and corrupt central government. The common petition—the lengthiest submitted to any medieval parliament— attacked failings and abuses in all ranks of society. Its recurrent complaint was of the corruption of local government, and it demanded annual parliaments where in future the errors and defects of the realm could be corrected.[65]

In the autumn of 1376 Gaunt consciously undid the acts of the Good Parliament: Latimer and Neville were pardoned, the new council was superseded, and an exemplary revenge was taken on the earl of March, Bishop Wykeham and the speaker, de la Mare. But the slavishness of the parliament of January 1377 which accepted this without murmur should not be overstressed. For the government had reverted to its traditional anti-papalism and was prepared to tax the church; Gaunt's control of the court removed the opportunity for unworthy men to accroach royal power, and the greater nobility were mustering to meet the threat of invasion.[66] The commons' grant of a poll tax symbolised a restored, if reserved, confidence in government, a remaking of that unity of political society on which government and the state itself rested.[67]

What conclusions from these crises can we draw about the character and purpose of parliament's opposition to the crown? The background to each was unusual economic and social strain, the burden and danger that war had brought to the realm, and the widespread conviction of an abuse of power in the daily practice of government. Although this reflected criticism of the king, blame was primarily placed upon evil counsellors, the expulsion and punishment of whom was the principal demand both of those they had displaced and those who suffered misgovernment. This coalescing of faction and popular discontent presented a serious challenge to the king, who could recover his authority

[64] For the commons' oath of unity at the start of their debates see *Anonimalle*, p. 81; for their importance, the remarks of Gaunt's retainers cited in *Chron. Angliae*, p. 74.

[65] The petitions are summarised by Stubbs, *Const. Hist.*, II, pp. 453–5.

[66] See the chancellor's speech in *Rot. Parl.*, II, pp. 361–2; also *Chron. Angliae*, pp. 112, 130, and *Anonimalle*, p. 101.

[67] This was less than the government had asked and it was to be placed under special treasurers; *Rot. Parl.*, II, p. 364.

only by restoring unity among the magnates and detaching them from leadership of an opposition. The magnates, for their part, had to be reassured of the crown's good will, its abandonment of partisanship, and the repudiation of the worst aspects of misrule which had provoked their followers. In short, the simple and single aim of opposition was to recall those in authority to their rightful and traditional functions as the source and means of good government. Opposition was intended to teach an exemplary lesson, not to challenge the hierarchy or practice of government or to achieve a constitutional advance. Even control of the king through magnate council was the means to a solution—just and effective royal government—not a solution in itself. For it was misgovernment and evil counsellors that were commonly recognised as provoking the turbulence of the peasantry and mob, and it was these that—in both crises—the landlord class feared beyond all. In this sense the commons saw themselves as the voice and conscience of the whole community, and it was this aspect of parliament that the political crises reinforced. It was no accident that in the thirty years following the Good Parliament its activities are better recorded and more widely chronicled than at any time before the age of Elizabeth. For most of the late middle ages parliament remained the essential agent through which the crown sought the co-operation of the local communities for the government of the realm, but it was also becoming the acknowledged voice of the common weal. Its role was at all times co-operative, critical and corrective; rarely if at all obstructive and sterile. That was why it commanded attention and survived.

J. R. MADDICOTT

3

Parliament and the Constituencies, 1272–1377

BETWEEN 1272 AND 1377 English political life was transformed. In Henry III's reign the stuff of politics had been the relationship between crown and magnates and its central thread the baronial claim to share in the king's patronage and in the making of his policies. Although the baronage had become increasingly responsive to pressure from below, from gentry and townsmen upon whom economic change and the agents of royal government bore with increasing severity, that pressure had not yet taken institutional shape. The 'community of the realm' was represented by its magnates. But by the time of the Good Parliament in 1376 it was the parliamentary commons, and not the baronage, who had come to be regarded as defending the interests of town and country. Their consent was necessary for grants of taxation and their requests were normally given legislative substance by the crown as the price of that taxation. New law was created mainly in response to the commons' petitions and as a remedy for popular grievances, grievances which originated with a well informed and demanding public opinion in the shires.[1] Members of parliament assembled at Westminster had become both the collective voice for the needs of their local communities and, through their control of taxation, the means for satisfying the fiscal needs of the crown. They were bound to be looked on with some ambivalence by those whom they left at home.

[1] Maddicott, 'County community', pp. 27–43.

Little of this had been true in Edward I's early years. Of the fifteen parliaments which met between 1272 and 1280 only three (so far as we know) included representatives of the commons and only one, that of April 1275, granted a subsidy to the crown. From 1275 customs revenues and Italian credit made it possible to finance royal policies without resort to direct taxation, even during the emergency of the Welsh war in 1277–8. Legislation there was in plenty, but its initiation lay with king, council and judges rather than with parliament. In the 1270s parliament's importance to the king's subjects stemmed not from these activities but rather from the occasion which it offered for the redress of individual grievances through the presentation of petitions. It was the written petition making a complaint or asking a favour which linked parliament with local opinion and which ultimately became the vehicle for the views of the whole community. The early history of the relations between parliament and provincial England is essentially the history of the petition.

The petition to the crown had contemporary parallels in France and Spain, and English precedents in the 'bills' (the current word for petitions) presented to the king's justices in eyre under Henry III.[2] But it was only in Edward I's reign that petitions came to be presented in parliament and that regular parliaments came to provide regular opportunities for redress. This was a momentous innovation, for it meant that for the first time the voice of the aggrieved and of the socially insignificant could be heard at the centre of government. The tenants of the abbot of Halesowen who had been wrongfully imprisoned by their lord; the widow of a London butcher to whom the king owed money; the man assaulted on the high road while travelling to join the royal army in Wales: in the 1270s these and many more sent their petitions to king and council.[3] They did not necessarily do so at parliament-time, though parliament was already seen as a particularly suitable occasion for the delivery of petitions. Nor can we yet show that members of parliament had any concern with the transmission of petitions; the apparent infrequency of their attendance at parliament makes this unlikely. Nevertheless the growth of petitioning in parliament may already have begun to create a wider public awareness of national politics and of the political remedies for complaint.

[2] A. Harding, 'Plaints and bills in the history of English law', in *Legal History Studies, 1972*, ed. D. Jenkins (Cardiff, 1975), pp. 66–70.
[3] PRO, Ancient Petitions, SC8/50/2483, SC8/65/3235, SC8/34/1700.

At the start of our period, then, the opportunity for petitioning provided by parliament forms a growing part of parliament's 'popular'
function. Why and how this had come to be so is an obscure but
fundamental question. It is reasonably clear that the petition delivered
in parliament originated during the 1270s. Before 1272 petitions are
very rare indeed, and in no case can they be identified with particular
parliaments.[4] By 1280, on the other hand, they are being presented in
such numbers that they threaten to disrupt the political work of king
and council; it was this danger which induced Edward I in that year
to decree that as many petitions as possible should be dealt with by
his chief ministers and that only the most important should be reserved
for the king himself.[5] The regulation of petitioning proved its popularity. Now the absence of petitions prior to 1272 is unlikely to be
explained by their mere failure to survive, for our earliest examples
vary so greatly in diplomatic style as to make us suspect that the
petition itself is a novelty. The sixty-one petitions presented to parliament in 1278, the earliest series for which there is evidence, contain
thirty-six different forms of address. By contrast, 120 of the 133 petitions presented in the parliament of 1305 begin with the words 'A
nostre segnur le roy', now plainly a standard formula for a standard
document.[6] But it is equally clear that the procedure for treating
petitions had already been worked out by this time. As with almost
all later examples, the petitions of 1278 bear official endorsements
directing them to the appropriate court or office, and one such endorsement mentions two men 'assigned to receive petitions'.[7] If the petitions
still bear the marks of their recent origins, the crown has already
provided the machinery for dealing with them.

The lack of petitions under Henry III, their diversity of style in 1278,
and the existence by then of officials appointed to receive them, all
suggest that the petitions which began to appear in the 1270s were the
product not of a long evolutionary process but of some sudden 'act
of creation' by which the crown may have invited the complaints of
its subjects in parliament. Just such an invitation was issued before the

---

[4] H. G. Richardson and G. O. Sayles, *Parliaments and Great Councils* (London,
1961), p. 36; Sayles, *King's Parliament*, pp. 64, 76, 78.
[5] *CCR 1279–88*, p. 56; Sayles, *King's Parliament*, p. 80.
[6] *Rot. Parl.*, I, pp. 1–14; Ehrlich, *Proceedings against the Crown*, pp. 84–5.
[7] *Rot. Parl.*, I, p. 10.

parliaments of 1305 and 1330,[8] and the meagreness of parliamentary records before the 1290s makes it unsafe to assume that the practice had not been normal for many years. But the motive for Edward's willingness to entertain the often tedious complaints of his people remains as yet unclear.

His main reason for receiving, and perhaps even for encouraging, petitions may have been to facilitate complaints against his ministers and to place the check of public opinion on their activities. This view, first advanced by Reiss in 1885, is now generally discounted, yet there is still much to be said for it.[9] The plaints delivered in eyre, the precursors of the parliamentary petition, were often laid against royal officials, and when it suited the government's needs they might be directly solicited, as in 1258–9. Similar practices, stimulated by similar needs, were developing elsewhere in Western Europe during the thirteenth century.[10] Statistics provide some limited support for the argument. Of the sixty-one petitions presented in 1278, twelve (20 per cent) spoke of the misdeeds of the king's officials. Of the twenty-three surviving petitions sent in by shire communities between 1298 and 1307, seven (30 per cent) contain complaints against officials, and of the forty presented by the boroughs three (7 per cent) are on this subject.[11] The last figure is predictably low, since the self-government enjoyed by most boroughs is likely to have given them some protection from the king's agents. The first two figures suggest that a substantial minority of early petitions were directed against officials; and the second of the two figures takes no account of the great bulk of petitions presented not by shires but by individuals, who were perhaps more likely than their communities to hold grievances of this sort. This does not mean that we should expect early petitions to be exclusively or even largely confined to officials' misdeeds, for as the value of the new procedure came to be generally appreciated its uses would inevitably proliferate.

In Edward II's reign firm evidence takes the place of speculation. At the Easter parliament of 1309 'the community of the realm' complained that knights and burgesses coming to parliament and 'having petitions

[8] *Cal. Chancery Warrants, 1244–1326* (HMSO, 1927), p. 246; *Memo. de Parl.*, p. 3; *Rot. Parl.*, II, p. 443; *Rot. Parl. Hactenus Ined.*, p. ix n. 1.

[9] L. Reiss, *The History of the English Electoral Law in the Middle Ages*, trans. K. L. Wood-Legh (Cambridge, 1940), pp. 3–5; Haskins, 'Petitions of representatives', pp. 9–13; Sayles, *King's Parliament*, p. 90 n. 54. And see above pp. 44–5.

[10] A. Harding, 'Plaints and bills', pp. 66–8.

[11] *Rot. Parl.*, I, pp. 1–14; Haskins, 'Petitions of representatives', pp. 9–11.

to deliver concerning wrongs and grievances which cannot be redressed by the common law nor in other manner without special warrant' could find no one to receive their petitions. The 'wrongs and grievances' remained unspecified, but in 1311 comes proof that they included complaints against royal officials. The twenty-ninth of the Ordinances of that year stated that 'many men are grieved by the king's ministers without right, which grievances cannot be redressed without common parliament' and it went on to demand that 'bills delivered in parliament should be dealt with there'.[12] The redress of grievances against officials through the delivery of petitions in parliament is very strongly implied here, if not directly stated. By 1309–11 it seems clear that members of parliament were putting forward the petitions of their constituents and that those petitions were frequently directed at the doings of royal ministers.

Were these procedures encouraged by the king? We have seen that in 1305 and in 1330, and possibly at other times, the king invited the submission of petitions in parliament. Occasionally he issued a more specific invitation for the delivery of complaints against his servants. This first happened when the notorious Adam de Stratton, the king's chamberlain, was disgraced in 1279. In June that year Edward I had it proclaimed throughout the counties that all wishing to complain against Stratton should appear at Westminster fifteen days after Michaelmas, a week prior to the autumn parliament.[13] The same method was used on a larger scale in October 1289, when a general enquiry began into the misdeeds of royal officials during the king's absence in Gascony. The aggrieved were told to appear at Westminster on 12 November, bringing with them a written statement of their complaints, to be heard by the king's appointed commissioners and reported to him at the next parliament.[14] It may have been used again in 1294, when William March, Edward's treasurer, fell from favour,[15] and it was certainly used in 1307, when another treasurer, Walter Langton, was

---

[12] *Rot. Parl.*, I, p. 444, 285; Edwards, ' "Justice" ', in Fryde and Miller, I, pp. 285–6.

[13] PRO, K.R. Memoranda Roll, E159/52 m. 7; *Cal. Fine Rolls 1272–1307* (HMSO, 1911), p. 120; N. Denholm-Young, *Seignorial Administration in England* (Oxford, 1937), pp. 81–2.

[14] *State Trials of the Reign of Edward I, 1289–93*, ed. T. F. Tout and H. Johnstone (CS, 3rd ser., IX, 1906), pp. xii–xiii; HMC, *Various Collections*, I (1901), p. 256.

[15] *Select Cases before the King's Council, 1243–1482*, ed. I. S. Leadam and J. F. Baldwin (Selden Soc., XXXV, 1918), pp. li–lii.

deposed. Proclamations were then to be made at Westminster, 'when the exchequer and bench shall be open', that all those with complaints against Langton should deliver their bills to the clerk of Chief Justice Bereford.[16] In 1305, when Edward I had asked for the delivery of petitions before the opening of parliament, proclamation had similarly been made before the bench and exchequer as well as in chancery. The resemblance of procedure in 1305 and 1307 not only points to the parallels between the normal business of petitioning and extraordinary action against particular officials; it also suggests one means by which those outside London might learn of the remedies provided by the crown, for proclamations in the courts may have been intended to ensure that the local attorneys who worked there took the news back to their home districts.[17]

On at least three occasions between 1279 and 1307 the crown thus solicited its subjects' grievances against its servants. In each case the disgrace of ministers was the prelude to the unleashing of popular complaint and in two cases the delivery of complaints seems to have been linked with a forthcoming meeting of parliament. The king's purpose here was threefold: to demonstrate his care for his people's interests, to acquire the evidence needed for the conviction of the accused and to let it be known that the same procedure might be used against future wrongdoers. It is arguable that the parliamentary petitions which developed in the same period may have served, and have been intended to serve, similar purposes.

The same decade that saw the inauguration of petitioning also saw rigorous enquiries by the crown into the conduct of local government and a much wider range of ministerial offences brought within the purview of the judicial eyre. Seventy-two new articles were administered by the eyres which began in 1278; most were based on the hundred roll inquests of 1274–5 and the resulting statutes of April and October 1275, and most concerned the conduct of the king's officials in the counties.[18] Though the scale of the crown's activity here was new, its

[16] *Records of the Trial of Walter Langeton, Bishop of Coventry and Lichfield, 1307–12*, ed. A. Beardwood (CS, 4th ser., VI, 1969), p. 138; A. Beardwood, 'The trial of Walter Langton, bishop of Lichfield, 1307–12', *Trans. American Philosophical Soc.*, new ser., LIV, part 3 (1964), pp. 12–13.
[17] *Cal. Chancery Warrants*, p. 246; R. C. Palmer, 'County Year Book reports: the professional lawyer in the medieval county court', *EHR*, XCI (1976), pp. 776–98.
[18] H. M. Cam, *The Hundred and the Hundred Rolls* (reprint, London, 1963), p. 230.

methods were those traditionally used to supervise the provinces and they had obvious disadvantages. The chief was that the crown's ministers themselves might successfully obstruct the working of justice. Hundred bailiffs could threaten juries which reported their misdeeds, as happened several times in 1274–5, and sheriffs, to whom bills in eyre seem to have been delivered before their hearing by the justices, were still better placed to impede complaint. This is perhaps why the dismissal of all or most of the sheriffs was sometimes seen as a necessary preliminary to a general eyre, as in 1258 and 1278.[19] The eyre itself was an infrequent visitor to the shires, and extensive though its articles were by 1278 they could hardly itemise every sort of official misconduct. As long as the abuses of local government remained a matter for determination in the localities, the scope for popular complaint would be limited.

The petition may have owed something of its immense and immediate popularity to its freedom from these limitations. It could state a grievance or claim of any kind, and its delivery in London, whether directed against highly placed wrongdoers like Stratton and Langton or against sheriffs and bailiffs, could be made more discreetly than in the counties and with less chance of interference. The risks which this process might circumvent were recognised by Edward III in 1340, when those with complaints against his ministers were told 'to bring written bills and present them in London, secretly if there was a danger to them from officials still in office'.[20] Edward I's motives in thus expanding the remedies for his subjects' complaints were part of a wider pattern of concern for the protection of local interests and the punishment of rapacious officials. The hundred roll enquiries of 1274–5 into local maladministration and the crown's rights; the wholesale dismissal of the sheriffs in 1274 and 1278; the codification of reform in the Statute of Westminster I and the elaborate arrangements for the publication and preservation of the statute in the provinces;[21] the two parliaments of 1275, to both of which the commons were summoned, and the concessions made to the financial claims of necessitous gentry by the

---

[19] *Ibid.*, pp. 43–4; R. V. Rogers, 'MS of eyre of Northampton, 3 Edw. III (1329)', *BJRUL*, XXXIV (1951–2), p. 411 n. 3; Treharne, *Baronial Plan of Reform*, pp. 121–5; 'Annales Dunstaplia', in *Annales Monastici*, III, ed. H. R. Luard (RS, 1866), p. 279.

[20] N. M. Fryde, 'Edward III's removal of his ministers and judges, 1340–1', *BIHR*, XLVIII (1975), p. 149.

[21] *Statutes*, I, p. 39; Richardson and Sayles, 'Early statutes', p. 545.

Statute of Jewry, passed at the second of those parliaments: all demonstrate the king's new-found regard for public opinion and for the local and knightly aspirations which had emerged during the period of baronial reform and civil war between 1258 and 1265 and which remained unsatisfied at his accession. Edward's policies at this time, including his readiness to hear petitions, may have owed much to the work of Simon de Montfort.[22]

The evidence suggests, then, that the use of petitions which began in the 1270s was deliberately fostered by the crown as a means by which redress might be offered to aggrieved subjects and particularly to those suffering from the malpractices of officials. Petitions had from the start been received at parliament-time (though not only then), and by 1309 or thereabouts they were being delivered by the representatives of the commons. It was perhaps during the 1290s, when the king's financial needs first brought the commons regularly to parliament, that they began to act as messengers for their constituents. Parliament had of course many other functions, legislative, political and taxative. But it 'was valued by the people at large . . . in so far as it afforded a means of obtaining relief which, for any reason, could not be obtained from the ordinary courts of the land'.[23] By the beginning of Edward II's reign the transmission of popular complaints by the knights of the shire and burgesses, and their regular consideration at Westminster, had brought the possibility of relief within reach of the unenfranchised.

It sometimes remained no more than a possibility. The petition did not automatically provide a remedy for oppression and misgovernment or a key to favour and privilege. Maitland was right when he wrote that the petitioner 'did not get what he wanted, he was merely put in the way of getting it'.[24] Nor, in the early days, was it used mainly by the disadvantaged. While many early petitions were from small men (and some have been cited), the sixty-one petitions of 1278 came chiefly from individuals and corporations of high standing: eleven were from religious houses, five from earls and countesses, and many of the remainder from substantial landowners. Not until the early fourteenth century do the potentialities of this method of approach to the crown seem to have been fully realised by the very humble. The point can hardly be quantified, since the standing of petitioners is often obscure

[22] I hope to say more on this subject on another occasion.
[23] *Rot. Parl. Hactenus Ined.*, p. vii.
[24] *Memo de Parl.*, p. lxviii.

and sometimes (we may suspect) deliberately misstated. Petitioners almost certainly exaggerated their lowliness in order to emphasise their afflictions, and if they call themselves 'poor', as they often do, it may be a mark of deference rather than of indigence. But when we find two 'poor men and threshers of corn in the grange of their lord' complaining that the reeve has revenged himself on them for their reporting his sharp practices to the auditors; or when the 'poor tenants' of two Derbyshire villages contend that they have been wrongfully distrained by the sheriff for the chattels of an indicted felon; or when the 'poor villeins' of Penrhos in Anglesey assert that their customs and services have been extortionately assessed by the sheriff:[25] then it is hard to doubt that we are listening to men of no great importance and men whose complaints would have gone unheard a hundred years earlier.

The scope of the petition was also widening in another direction: it was becoming the regular vehicle for the needs of local communities. In the 1270s petitions submitted by shire communities had been rare. Only two have been found from that decade, one of them, from Cheshire, presented in the parliament of 1278.[26] By the end of Edward I's reign petitions of this sort were becoming more common: between 1290 and 1307 twenty-three surviving petitions were sent into parliament by shires and another forty by boroughs.[27] But in the single parliament of January 1315 nine of some 220 petitions were presented by shires and fourteen by boroughs, and in that of October 1320 eight from a mere 115 petitions came from shire communities.[28] The expansion of the 'community' petition seems to have come mainly in the middle and later years of Edward II, years which also saw the emergence of the 'common petition' containing requests put forward in the name of the whole commons in parliament.[29] The demands which the petition is beginning to embody are broader than those of individuals. They mark the growing political cohesiveness of local communities and of the national community and the opportunities which parliament gave for the voices of both to be heard.

The claims both of communities and of individuals suggest that men

[25] PRO, SC8/60/2971/ (*c.* 1330?), SC8/78/3871 (*c.* 1332); *Rot. Parl.*, I, pp. 308–9 (1315).

[26] *Rot. Parl.*, I, p. 6; PRO, Ancient Correspondence, SC1/20/179.

[27] Haskins, 'Petitions of representatives', pp. 9–11.

[28] *Rot. Parl.*, I, pp. 287–333, 371–86.

[29] Harriss, *King, Parliament and Public Finance*, p. 118; Rayner, ' "Commune petition" ', pp. 553–6.

did not go to parliament merely to treat the matters put before them by the king. They went also (perhaps primarily) to defend the affairs of their communities and their constituents and to do local business. Petitions and accounts show us something of the interests of townsmen. Burgesses from Winchester, for example, went to parliament in 1311 to ask the king for a judicial commission to bring to trial various malefactors within the city;[30] while the Leicester accounts record payments to the town's members in 1312–13 and 1350–1 for their stay at parliament 'on the business of the community'. Occasionally they are more particular. The elected men paid £1 6s 8d for a writ while at the Westminster parliament of 1309; 'bills ... for obtaining pontage' were taken to parliament in 1324; 'a certain commission' and a writ of supersedeas were purchased at the York parliament of 1335.[31] In the previous year the members for Lynn in Norfolk had been paid by their town for 'asserting the liberty' in parliament at York, and in the first parliament of Richard II's reign in 1377 the members for Norwich petitioned for confirmation of their charters and privileges.[32] It was another Norwich record which epitomised the role of all these parliamentary burgesses: 'to increase our liberties as they may be able'.[33]

The local interests of the shire knights were rather different. Like the burgesses, they brought up the petitions of their constituents and they may already have had an advertised duty to do so. We do not know the antiquity of the procedure which followed the Norfolk election of 1461, when the sheriff had it proclaimed that all those with business to prosecute in parliament should approach the elected knights.[34] But the shires' corporate concerns were distinct from those of the towns, for few held privileges and liberties. The men of Cornwall were exceptional in petitioning about 1302 for the confirmation of their charter from King John relating to the county shrievalty, and the men of Devon in asking for the unimpeded enjoyment of their 'liberties and customs' in 1318.[35] The main preoccupation of the shires

[30] PRO, SC8/327/E808, E810.
[31] *Records of the Borough of Leicester*, ed. M. Bateson, I (London, 1899), pp. 278, 267, 345, II (1901), pp. 75, 17.
[32] HMC, *Eleventh Rep.* (1887), p. 214; McKisack, *Borough Representation*, p. 134.
[33] McKisack, *Borough Representation*, p. 119.
[34] C. H. Williams, 'A Norfolk parliamentary election, 1461', *EHR*, XL (1925), p. 85.
[35] PRO, SC8/323/E562; *Documents illustrative of English History in the Thirteenth and Fourteenth Centuries*, ed. H. Cole (London, 1844), p. 26.

was with office-holding and with the behaviour of office-holders, and here they did more than reiterate the traditional grievances of individuals against extortion and maladministration. Individuals complained; counties sought reform through the exercise of influence on appointments. Some of the earliest petitions from the counties requested the dismissal of officials and their replacement by others. Among the petitions of 1320, for example, we find the community of Buckinghamshire asking for the appointment of two named men as keepers of the peace in the county and the community of Norfolk demanding the removal of Thomas Ynglesthorp from that post;[36] while from about 1340 there survive petitions from the communities of Dorset, Herefordshire and Shropshire, all putting forward candidates for keeperships of the peace.[37] Often petitions of this kind were delivered by the county's representatives in parliament. It was the members for Cornwall who asked king and council about 1325 for the appointment of six knights as keepers of the peace and of the coast, and the members for Devon who named four men for similar work in 1334.[38]

These requests represent the ambitions of county communities for a greater say in the appointment of local officials, and they rapidly became the ambitions of the commons in parliament. In 1343 and 1352 the commons asked for the election in parliament of justices of oyer and terminer; in 1354 they asked for the names of those chosen as justices of labourers to be submitted to the knights of the counties; and in 1363, 1365 and 1376 they went a step farther by asking for the right to choose justices of labourers and of the peace.[39] This was merely symptomatic of the increasing regulation of all local offices by and in parliament. By the start of Richard II's reign, for example, persistent pressure from the commons had gained for the JPs the right to determine cases, which they never afterwards lost,[40] and had succeeded in enforcing a local land-holding qualification on sheriffs and in limiting their tenure of office to a year.[41] In the long term it was these corporate interests of the shires rather than of the boroughs which most affected

[36] *Rot. Parl.*, I, pp. 373, 379.
[37] PRO, SC8/107/5327, SC8/115/5741, SC8/142/7077. For the circumstances of these petitions see Putnam, 'Transformation of keepers of the peace', pp. 35–8.
[38] PRO, SC8/35/1714, SC8/264/13186.
[39] *Rot. Parl.*, II, pp. 136, 238, 257, 277, 286, 333.
[40] Putnam, 'Transformation of keepers of the peace', pp. 46–7; J. B. Post, 'The peace commissions of 1382', *EHR*, XCI (1976), pp. 98–101.
[41] N. E. Saul, 'The Gloucestershire gentry in the fourteenth century' (Oxford University D.Phil. thesis, 1978), pp. 125–7.

English government. The boroughs' petitions in parliament were mainly conservative in tone: they chiefly wanted the confirmation and extension of ancient liberties. The shires, by contrast, were asserting claims to some degree of self-government which were largely novel. The growing autonomy of the shire community owed much to the development of petitioning, the pressing of corporate claims by shire representatives in parliament, and the transformation of those claims into the requests of the whole commons.

If parliament in this way came to meet the communal needs of shires and boroughs, it also served the particular ambitions and interests of those who attended it. Some have implicitly denied this, arguing that in the fourteenth century men were reluctant to go to parliament and that election was regarded as an affliction rather than a privilege.[42] It is as hard for us as it may have been for contemporaries to weigh up the burdens and benefits of parliamentary service, but the probability is that it brought pleasure more often than distress. The evidence, inferential rather than direct, derives mainly from elections.

Elections for county seats took place in the county court, where the suitors of the court were (in theory) the electors and the sheriff the returning officer. Borough procedure was more varied, but generally the electorate was small and consisted of the more important men of the town.[43] It is clear that in the shires election was a matter for the whole community. Phrases such as 'by the assent of the aforesaid county court' or 'in the county court of Dorset by the whole community of the same county' or 'the whole county court of Middlesex has elected . . .' are common enough on sheriffs' returns to imply that the choosing of the county's members entailed consultation and not mere nomination.[44] No doubt the wishes of great men counted for more than those of small, but even when the choice lay with them (as it appears to have done in Crowthorne's case, discussed below) it had to be backed by more general support. Without a properly constituted assembly those present sometimes felt inhibited from proceeding. The knights and landholders of Sussex, called upon to elect in 1297, refused to do so in the absence of 'the archbishop of Canterbury and other

[42] Stubbs, *Const. Hist.*, III, p. 421; H. G. Richardson, 'John of Gaunt and the parliamentary representation of Lancashire', *BJRUL*, XXII (1938), pp. 17–25.

[43] McKisack, *Borough Representation*, pp. 30–43.

[44] L. Reiss, *History of English Electoral Law*, pp. 51–2. For the composition of the county court see Maddicott, 'County community', pp. 28–33.

persons, bishops, earls, barons, knights and others';[45] while the sheriff of Westmorland claimed in 1306 that short notice and the absence of all the knights and free tenants on the Scottish border prevented his making an election.[46] This by itself does nothing to prove that election was welcomed by the elected, but it does go half-way to that conclusion by showing that the business was taken seriously and was not to be managed without the assent of the community.

The absence of contested elections in the fourteenth century, it has been tentatively argued, may indicate that serving in parliament is more likely to have been considered a burden than an honour. But contested elections remained unusual until the nineteenth century, by which time a place in parliament had long been regarded as worth having,[47] and if they were unknown in our period, disputed elections (that is, those in which the results were called into doubt) were relatively common. The evidence for electoral sharp practice points as strongly to the desirability of a seat as would the evidence of open competition. The first such evidence comes in 1318, when Matthew Crowthorne, chosen (according to his own petition) as member for Devon 'by the bishop of Exeter and Sir William Martin, with the assent of the other good men of the community', was displaced by another man, whom the sheriff returned against the wishes of the community. Crowthorne would hardly have troubled to complain about this injustice, nor subsequently to have secured his own return for Exeter, as he did, had he not valued his place in parliament.[48] In such cases as this the sheriff was almost invariably the culprit. It was William le Gentil, sheriff of Lancashire, according to a local jury, who in 1320 had chosen two knights for parliament without the county's assent, when they should have been the choice of the whole county.[49] More striking still was a presentment made before the king's bench by the jurors of two Cambridgeshire hundreds in 1338. The ancient custom, they said, was for election to be made 'by the *probiores* of the county in full county court', but for seven years past the sheriffs had returned themselves and their friends without the election of the county and

---

[45] *Parl. Writs*, I, p. 60; L. Reiss, *History of English Electoral Law*, p. 53.

[46] *Return of Members*, p. 23.

[47] J. G. Edwards, 'The emergence of majority rule in English parliamentary elections', *TRHS*, 5th ser., XIV (1964), pp. 179, 185.

[48] *Parl. Writs*, II, ii, appendix, p. 138; *Return of Members*, p. 55; H. G. Richardson, 'John of Gaunt', p. 18.

[49] *Parl. Writs*, II, ii, p. 315.

outside the county court, contrary to custom.[50] In the same decade the sheriff of Lancashire was accused of returning to parliament his clerks and other members of his following, who were not elected with the county's assent.[51] It was the deputies of another sheriff of Lancashire (a county peculiarly subject to interference) who in 1362 were found simply to have returned themselves for parliament without election.[52] Nor were borough elections immune from similar malpractices. In 1338 the indenture which contained the names of those elected for the city of Lincoln was tampered with by three men, including the sub-sheriff and the sheriff's clerk, and the names of two of the three were substituted for those of the citizens.[53]

There was thus already a strong and well defended tradition that in county elections the right to elect lay with the men of the county. Elections, governed by 'ancient custom', were a cherished communal privilege, and their hindrance was seen as an infringement of the county's liberties and a proper subject for complaint by local juries. Though it is possible that sheriffs and their underlings had special reasons for wishing to be returned, as will be shown, interference in elections is unlikely to have been attempted or resented had men been indifferent or hostile to parliamentary service.

Before the end of Edward III's reign there is little to show that such interference had a direct political purpose. So far as can be seen, neither kings nor particular magnates tried to have their own men returned to parliament with any regularity, and electoral manipulation was more often the result of private enterprise than of attempted supervision from above. Evidence of politically motivated meddling in elections, largely lacking under Edward II,[54] begins to appear only in the 1370s. In the Good Parliament of 1376 the commons asked that knights should be elected 'by common election of the best men of the said counties and not returned by the sheriff alone without due election'.[55] And in the next assembly of January 1377 John of Gaunt was said by the St

[50] M. M. Taylor, 'Parliamentary elections in Cambridgeshire, 1332–38', *BIHR*, VIII (1940–1), pp. 21–6.

[51] H. G. Richardson, 'John of Gaunt', p. 19 n. 2.

[52] *Dignity of a Peer*, III, pp. 633–4; Stubbs, *Const. Hist.*, III, p. 436; H. G. Richardson, 'John of Gaunt', p. 7.

[53] PRO, Just. Itin. 1, Assize Rolls, 521 m. 15d.

[54] G. Lapsley, *Crown, Community and Parliament*, pp. 111–40; J. R. Maddicott, *Thomas of Lancaster, 1307–22* (Oxford, 1970), pp. 51–2.

[55] *Rot. Parl.*, II, p. 355; J. G. Edwards, 'Emergence of majority rule', pp. 177, 194–6.

Albans chronicler to have procured the removal of the knights who had 'stood for the community' in the Good Parliament, so that only twelve (actually eight) of those present earlier were returned in 1377. The chronicler's word has been doubted on the grounds that the small number of knights re-elected to the second parliament was hardly fewer than the numbers common to other consecutive parliaments in the 1370s. K. L. Wood-Legh's figures, however, suggest the opposite conclusion. We have to go back through eighteen parliaments to 1353 before we find a smaller number of attendances (four) at two con-secutive parliaments. The average betwen 1353 and 1377 was some fifteen and even the long gap between the parliaments of 1373 and 1376 left twelve knights common to both meetings.[56] Taken together, petition and chronicle imply that interference in elections was becom-ing more frequent, a testimony both to the bitter factional conflicts of Edward III's last years and to the rising power of the commons.

By 1377, then, the return of the unqualified for parliament was sufficiently common to provoke a general protest, while seats were valued enough for a great magnate to attempt to control them. The evidence of re-election to parliament, already touched on, points in a similar direction. During Edward III's reign the re-election of knights to parliament became common and in a majority of Edward's parlia-ments knights with previous parliamentary experience outnumbered those who lacked it. About three-fifths of his parliaments had a majority of the experienced, compared with just over one-third of the parliaments between 1290 and 1307.[57] More revealing still are the large numbers of those attending a series of consecutive parliaments. This had never been rare, and under the first two Edwards sixty knights were returned to three consecutive parliaments, fourteen to four, five to five, one to six and one to seven. But under Edward III 124 knights served in three consecutive parliaments, forty-two in four, nineteen in five, nine in six, four in seven and one in eight.[58] If we take the total number of parliaments, not necessarily consecutive, in which knights served, we find that between 1290 and 1327 only three knights served in ten or more parliaments, while under Edward III twelve were in this

---

[56] *Chron. Angliae*, p. 112; H. G. Richardson, 'John of Gaunt', pp. 29–33; K. L. Wood-Legh, 'The knights' attendance in the parliaments of Edward III', *EHR*, XLVII (1932), pp. 406–7.

[57] K. L. Wood-Legh, 'The knights' attendance', pp. 404, 407–8.

[58] *Ibid.*, pp. 410–11.

position.[59] Even when allowances have been made for the greater number of parliaments under Edward III, the statistics show that re-election then became more common. The apparent willingness of men powerful in their own localities to attend repeatedly at Westminster does not suggest any general reluctance to serve.

Though they were doubtless actuated partly by public-spiritedness, it is the personal and material advantages brought by election that are most in evidence. The way to those advantages often lay through the petition, for a seat in parliament allowed members to forward their own petitions and those of others in which they had some financial stake. A few members can be found presenting their own petitions in almost every parliament from the 1290s onward; four, for example, acted thus in 1307 and three in 1328.[60] Since claims could be advanced orally, as well as in writing, without leaving much trace on the records these figures almost certainly underestimate the number of requests put forward by members. In the parliament of March 1340 four knights attending for Nottinghamshire, Kent, Cumberland and Staffordshire secured pardons of their debts to the crown, but in no case does a written petition survive and probably none was made.[61] A word in the ear of the king or chancellor may have been equally efficacious.

It was not only for themselves and their constituents that members put forward petitions, but also for their friends and clients. Certain evidence of this comes only in 1372, when an ordinance, probably originating with the commons, barred lawyers conducting cases in the royal courts from attendance at parliament as shire representatives. The stated reason for their exclusion was that 'they procure and put forward many petitions in parliament in the name of the commons, which are no concern of the commons, but touch only the particular persons by whom the lawyers are retained'. Clearly the commons' petitions might be manipulated by lawyer members for their own advantage and did not always represent the common interest.[62] Nor was it only the lawyers who had clients with interests to be defended in parliament. The writs for the parliaments of the early 1350s had laid

[59] *Ibid.*, p. 405; Edwards, 'Personnel of the commons', p. 199.

[60] Haskins, 'Petitions of representatives', p. 16; *Rot. Parl.*, II, pp. 13 (Andrew de Seint Liz, MP for Bucks), 14 (Geoffrey Stace, MP for Ipswich), 23 (Richard de Emeldon, MP for Newcastle on Tyne).

[61] *Rot. Parl.*, II, p. 115; *Return of Members*, pp. 130–1.

[62] *Rot. Parl.*, II, p. 310; K. L. Wood-Legh, 'Sheriffs, lawyers and belted knights in the parliaments of Edward III', *EHR*, XLVI (1931), p. 377.

down that those elected should not be 'persistent litigants [*perlitatores*] or maintainers of plaints or those who live by such gains'. These men are unlikely to have been professional lawyers, as has been supposed.[63] They were rather the paid supporters of other men's quarrels, rogues found in every county and denounced at every trailbaston session, whose practice of maintenance was coming to threaten parliament just as it already threatened the king's other courts.

As well as promoting petitions, members of parliament could suppress them. This is directly stated in Edward III's orders to the sheriffs in November 1330, by which they were to ensure that two of the 'most loyal and sufficient knights or serjeants' were sent from each county to the forthcoming parliament. Previously, the king said, some of those returned to parliament had been partisans (*gens de coveigne*) and maintainers of false quarrels, and had prevented 'good men' from 'showing the grievances of the common people' and from finding redress in parliament.[64] Edward's instructions came, of course, after a long period of political instability during which the country had been managed in the interests of Roger Mortimer and Queen Isabella, and it is hard to tell whether this abuse was common in more normal times. But it may have been by no means unusual and have been linked with a second abuse: the 'election' to parliament of serving sheriffs.

This practice first emerges in 1302, when the sheriff of Herefordshire was returned to parliament for his own county, and it continued until its prohibition in 1372 by the same ordinance which demanded the exclusion of lawyers. The ordinance was effective for the rest of Edward III's reign, though less so under Richard II.[65] The aim of sheriffs in securing election was very probably to suppress petitions against their misbehaviour and the misbehaviour of their subordinates. We have already seen that petitions against ministerial abuses were common and that the petition itself may have owed much of its early popularity to its being a form of complaint less easy to silence than the grievances of individuals and the presentments of juries delivered to the king's judges in the localities.[66] A popular sheriff (if such existed) may occasionally have been the unfettered choice of the county, but it is

[63] *Dignity of a Peer*, III, pp. 590, 593, 603, 605; Stubbs, *Const. Hist.*, III, pp. 412–13; K. L. Wood-Legh, 'Sheriffs, lawyers and belted knights', p. 377.
[64] *Rot. Parl.*, II, p. 443; K. L. Wood-Legh, 'Sheriffs, lawyers and belted knights', pp. 376–7.
[65] K. L. Wood-Legh, 'Sheriffs, lawyers and belted knights', p. 373.
[66] Above, pp. 64–7.

more likely that sheriffs jobbed themselves into parliament in an attempt to limit complaint by petition. It was, after all, they and their staffs who were the guilty parties in almost all election disputes. It is very significant that during Edward III's minority, when *gens de coveigne* sat in parliament and 'the grievances of the common people' went unheard, there should have been ten sheriffs in two successive parliaments, those of York and Northampton in 1328; while under Edward II there had never been more than six in any one parliament and usually only two or three.[67] Few can have been so foolish or fool-hardy as to deliver petitions directed against local officials to a shire knight who was also a sheriff.

We ought to view parliament, then, not only as a political assembly and a court but as an occasion for the complex interplay of private hopes and fears—for the seeking of royal favour, the promotion and suppression of petitions, the maintenance of friends and the thwarting of enemies. These things are revealed to us only fragmentarily, mainly in the attempts made by the king and by parliament itself to regulate membership of the commons, yet they are suggestive of many currents of personal conflict and ambition which ran beneath the political sur-face of parliamentary life. But not all can have regarded parliament in this way, for in no parliament are private petitioners, lawyers, sheriffs and maintainers likely to have predominated. A more widely shared incentive for election may have lain in the wages to which the elected man was entitled. After some fluctuations these were fixed in 1327 at 4s a day for a knight and 2s for a burgess, rates which remained stable for the rest of the middle ages.[68] By comparison with other contem-porary wage scales this was handsome remuneration. A knight attend-ing parliament drew twice the 2s a day which he received on campaign and as much as the military wage of a banneret.[69] The setting of wages at a relatively high level may have been intended to encourage men of substance to put themselves forward for parliament, but it almost certainly had the concomitant effect of making parliamentary service attractive and of tempting the unscrupulous. In the majority of dis-puted elections already discussed some financial motive is alleged

[67] K. L. Wood-Legh, 'Sheriffs, lawyers and belted knights', p. 373. The number of sheriffs in any parliament may be deduced by comparing the *List of Sheriffs* (PRO, *Lists and Indexes*, IX, 1898) with the *Return of Members*.

[68] Cam, *Liberties and Communities*, p. 237.

[69] For army wages see A. E. Prince, 'The strength of English armies in the reign of Edward III', *EHR*, XLVI (1931), p. 362.

against the usurper. In 1320 £20 was levied for the wages of the two knights returned singlehandedly by the sheriff of Lancashire, although it was claimed that the county could have had knights of its own choice for only £10. Even when allowance has been made for the cost of travel, £10 a head for a parliament lasting only twenty days hardly fell within the definition of the 'reasonable expenses' which the king had ordered the counties to provide for their representatives.[70] In the Lancashire case of 1335 the sheriff was accused not only of returning his own followers but of taking a share of their expenses when they returned home;[71] and the two men who forced themselves upon the electors of Lincoln in 1339 had attached the citizens' goods in payment of their expenses.[72] Finally, it was the levying of wages which provided the chief grievance against the lieutenants of the sheriff who apparently returned themselves for Lancashire in 1362.[73]

The evidence of disputed elections and of the sheriff's interest in them suggests that profits were to be made from going to parliament. Their size remains obscure, since it depended on two unknowns: the cost of travel and accommodation, and the ability of the representative to extract more than the standard wage from his constituents. But we ought in any case not to think of profits in a purely material sense, for the benefits brought by attendance at Westminster were not always direct or tangible. Parliament was a social gathering, a season for conviviality, display, the exchange of news and the doing of business. It was a time when a king's bachelor might meet the treasurer to discuss his accounts and a knight attending for Bedfordshire might conveniently do homage for his father's lands.[74] More than wise words in debate contributed to the winning of a reputation there, as John Bromyard's slighting reference to those who 'came to parliament or to the tournament with so many horse' reminds us.[75] In such public gatherings a train of good horses helped to establish a man's value. So too no doubt did his exploits during the session. In the Good Parliament of 1376 two shire knights, Sir John de la Mare of Wiltshire and Sir John Kent-

---

[70] *Parl. Writs*, II, ii, pp. 229, 315.
[71] H. G. Richardson, 'John of Gaunt', p. 19 n. 2.
[72] PRO, Just. Itin. 1/521 m. 15d.
[73] *Dignity of a Peer*, III, pp. 633–4.
[74] H. G. Richardson and G. O. Sayles, 'The parliament of Lincoln, 1316', *BIHR*, XII (1934–5), pp. 106–7; M. Bassett, *Knights of the Shire for Bedfordshire during the Middle Ages* (Beds. Hist. Rec. Soc., XXIX, 1949), p. 73.
[75] G. R. Owst, *Literature and Pulpit in Medieval England* (2nd edn., Oxford, 1961), p. 334.

wode of Berkshire, tricked a suspected accomplice of Alice Perrers, the king's mistress, into giving himself up. The suspect was a Dominican friar, known both as a physician and a magician, whom the knights approached at Alice's manor of Pallenswick under the pretext of seeking advice about their health. The phials of urine which they carried deceived the friar into receiving them, thus effecting his own capture, and it was only the subsequent intervention of the archbishop of Canterbury that saved him from burning.[76] It is a good story, which may have sounded as improbable to a home audience in Wiltshire or Berkshire as it does to us; but it is likely to be true. It reveals something not only of knightly attitudes at a time of political crisis but of the pleasurable encounters with the unexpected which parliamentary service might provide.

The rewards and diversions which came the way of a member of parliament may not always have compensated for the discomforts of his position. Chief among these was his standing as the servant of two masters. If he took wages from his constituents and went to parliament 'to show what grieves them and to speak for their profit' (as the author of *Mum and the Sothsegger* wrote),[77] he had also to recognise the crown's claims to taxation. From the crown's standpoint knights and burgesses were present in parliament to bind their communities to the measures which they accepted and above all to bind them to the payment of taxes. Since 1295 they had come with full power (*plena potestas*) to make grants on their constituents' behalf.[78] But these constitutional doctrines did not preclude resentment and criticism from provincial audiences lacking the tuition in the government's needs and claims to which their representatives had been exposed in parliament. From the 1330s the crown used various devices to nourish the commons' compliance in the granting of taxes: an opening speech from the chancellor or chief justice setting out the king's requirements; the parliamentary publication of reports on military progress; the regular undertaking to consider the reforms asked for in the commons' petitions. But the commons in the counties were less directly exposed to pressure from above, nor was their sense of responsibility so directly cultivated. They could not always have welcomed the returning knights and burgesses who had granted taxes on their behalf. Concessions which

---

[76] *Chron. Angliae*, pp. 98–9; Holmes, *Good Parliament*, pp. 136–7.
[77] Cam, *Liberties and Communities*, pp. 230, 234.
[78] Edwards, '*Plena potestas*', in Fryde and Miller, I, pp. 136–49.

seemed justifiable at Westminster may have been seen in a different light in Cumberland or Cornwall.

There were ways in which local opinion could be mollified. Under Edward III it became quite common for MPs to take back to their counties some record of parliament's doings, usually a record of the grant which they had made to the king and of the conditions attached to it. The practice may have begun in an earlier period (the inadequacies of the early rolls of parliament make it impossible to tell), but only in Edward III's opening parliament do we first hear it. In January 1327 the commons asked to be allowed to carry back for publication in their counties a written account of their petitions and of the answers proposed by king and council. The resulting statute, which embodied the substance of the commons' requests, was presumably transmitted in this way.[79] Not until the political crisis of 1339–40 and the decade of high taxation which followed did this procedure come to be linked with the grant of a subsidy. In the parliament of October 1339 the commons took the quite exceptional step of asking for time to consult 'the commons in their counties' before they would meet the king's demand for a large aid. If the king would summon another parliament, they said, they meanwhile would do all they could in their counties to see that he should have his aid.[80] They subsequently agreed in July 1340 to a loan of 20,000 sacks of wool for the king, the terms for which were to be delivered to the knights 'to report in their counties'.[81] In 1344 and 1348 they asked that their grants and the conditions on which they had been made should be drafted as letters patent and sent into the counties. The same may have been done in the parliament of 1352[82] and was certainly done in that of 1373, when the commons again secured the despatch to each county of 'commissions' concerning the grants made in parliament and the conditions attached to them.[83]

These schedules of taxation and its attendant conditions were both a form of propaganda and a public recognition by the king of his statutory obligations, to which the grant of a subsidy had bound him. But they also allowed the knights of the shires to vindicate their actions

[79] *Rot. Parl.*, II, p. 10; Richardson and Sayles, 'Early statutes', p. 546; Harriss, *King, Parliament and Public Finance*, p. 122.
[80] *Rot. Parl.*, II, p. 104; Harriss, *King, Parliament and Public Finance*, pp. 255–6.
[81] *Rot. Parl.*, II, p. 119; Harriss, *King, Parliament and Public Finance*, p. 279.
[82] *Rot. Parl.*, II, pp. 150, 201; Harriss, *King, Parliament and Public Finance*, pp. 326, 365.
[83] *Rot. Parl.*, II, p. 317.

before the bar of local opinion and to bring to bear on their constituents some of the same responsibilities and obligations under which they themselves had worked in parliament. In 1348 they asked specifically that the letters patent concerning their grant should make mention of the king's 'great necessity' (an allusion to his financial difficulties), and they tried in 1327 and 1344, and probably on other occasions, to ensure that proclamations gave publicity to the concessions which they had obtained from the crown. Proclamations in the counties, the normal mechanism by which the government made its will known, were thus used to explain and justify the knights' parliamentary activities. The wide audience which they found, in county courts, boroughs and market towns, must have been made well aware of the novel importance of parliamentary politics.[84]

These self-defensive measures marked the effect of taxation in setting MPs at odds with their constituents. As they showed by referring the king's demands to their communities in 1339, they were very conscious of the burdens imposed by their grants and occasionally reluctant to act without local support. Their concern to escape nomination as collectors of taxes, an exemption for which they petitioned in 1352, 1373 and 1377, may have been partly due to their wish to avoid the double odium of responsibility both for the granting and for the levying of subsidies.[85] There may even have been some feeling in the provinces that when taxes were raised the representatives escaped more lightly than the represented. 'It is no trouble to the great thus to grant the king a tax,' wrote a satirist about 1339. 'The simple must pay it all . . . those who make the grant give nothing to the king.'[86] This was not, of course, true: in England none had *de iure* exemption from taxation. But the high social position of the knights of the shires, 'the more worthy . . . of the county' as they were often described in the writs for election, and the increased possibilities for such men to evade taxation after the reform of the tax system in 1334,[87] gave the accusation the credibility of a half-truth. At times of particularly heavy taxation these discontents may have been reflected in an unwillingness to re-elect the men who had agreed to such impositions. The parliament

[84] *Rot Parl.*, II, pp. 201, 10, 150. For proclamations and their audience see Maddicott, 'County community', pp. 32–6.
[85] *Rot. Parl.*, II, pp. 240, 317, 368.
[86] *Political Songs*, ed. T. Wright (CS, old ser., 1839), p. 184.
[87] Stubbs, *Const. Hist.*, III, p. 412; J. R. Maddicott, *English Peasantry*, pp. 50–2.

of April 1341, the first after that of July 1340 which had conceded a large loan of wool to the king, contained only three knights who had sat in the previous parliament, and throughout the years of high taxation in the early 1340s re-election remained relatively uncommon. By contrast, the ten-year respite from the lay subsidy in the 1360s saw a much higher number of men returned to successive parliaments.[88] When MPs returned to their constituencies it may have been by their readiness or reluctance to make grants of taxation that they were chiefly judged.

On matters of taxation the county thus had its own opinion. Its court, where that opinion was voiced, theoretically lacked the right to grant, refuse or bargain over taxation, but the limitation sometimes went unrecognised; the actions and attitudes of the county court were not always very different from those of the French provincial estates, with which they are often contrasted. When the king's agents in Shropshire attempted to levy the sum of wool at which the county had been assessed in the parliament of April 1341 it was the county court which resisted them. The magnates and commons assembled there told the collectors that they were to raise only two-thirds of the shire's quota, causing them to write back lamely to the chancellor to ask for the issuing of a new commission to three local knights, 'whom the community of the county dare not go against'.[89] Though the modification in the locality of a grant made in parliament probably owed more to the exceptionally harsh economic conditions of 1340–1 than to normal practices, the county was at all times disputatiously stubborn in protecting its financial resources. The 'commune' of Shropshire once told Edward II's commissioners of array that they could not meet the cost of the archers which the county had been told to raise, since the local magnates were currently out of the district and nothing could be done without their assent. The community of Worcestershire refused to meet similar costs in 1338, arguing that the arrayers' commission did not state at whose expense the county's archers were to be equipped and transported.[90] It is hardly surprising that members of parliament should have been as conscious as the government of the need to conciliate and inform local communities which were so alert to their own interests and so adept in their defence.

By the 1320s, if not earlier, those communities were beginning to

[88] K. L. Wood-Legh, 'The knights' attendance', pp. 406–7.
[89] PRO, SC1/28/149. For the date see *Rot. Parl.*, II, p. 131.
[90] PRO, SC1/28/168, SC1/39/48.

learn about the work of parliament not only from the proclamations occasioned by statutes and tax grants but from the less formal reports of their members, sometimes despatched in written form during the session and sometimes made orally on the members' return. As far as we know, newsletters were first sent out from the Carlisle parliament of 1307, but they dealt mainly with the assembly's ecclesiastical business and catered for an ecclesiastical readership.[91] There is little sign of a wider audience for parliamentary news until the time of Edward III's accession, the manner of which may in itself have done much to promote public discussion. We have already seen how the statutes drafted in Edward's first parliament were despatched to the shires at the commons' request. The same parliament probably saw the distribution of unofficial rolls containing a draft version of the commons' petitions, William Trussell's renunciation of homage to Edward II, and the form of judgement on Hugh Despenser the younger; and yet another version of these same petitions found its way to the archives of Bridport in Dorset, a borough represented in the parliament.[92]

The appetite for news which these documents suggest is equally well illustrated by other local records about this time. The first evidence of individual members reporting to their constituents comes from 1328, when the representatives of London twice wrote home from the York parliament to tell the mayor and commonalty of parliamentary negotiations over the location of the staple, of the doings of the French and Scottish envoys and of the announcement of the death of the king of France.[93] Smaller towns had a similar interest. When one of the members for Leicester returned from the York parliament of 1332 wine was bought for him while he told the news (*narrand' rumores*), and there were similar payments in 1351–2.[94] Other borough records, particularly those for Lynn, suggest that such reports were regularly made in the late fourteenth century and probably earlier.[95] We cannot expect to

[91] H. G. Richardson and G. O. Sayles, 'The parliament of Carlisle, 1307; some new documents', *EHR*, LIII (1938), pp. 425–37.

[92] Above, pp. 81–2; *Rot. Parl. Hactenus Ined.*, pp. 100–1; Dorset County Record Office, Dorchester: Bridport Borough Archives, B1/G1 ('The Old Doom Book of Bridport'), f. 149.

[93] *Calendar of Plea and Memoranda Rolls of the City of London, 1323–64*, ed. A. H. Thomas (Cambridge, 1926), pp. 52–3, 56–7; McKisack, *Borough Representation*, p. 140.

[94] *Records of the Borough of Leicester*, ed. M. Bateson, III, pp. 11, 75; Tout, *Chapters*, III, p. 291 n. 1.

[95] McKisack, *Borough Representation*, pp. 139–44.

learn so much from local sources about the reception of news in the counties, for counties kept no records. But it is hard to think that wine and gossip flowed less freely in the shires than in the boroughs when parliament was over.

Whether this lively and often critical interest in parliament and its activities produced anything like a general attitude to parliament is hard to tell. Provincial opinion doubtless fluctuated from one parliament to another, varying with the financial burdens which the assembly imposed, the legislative benefits which it offered, and the success of the community's members in promoting local interests. Only preachers were prepared to generalise, often in no favourable terms. John Bromyard, writing about 1348, commented that much advice was given in contemporary parliaments but little was done; matters ordained there were afterwards ignored. Bishop Brinton of Rochester, preaching in 1378 or 1379, held similar views: 'In the realm of England so many laws abound and yet there is no execution or observance of the laws.' And a later versifier agreed: 'Many acts of parliament, And few kept with true intent.'[96]

It was the business of preachers and poets to moralise. But they may nevertheless provide a better witness to public opinion than their professional interests would suggest, for there was much truth in their attack. Parliament lacked the regular control over the executive which might have transformed legislation into law enforcement. Statutes might promise reform, but the crown could occasionally repeal them and often ignore them; the recurrent statutes limiting purveyance and military obligation under Edward III suggest the ineffectiveness of much law-making. In these circumstances the misgivings of the preachers may have been widely shared. In January 1341, shortly after the king had appointed judicial commissions to punish the crimes of his officials, he asserted his good intentions in the face of a mistrustful public. 'We have heard,' he said, 'that many men of our realm greatly fear that such wrongdoers will be reconciled with us and will escape lightly . . . and will afterwards be as great masters and maintainers as they have previously been'—fears which in the event were well justified.[97] A similar and related scepticism about the possibilities of change

[96] G. R. Owst, *Literature and Pulpit*, pp. 340, 584; *The Sermons of Thomas Brinton, Bishop of Rochester* (1373–1389), ed. M. A. Devlin, II (CS, 3rd ser., LXXXVI, 1954), p. 390.
[97] PRO, SC1/62/85.

may have met the statutes and concessions obtained in parliament when these were announced in the counties. Provincial Englishmen took a less whiggish view of parliamentary development than some modern historians have done. They did not think in terms of 'the rise of the commons' or of the commons' 'growing political maturity'; and they were all too well aware that the redress of grievances made possible by parliament was a less certain prospect than the taxation which parliament imposed.

By the 1370s parliament had become the chief intermediary between the crown and its subjects. The commons' petitions told the government of the grievances of the provinces, while statutes, ordinances and tax schedules marked the quickening flow of information and instruction in the reverse direction, from centre to localities. Representatives reported both to their constituents, as we have seen, and to the king, who may have learnt much through conversation with individual knights and burgesses. It is only incidentally that a petition of about 1339 from the community of Cumberland mentions that the county's 'knights for parliament' will tell the king of the dangerous state of the Marches,[98] and many similar communications are likely to have gone unrecorded. Behind this widening range of contacts between government and governed lay the fiscal pressures engendered by war and taxation. Yet if there is a point at which parliament and provinces moved sharply into closer alignment it seems to be neither in 1294–5, when the country was first committed to large-scale war and the commons first began to appear regularly in parliament, nor in 1337, at the opening of the Hundred Years War, but in 1327. That year saw the presentation of the first full set of commons' petitions; the first comprehensive statute to derive from such petitions; the first known request from the commons for the publication of the king's concessions in the provinces; and the first instance of the circulation of an unofficial version of parliamentary proceedings. All were precedents taken up again in the parliaments of the 1330s and 1340s. This sudden expansion in the public role of parliament was rooted both in the misgovernment of Edward II, which produced many of the abuses enumerated in the commons' petitions and reformed by the ensuing statute, and in the part played by parliament in the king's deposition. Parliament was now no longer valued by the localities chiefly as an occasion for the submission of private complaints, a part of its business which

[98] PRO, SC8/206/10289.

declined rapidly under Edward III.[99] It had become instead a meeting place for broader interests : for the grievances of particular communities and of the national community and for the concerns not merely of king, council and aristocracy but of the political nation.

[99] Sayles, *King's Parliament*, pp. 110–11.

J. H. DENTON

4

The Clergy and Parliament in the Thirteenth and Fourteenth Centuries

THE EMPHASIS NOW OFTEN GIVEN to the specifically lay features of the organisation and work of parliament during the first two centuries of its development calls for scrutiny. The description of parliament as 'an omnicompetent organ of government at the summit of lay affairs in England' is perhaps unexceptionable.[1] Even so, we must assume no intention here to imply the exclusion from parliament either of the clergy or of clerical interests. Important developments took place during this period concerning the position of the clergy in parliament. To attempt to understand these developments is to be made aware of many gaps in our present knowledge. What follows is intended not only to indicate the marked disregard of the clergy by some historians of parliament but also to serve as a guide to areas in need of more detailed study.

Let us begin with a brief survey of the categories of churchmen who were present when parliament was in session. In the first place, royal clerks, alongside judges and lay officers, were responsible for the administrative and judicial work of parliament; and a number of royal officials, lay and clerical, including masters, or principal clerks, of chancery, were summoned personally to be present with the king and 'with the others of our council'.[2] While we may consider that the

[1] Edwards, ' "Justice" ', in Fryde and Miller, I, p. 297, and cited in E. Miller, *The Origins of Parliament* (Historical Assoc. pamphlet, 1960), p. 23.
[2] See Richardson and Sayles, 'King's ministers in parliament'; Plucknett, 'Parliament', in Fryde and Miller, I, pp. 209–11; and *Memo de Parl.*, pp. xxxxvii–xxxxviii (Fryde and Miller, I, pp. 93–4).

clerical interest *per se* was the concern not of these royal clerks but rather of the directly summoned prelates and of the indirectly summoned ecclesiastical dignitaries and lower clergy, it must none the less be remembered that the clerks working in parliament and the clerical councillors were, of course, themselves either prelates, ecclesiastical dignitaries or members of the lower clergy.[3] This simple factor is an indication of the two-sided nature of the duties and responsibilities of the clergymen who served the crown. But more striking in fact than this intermingling of roles is the existence of a division and distinction of outlook and activity between the royal clergy and the clergy outside royal government, a division and distinction which was visible at many points in the thirteenth and fourteenth centuries and was of deep political and social significance.[4] The clerks who served the king were sometimes classed as 'laymen' by other clerks. But this was abuse.

The spiritual lords, personally summoned, though often in fact present only by proxy, were bishops and abbots or priors.[5] Although the composition of neither councils nor parliaments was determined by tenurial considerations alone, and although the king could veto, as for political reasons, the summons of particular prelates or grant individual privileges of exoneration from attendance, yet there is no question of the central importance for the prelates summoned to parliament of their binding tenurial relationship with the crown. As specified in 1164 ecclesiastical tenants-in-chief were bound as 'barons' to be 'present at the judgements of the king's court unless a case shall arise of judgement concerning life and limb' (Constitutions of Clarendon, cap. 11). All twenty-one bishops of England and Wales were, as a rule, summoned,

[3] The diffusion of royal clerks as deans, archdeacons and canons of cathedral churches *c.* 1321 is effectively demonstrated in J. S. Roskell, 'A consideration of certain aspects and problems of the English *Modus Tenendi Parliamentum*', *BJRUL*, L (1967–8), pp. 423–31.

[4] See, for example, the point of view of the royal clerks elaborated in complaints against Archbishop Pecham's canons promulgated at Reading in 1279; *Councils & Synods with other Documents relating to the English Church, II, 1205–1313*, ed. F. M. Powicke and C. R. Cheney (2 parts, Oxford, 1964), pp. 853–4.

[5] For what follows see Roskell, 'Attendance of the lords', especially pp. 153–62, 202–4; M. Howell, *Regalian Right in Medieval England* (London, 1962), pp. 61–2; Plucknett, 'Parliament', in Fryde and Miller, I, pp. 207–8; H. M. Chew, *The English Ecclesiastical Tenants-in-Chief and Knight Service* (London, 1932), pp. 168–79; and (to be used with care) A. M. Reich, *The Parliamentary Abbots to 1470* (*Univ. of California Publications in History*, XVII, no. 4, 1941). On the precedence of bishops see E. Kemp, 'The Canterbury provincial chapter and the collegiality of bishops in the middle ages', in *Études d'Histoire du Droit Canonique dédiées à G. le Bras* (Paris, 1965), I, pp. 185–94.

though five of them (the Welsh bishops and the bishop of Carlisle) held of the king in chief by free alms rather than by military service, and thus not technically by barony. The bishop of Rochester held his lands of the archbishop of Canterbury; but it is interesting that by 1291 Edward I appears to have established that three of the bishop's manors were actually held in chief of the king, and, after this time, lands held of the king were certainly taken into royal custody during vacancies at Rochester. There is little strength to the argument that the summons of vicars-general for bishops who were absent from the realm and the summons of guardians of the spiritualities during episcopal vacancies imply that the bishops attended parliament by reason of their 'spiritual' position. The work of administering sees fell to vicars-general and guardians of spiritualities: as Pike pointed out, *they* had the authority to summon the other clergy of the diocese.[6] We must not imagine that the status of bishops as clergymen was in any way weakened by the fact that they held land of the crown. But their role in parliament was not, in essence, a spiritual role.

As for abbots and priors, the full official record for the parliament of January 1265 shows that the summons, on this occasion of a total of 102 religious superiors, was not governed by strict or consistent feudal principles. The monastic changes of the twelfth century had drastically altered the list of wealthy and politically important houses. The number of heads of religious houses summoned, though varying considerably in composition, remained high during Edward I's reign, but declined rapidly in Edward II's reign.[7] For example, of the many Cistercian and Premonstratensian abbots summoned by Edward I only Beaulieu remained after 1322; and Beaulieu soon successfully claimed release from the duty of attendance. The evidence for the period from

---

[6] Pike, *House of Lords*, p. 155.

[7] There are sometimes perplexing omissions in the lists of prelates summoned. Why was the bishop of Worcester omitted from the lists for parliaments in 1295, 1296 and 1300 (*Parl. Writs*, I, ii, pp. 32, 47, 83)? Although the bishop of Winchester was omitted from the close roll list for the Carlisle parliament in 1307, he was certainly summoned (*Parl. Writs*, I, ii, 182–4 and *Registrum H. Woodlock*, ed. A. W. Goodman (CYS, 1940–1), pp. 158–9). Conversely, why did twelve abbots who were not included among those summoned to the Carlisle parliament send their proctors (*Rot. Parl.*, I, pp. 188–91, and *Parl. Writs*, I, ii, pp. 182–4)? These were the Cistercian abbots of Bindon, Netley, Quarr, Stoneleigh, Swineshead, Warden and Waverley, the Benedictine abbots of Abingdon, Chertsey, Crowland and Hyde and the Premonstratensian abbot of Easby. Perhaps they wished to be present because of their interest in the king's statute 'De asportis religiosorum' (see *Councils & Synods II*, ed. F. M. Powicke and C. R. Cheney, p. 1232).

the second half of Edward II's reign up to 1341 demonstrates that the regular clergy had no wish to attend parliament and many secured release on the grounds that their tenure was not baronial. Of those who continued to be summoned, however, many held of the king by alms rather than by knight service, and others whose tenure was baronial were not summoned. A class of ecclesiastical barons 'by writ' had emerged. On average only twenty-seven abbots and priors were summoned after the middle of the fourteenth century, though we should add to these the ten priors of monastic cathedral churches, who were summoned indirectly, that is, by their bishops. It is important to note in this respect that the difference between the number of regular clergy summoned to parliaments and the number summoned to convocations of clergy was now considerable and, indeed, had become the major distinction in the clerical composition of the two assemblies. This factor must be borne in mind, not least because a very large proportion of the estates or 'temporalities' of the English church were in the hands of the monasteries.

Beneath the spiritual lords were the ecclesiastical dignitaries and diocesan clergy, summoned by each individual bishop. This whole group are on occasion classified as the 'lower clergy', though it is hard to find the reasons for putting them in a single category. Considering the emphasis given to the representatives from the shires, it is surprising that so little interest has been shown in the representatives from the dioceses. Many matters concerning the clergy from the dioceses are yet to be fully explored, including their particular contribution to decisions taken by the assembled clergy and the changing procedures of their summons in the period 1294 to 1340. As to attendance, it must be stressed from the first that the usual summons by use of the *premunientes* clause in each bishop's writ was an indirect summons which was not regarded as legally enforceable. The clergy, *qua* clergy, would not accept summons by enforceable writs to a lay court. Those summoned by the *premunientes* clause remained unchanged from the time the diocesan clergy were first summoned to parliament in 1295. The ecclesiastical dignitaries, all deans or priors of cathedral churches and all archdeacons, were summoned individually, and the cathedral and parish clergy were summoned by representatives, one to be chosen by each cathedral chapter or priory and two by each diocese. As a result, remembering that the dioceses of Bath and Wells and Coventry and Lichfield possessed two cathedral churches, a full summons comprised ten cathedral priors, thirteen cathedral deans,[8] sixty archdeacons, twenty-three proctors of cathedral churches and forty-two proctors of the parish clergy. The question of actual attendance is complicated by several matters, not the least of which is the fact that proctors of absent individuals and proctors appointed to represent cathedral and parish clergy often served in more than one proctorial capacity.

However much, in the end, it may be necessary to emphasise that parliament was a lay court and that the clergy were a class apart from the laity, there is no doubt that students of the early growth of parliament, with its large complement of clergy in attendance, must avoid a narrow or limited approach. Can we wholeheartedly accept generalisations about parliament reflecting the needs of the whole community and about shire representatives providing vital links between central government and the localities when little or no account is taken of members of that wealthy and influential section of society who were probably best able throughout this period to act as agents of communication? It is no answer to argue that the clergy's contribution to the affairs of the realm has been studied by historians of convocation, for, although this may be partly true, the assumption that convocation can and should be studied as an institution quite separate from parliament is questionable.

The keen interest of former times—especially of the late seventeenth and early eighteenth centuries—in the historical relationship of convocation and parliament has long since died away. William Wake's erudite work on *The State of the Church and Clergy of England, in their Councils, Convocations, Synods, Conventions and other Publick Assemblies* (London, 1703) is now consulted mainly for its appendix of documents; but as a detailed examination of all clerical assemblies of the medieval and early modern periods it has not yet been completely replaced.[9] There is no denying the political importance of the clergy in the thirteenth and fourteenth centuries and no denying the reliance within the king's government upon churchmen of all ranks; and yet it is generally assumed that the development of parliament, with its

---

[8] Thirteen were summoned, but it is not clear how the *premunientes* clause was interpreted by the bishops of Llandaff and St David's: they were asked to summon the deans, but neither of their cathedral churches possessed a dean as such (see J. le Neve, *Fasti Ecclesiae Anglicanae*, XI (The Welsh Dioceses), compiled by B. Jones (London, 1965), p. 86).

[9] For an important survey see, however, E. W. Kemp, *Counsel and Consent* (London, 1961).

political and governmental aspects, was separate and distinct from the concurrent development of ecclesiastical assemblies. Arguments that the clergy, for example the Dominicans,[10] had a particular influence in respect of representation upon parliament as it developed in the thirteenth century have foundered for lack of convincing evidence. To suggest that churchmen may have influenced the laity is itself to imply that the clergy had no *direct* part to play in the major assemblies of the day. Despite her own pioneering work, Maude Clarke's strictures about the gulf between ecclesiastical and secular historians are still largely relevant.[11] With few exceptions recent historians of parliament have been little concerned with clerical assemblies, and historians of convocation not sufficiently concerned with parliament. Is this division of interests a fair reflection of a demonstrable historical division between the twin institutions during the early stages of their growth ?

The question is not easily answered. One factor, however, stands out : although the ecclesiastical council (occasionally under the unambiguous designation *provinciale concilium*)[12] was at times specifically committed to the reform of the church and of the clergy and was at times clearly summoned in obedience to the prescriptions of canon law, yet the clergy met with increasing frequency during the thirteenth century in direct response to demands for taxation, made by the pope, then by pope and king and then, under Edward I, by the king separately.[13] Thus taxation, one of the primary reasons for the assembling of the barons and representatives from the shires and towns, was also a primary reason for the assembling of the clergy. Evidence relating to the clerical

[10] E. Barker, *The Dominican Order and Convocation* (Oxford, 1913).

[11] M. V. Clarke, *Medieval Representation and Consent* (London, 1936), p. 16. There is, however, recognition of the importance of the clergy's relations with parliament in D. B. Weske, *Convocation of the Clergy* (London, 1937).

[12] See E. W. Kemp, 'The origins of the Canterbury convocation', *JEccH*, III (1952), especially pp. 137–8, referring to the provincial councils of 1222, 1261, 1281, 1313, 1341, 1342, 1356, 1414 and 1417. And see *id.*, 'The archbishop in convocation', in *The Lambeth Lectures: Medieval Records of the Archbishop of Canterbury* (London, 1962), pp. 21–34; and B. Bolton, 'The council of London of 1342', in *Councils and Assemblies* (*Studies in Church History*, VII), ed. G. J. Cuming and D. Baker (Cambridge, 1971), pp. 147–60. Kemp has shown that convocation, that is, the assembly for granting taxes, and the provincial council became as one during the fourteenth century.

[13] See E. W. Kemp, 'Origins of convocation', pp. 138–43, and *Counsel and Consent*, pp. 67–86. Papal taxation, although it benefited in large measure the coffers of Edward I and Edward II, had become mandatory and not subject to consent : see especially W. E. Lunt, *Financial Relations of the Papacy with England to 1327* (Cambridge, Mass., 1939), pp. 175–418.

assemblies in two important parliaments (the Bury parliament of 1296 and the Lincoln parliament of 1316) demonstrates that we must take care not to suggest too clear-cut, or too early, a distinction between clerical meetings in and clerical meetings out of parliament.[14] The chronicler Bartholomew Cotton provides a valuable description of the congregation of clergy in the parliament at Bury St Edmunds in November 1296. The churchmen met separately from the laity (as they had done in the 'model' parliament of 1295)[15] to hear from Archbishop Winchelsey the request of a subsidy from the king. To discuss the matter they then divided into four groups: the bishops; the religious; the ecclesiastical dignitaries; and the proctors of the parish clergy ('procuratores communitatis cleri'). It is notable that exactly the same procedure was adopted when the Canterbury clergy reassembled to discuss the subsidy further in an ecclesiastical council in January 1297. There are no grounds for believing in practical differences in procedure or in powers between the two assemblies in respect of the clergy of the southern province, even though the new assembly summoned by the archbishop was of wider composition than the parliamentary assembly. Having brought the diocesan clergy into parliament, the crown no doubt hoped that clerical meetings would regularly convene in answer to the parliamentary summons. This policy came near to success during the archiepiscopate of Walter Reynolds (1313–27). The assembling of the clergy at the parliament of Lincoln in January 1316 has never been listed among the ecclesiastical councils of the English church. But it should be. The clergy of the southern province were, in fact, summoned by their archbishop to meet three days before the parliament ('as though at the doors of parliament'), but the evidence relating to their assembly suggests that there was confusion about whether they were meeting in an ecclesiastical council or in a parliament. The confusion is hardly

---

[14] *Bartholomaei de Cotton Historia Anglicana*, ed. H. R. Luard (RS, 1859), pp. 314–17, and *Councils & Synods II*, pp. 1150, 1158–9; and J. H. Denton, 'Walter Reynolds and ecclesiastical politics, 1313–1316: a postscript to *Councils & Synods II*', in *Church and Government in the Middle Ages: Essays presented to C. R. Cheney*, ed. C. N. L. Brooke *et al.* (Cambridge, 1976), pp. 263–4.

[15] See *Flores Historiarum*, ed. H. R. Luard (RS, 1890), III, p. 283 and 'Annales de Wigornia in *Annales Monastici*, ed. H. R. Luard, IV (RS, 1869), p. 524. It is interesting that the procedure for the discussion of taxation upon lay movables in the parliament of 1306 was for the knights and burgesses to deliberate apart from each other, granting aid, as they so often did, at different rates; the knights met with the prelates, earls, barons and other magnates, and the citizens and burgesses met with others of the king's demesne. For the evidence see D. Pasquet, *An Essay on the Origins of the House of Commons* (Cambridge, 1925), pp. 235–6.

surprising, since Archbishop Reynolds had been issuing provincial summonses for the clergy to assemble in parliaments very much as though they were councils of his province. The frequent variation of terminology for clerical meetings, in documentary as well as chronicle evidence, as between *concilium, parliamentum, congregatio, convocatio* and *tractatus,* certainly reflects at times a confusion of attitude.[16] It should come as no surprise that we must beware of assuming an early emergence of hard constitutional forms, for those who have studied the first phases of the history of parliament have long ago learned that categories or terms which imply rigid specifications, like 'commons' and, indeed, 'parliament' itself, must be used with the greatest care.

Two areas of study have been given some prominence in recent years: the *plena potestas* of representatives and the presentation of petitions. Both matters were of importance to the clergy, and consideration of them will serve to show that there has been a continuing tendency to stress unduly the early development of a lay commons. The influential article by J. G. Edwards about the writs of summons requiring the elected knights and burgesses to come to parliament with full powers to bind their counties and boroughs left the summons of the clergy completely out of account. Edwards pointed, for example, to the emphasis upon the full powers of the knights and burgesses in the *Modus Tenendi Parliamentum* of *c.* 1321, but he did not note that there is the same emphasis in the *Modus* upon the full powers of the representatives of the lower clergy.[17] The strong implication of the case presented by Edwards is that it was during the second half of the thirteenth century that a lay commons became a distinct and institutionalised reality. To view the principle of *plena potestas* narrowly and in relation only to the elected knights and burgesses is to give an

[16] See the ecclesiastical councils of January and March 1297 as *parliamenta* (*Councils & Synods II*, p. 1151 n. 2, and D. Wilkins, *Concilia Magnae Britanniae et Hiberniae* (London, 1737), II, p. 225); the clergy in the parliament of November 1296 as a *congregatio seu convocatio* (*Councils & Synods II*, p. 1149 n. 1) and the clergy in the parliament of April 1309 and in the parliament of November–December 1311 as a *convocatio* (PRO, Chancery Ecclesiastical Misc., C270/35/17 and *Registrum S. de Gandavo*, ed. C. T. Flower and M. C. B. Dawes (CYS, 1934), p. 417); and the ecclesiastical assembly of May 1314, summoned directly by the king, as a *tractatus* (J. H. Denton, 'Walter Reynolds and ecclesiastical politics', p. 257 n. 54).

[17] Edwards, *'Plena potestas'*, in Fryde and Miller, I, pp. 139–40, and M. V. Clarke, *Representation and Consent*, pp. 374, 376. In the Record Commission edition of the *Modus*, used by Edwards, there is no separate heading for the section on the clergy: *Modus Tenendi Parliamentum*, ed. T. D. Hardy (London, 1846), pp. 1–7.

exaggerated importance to the legal procedure of their summons.[18] The procedure for the summons of the clergy in the thirteenth century deserves a brief examination.

Setting aside the proctors of absent individual churchmen, the proctors of the clergy represented either chapters or parish clergy. As the summons of these proctors to assemblies became more frequent, so there was an increasing awareness that they must be in a position to act responsibly and with authority.[19] When proctors of cathedral and collegiate churches and religious houses had been summoned to an ecclesiastical council in May 1226, apparently for the first time, they were enjoined to come fully instructed about how they wished to reply to Honorius III's request of financial assistance. Proctors of cathedral churches were summoned to another council later in the same year, convoked at the request of the chapter of Salisbury and concerned with the granting of an aid to the king: the precise instructions given to the proctors of the Salisbury chapter have survived.[20] Later in Henry III's reign, in 1265, the dean and chapter of York were ordered to send two proctors having *plena potestas* to a parliament at Winchester.[21] Representation of the parish clergy, of rectors and vicars, in assemblies was also developing. In 1240, 1257 and 1258 it is clear that archdeacons were regarded as representing the interests of these lower clergy.[22] The archdeacons were on occasion required to present letters of proxy from the clergy subject to them; and allied to this process was an emphasis upon diocesan assemblies prior to provincial assemblies.

[18] See G. Post, *Studies in Medieval Legal Thought* (Princeton, 1964), especially pp. 108–10 (this chapter is a revised version of '*Plena potestas* and consent in medieval assemblies', *Traditio*, I (1943), pp. 355–408).

[19] See *Councils & Synods II*, pp. 157–8, 163–4, 285–93, 481–3, 504–5, 531, 571–2, 797–8, 826, 947. Some of the important writs of summons had been collected in Stubbs, *Select Charters*, pp. 445–7, 459–60.

[20] *Vetus Registrum St Osmundi*, ed. W. H. Rich Jones, II (RS, 1884), pp. 63–5 (D. Wilkins, *Concilia*, I, p. 605).

[21] Stubbs, *Select Charters*, pp. 406–7 (CCR 1264–8, pp. 116–17), for 1 June, but the parliament was apparently postponed until September.

[22] Matthew Paris's interesting statement (*Councils & Synods II*, p. 287) about the 1240 assembly was noted by J. Armitage Robinson, 'Convocation of Canterbury: its early history', *Church Quarterly Rev.*, LXXXI (1915–16), pp. 89–90: 'When in 1240 the papal legate had assembled the bishops at Northampton and made a fresh demand for money, "taught by the case of the abbots", as Matthew Paris says, they replied: "We have archdeacons under us, who know the resources of the beneficed clergy under them; but we do not know. The matter touches all ('omnes tangit hoc negotium'), therefore all should be assembled: without them it is neither fitting nor expedient to reply."' Also see E. W. Kemp, *Counsel and Consent*, p. 69.

The opinions of the lower clergy were being represented and, to some extent, their voice was being heard, as the protest of the rectors of Berkshire in 1240 bears witness. Proctors of the parish clergy attended an assembly in April 1254 (designated a 'parliament' in some official sources) and were summoned, separately from the archdeacons, to an ecclesiastical council in 1256. They were present to discuss a proposed royal subsidy in 1269 and were summoned again in 1278. In 1283, when a royal subsidy was once more in question, one proctor from cathedral churches and two proctors from each diocese were required to attend an ecclesiastical council with 'plena et expressa potestas'. This became an established procedure for many assemblies, as when this same number of proctors were summoned, through the *premunientes* clause, to come to parliament with 'plena et sufficiens potestas' in 1295. Edwards wrote: 'But shires and boroughs are not the only communities in England: around and above them there towers another community—the community of the realm, the community of England, which blends, transcends them all.'[23] Where, in this scheme of things, should we place the community of the clergy?

A similar disregard of the clergy is to be found in a second major area: the presentation of petitions in parliament. Much of the work that has been done on petitions has been about the petitions from the shires and towns, for a central aim has been to understand the origin of the commons' petitions.[24] Yet, as the petitions printed in *Rotuli Parliamentorum* alone show, ecclesiastical corporations—religious houses and cathedral churches—presented large numbers of petitions in parliament, seeking, like the burgesses, to protect their privileges and liberties. Individual churchmen also, of both high and low standing, petitioned the king, as when in 1278 two royal clerks sought royal support in disputes about their presentations to churches and as when in 1307 a poor chaplain from Llandaff sought protection for tithes granted to him from lands which were extra-parochial.[25] We have the record for the appointment of the triers of clerical petitions for the parliament of January 1348.[26] Pollard stressed a question of fundamental import

[23] Edwards, *'Plena potestas'*, in Fryde and Miller, I, p. 146.
[24] See G. L. Haskins, 'Three early petitions of the commonalty', *Speculum*, XII (1937), pp. 314–18; Haskins, 'Petitions of representatives'; Rayner, ' "Commune petition" '; and other references in Harriss, *King, Parliament and Public Finance*, p. 118.
[25] *Rot. Parl.*, I, pp. 5–6, 200.
[26] *Ibid.*, II, p. 164.

when he wrote that 'parliaments provided no remedy for abuses in the clerical courts'; but he went too far in suggesting that it was the papal court rather than parliament that was 'the final resort for matters in which the affections of churchmen were mainly involved'.[27] The king and his council in parliament could provide no immediate remedy for abuses in court Christian, but abuses, and supposed abuses, in the lay courts and the actions of royal justices and ministers were a major cause of clerical discontent.

The many sets of clerical grievances of the thirteenth and fourteenth centuries contain in the main complaints about the procedures of the king's courts. These *gravamina* presented to king and council have been usually studied with the intention of understanding the juridical relations of the English church and the crown and not with the intention of understanding the constitutional and political position of the clergy in parliament.[28] Richardson and Sayles, writing about the clerical petitions of 1285, perhaps stressed a little too firmly, for this early date, the 'essential incompatibility' of the ecclesiastical organisation with the secular. The force of clerical opinion proved to be one of the primary reasons for the crown's failure to bring together clerical and lay assemblies. Richardson and Sayles suggested that 'in parliament the representatives of the Church came only to complain and to consider the king's demands for taxes'.[29] But both these functions were of great importance. It is clear that clerical *gravamina* were often derived from the complaints of the lesser clergy of the diocese.[30] The usual procedure, so it seems, was that the grievances—and also the conditions attached to the granting of taxes[31]—were drawn up in ecclesiastical councils and

[27] Pollard, *Evolution of Parliament*, pp. 196–7.

[28] See, especially, the useful survey by W. R. Jones, 'Bishops, politics and the two laws: the *gravamina* of the English clergy, 1237–1399', *Speculum*, XLI (1966), pp. 209–45. For the grievances of 1399 see R. L. Storey, 'Clergy and common law in the reign of Henry IV', in *Medieval Legal Records in Memory of C. A. F. Meekings*, ed. R. F. Hunnisett and J. B. Post (HMSO, 1978), especially pp. 342–3.

[29] H. G. Richardson and G. O. Sayles, 'The clergy in the Easter parliament, 1285', *EHR*, LII (1937), p 231.

[30] For the formulation of grievances see, notably, the memorandum of the council of 1309 (*Councils & Synods II*, pp. 1266–8), the evidence from the Exeter diocese for 1328–9 (D. Wilkins, *Concilia*, II, pp. 548–9, and *Register J. de Grandisson*, ed. F. C. Hingeston-Randolph, I (London, 1894), pp. 446–8), and the memorandum of the council of 1399 (D. Wilkins, *Concilia*, III, pp. 239–40).

[31] See M. V. Clarke, *Representation and Consent*, p. 24 n. 3.

then presented by the prelates to the king in parliament, as in 1280, 1285, 1300, 1301, 1309, 1316, 1327, 1328–9, 1341, 1344, 1352, 1376, 1377 and 1399. Certain clauses in these grievances against the secular power were at times closely associated with legislation of the English church,[32] and some were also associated at times with petitions which were put forward separately by individual churches or churchmen.[33] In addition, as with the petitions of the lay commons, the clerical *gravamina* of the fourteenth century were frequently embodied in royal statutes, as in 1316, 1344, 1352 and 1377.

The role played by the spiritual lords in parliament was no doubt largely determined by their individual political position. It is interesting, for example, that the bishops who supported and the bishops who opposed the crown in 1297 were summoned, as were the magnates, by separately enrolled and differently dated writs to the autumn parliament in which *Confirmatio Cartarum* was conceded.[34] The constitutional development of parliament cannot, of course, be set apart from *realpolitik*. Although further examination of the activities of the prelates in parliament will no doubt be illuminating,[35] the position of the lesser clergy is still in greater need of clarification. Historians have been especially perplexed about the role of the lesser clergy who continued to be summoned by the *premunientes* clause to parliament. They were summoned, and often attended, after the 1330s even though it is clear that clerical assemblies, notably for the granting of taxes, met as provincial meetings quite distinct from parliament and were convoked separately by the archbishops of Canterbury and York. Why should the lesser clergy send proctors to both convocation and parliament? The two often met consecutively, but usually separate proctors appear

---

[32] For example, the canons of Archbishop Boniface: see C. R. Cheney, 'Legislation of the medieval English Church', *EHR*, L (1935), pp. 402–4, and *Councils & Synods II*, pp. 661–85.

[33] As in 1301: the general complaint against the king's treatment of alien priories coincided with individual petitions from priors (see *Councils & Synods II*, p. 1218, *Rot. Parl.*, I, p. 144, and PRO, King's Memoranda Rolls, E159/74 mm. 63r–64r).

[34] *Parl. Writs*, I, ii, pp. 55–6.

[35] We learn of the archbishop of Canterbury's responsibility for examining clerical proxies and excuses for absence, and for imposing penances on those 'not caring to attend', from Winchelsey's delegation of some of his authority to the bishops of Salisbury and Chichester for the parliament of November–December 1311 (*Reg. Gandavo* (CYS), p. 417).

to have been appointed for each.[36] Before the list of parliaments in the *Handbook of British Chronology* it was noted that the matter of the presence or absence of the representatives of the diocesan clergy demanded further research.[37] A commonly held view has been that the proctors of the diocesan clergy gradually withdrew from parliament in the course of the fourteenth century. For example, following a comment by E. C. Lowry about the proctors of the Ely diocese, A. M. Reich concluded that after 1341 only a few of these proctors were present in parliament for the next thirty years and then their class disappeared. This did not run counter to the view expressed by Tout that 'there is little evidence that the lower clergy had "representatives" in the parliaments of the later fourteenth century'.[38] More recently A. K. McHardy has surveyed the evidence, which, although in no sense complete, suggests in fact that the cathedral chapters and parish clergy continued to send proctors to parliament at a roughly even rate during, and perhaps beyond, the fourteenth century.[39]

Nevertheless there is no denying that convocation was divorced from parliament after the 1330s. The division had taken place by stages and resulted from a long struggle which had lasted more than forty years; and, even after the decisive separation, clerical assemblies continued to be summoned at the king's request and to be attended by the king's agents.[40] The break, associated with the events of 1340 and 1341, proved

---

[36] Yet the bishop of Lincoln advised the clergy of his diocese to appoint the same proctors for the clerical assembly of 16 January 1327 at St Paul's as had been appointed for the parliament of 7 January at Westminster; D. Wilkins, *Concilia*, II, p. 534, cited by D. B. Weske, *Convocation of the Clergy*, p. 112. Chapter 3 of Weske's book is a reprint with few changes of 'The attitude of the English clergy in the thirteenth and fourteenth centuries towards the obligation of attendance on convocations and parliaments' in *Essays in History and Political Theory in Honor of C.H. McIlwain* (Cambridge, Mass., 1936), pp. 77–108.

[37] *HBC*, p. 496.

[38] E. C. Lowry, 'Clerical proctors in parliament and knights of the shire, 1280–1374', *EHR*, XLVIII (1933), p. 454; A. M. Reich, *Parliamentary Abbots to 1470*, p. 361; and Tout, *Chapters*, IV, p. 18 n. 2.

[39] A. K. McHardy, 'The representation of the English lower clergy in parliament during the later fourteenth century' in *Sanctity and Secularity: the Church and the World* (Studies in Church History, X), ed. D. Baker (Oxford, 1973), pp. 97–107. Also see D. B. Weske, *Convocation of the Clergy*, pp. 57–79, and E. W. Kemp, 'Origins of convocation', p. 142.

[40] For the attendance of royal envoys see J. R. L. Highfield, 'The Relations between the Church and the English Crown, 1349–78' (Oxford D.Phil. thesis, 1951), pp. 254–8, 451–2. The minutes of the convocation of 1406 illustrate, as E. F. Jacob pointed out, the close connection of convocation with parliament: 'The Canterbury convocation of 1406' in *Essays in Medieval History presented to Bertie Wilkinson*, ed. T. A. Sandquist and M. R. Powicke (Toronto, 1969), p. 348.

to be of long-term significance. The methods of summoning the clergy to parliament had gone through a number of changes. Since 1314 one of the means of enforcing the crown's desire to gain the attendance in parliament of the lower clergy had been to supplement the *premunientes* clause to each bishop with a writ enjoining the archbishops of each province to issue provincial writs. As a result, the archbishops themselves had often been ordering the attendance of the clergy. The last attempt by the crown to secure the presence of the clergy by provincial writs was made for the parliament of March 1340. The clergy had stated early in the fourteenth century, and would state again, that the king had no customary right to cite them by enforceable mandates to assemble in a lay court. They were often to choose to be present in parliament but strongly opposed the legal requirement. In 1341 Archbishop Stratford made a clear statement that the clergy—other than the spiritual lords—were in no way bound to attend parliament.[41]

In some measure the crown continued to want the presence of the diocesan clergy. Edward III, for example, appears to have been trying to gain the support of the clerical proctors when he asked that they should attend the February parliament of 1371 two days in advance of the prelates and laymen.[42] The parish clergy themselves must have felt that there were times when their interests needed to be safeguarded in parliament, for otherwise they would have shunned altogether the elaborate process of electing diocesan representatives, through the rural deans and the archdeacons, and shunned the necessity of paying expenses chargeable upon the income of each rector or vicar.[43] It is possible that at times the lower clergy wished to present petitions in parliament, as when a proctor for the clergy of the York diocese peti-

[41] See A. K. McHardy, 'Representation of lower clergy', pp. 97–9, 105; J. H. Denton, 'Walter Reynolds and ecclesiastical politics', especially pp. 257–63; M. V. Clarke, *Representation and Consent*, pp. 22–3, 126–40; and H. M. Chew, *Ecclesiastical Tenants-in-Chief*, pp. 173–5.

[42] *Dignity of a Peer*, IV, pp. 646–7, and Tout, *Chapters*, III, pp. 266–8.

[43] See the manorial accounts cited in A. K. McHardy, 'Representation of lower clergy', p. 99 (and see p. 105); and see D. B. Weske, *Convocation of the Clergy*, pp. 115–16, *Reg. Woodlock* (CYS), pp. xxx, 194–5, 206–7, and *Councils & Synods II*, pp. 1363–4. Durham, Dean and Chapter Muniments, Locellus XIX, no. 90, is a patent letter of 2 January 1331 recording the receipt, by the collector, of payments from some of the benefices of the archdeaconry of Durham for the expenses of the clergy's proctor (Master John de Bochingham) at parliament 'pro nova taxatione querenda'.

tioned in 1368.[44] Yet any clergyman could petition in parliament, and there appears to be no evidence that the clerical proctors petitioned there in concert. The clergy may well have been concerned about the 'lay' taxes granted in parliament, for they apparently contributed to these taxes for their goods upon lands acquired since the assessment of ecclesiastical wealth in 1291.[45] Yet most of the income which they derived from their parochial benefices, classed as spiritual income, was included in the 1291 assessment, and taxation upon that income came to be always granted in convocation, even if, as at Westminster in 1376 and at Northampton in 1380, the request was made in parliament.[46] While both petitions and taxation demand more thorough investigation, it seems likely that the place of clerical proctors in parliament will not be seen in perspective until we understand better their place in convocation. Certainly their function in the one should not be studied in isolation of their function in the other.

We can be sure that the representatives from the dioceses often acted as a coherent group. The term *communitas cleri* must always have included the lower clergy and at times referred specifically to the parochial representatives.[47] The crown's point of view about the clergy had been clearly expressed in a letter of Edward I in 1279 to the bishop of Worcester: 'the *communitas cleri* live under our rule no less than the rest of the people and enjoy our defence and protection of their temporalities and for the most part of their spiritualities'.[48] The inferior clergy established quite early in the thirteenth century the principle that taxation upon their income by the king required their consent, and there can be no doubt that it was this factor above all others that explains both the need and the desire for their representation in

[44] Sayles, *King's Parliament*, pp. 114–15.

[45] J. F. Willard, 'The English church and the lay taxes of the fourteenth century', *University of Colorado Studies*, IV (1906–7), pp. 217–25; and see *The Lay Subsidy of 1334*, ed. R. E. Glasscock (London, 1975), pp. xvii–xxii.

[46] *Anonimalle*, p. 80, and *Rot. Parl.*, III, p. 90. A convocation assembled at Northampton in 1380 while parliament was in session (see references in *HBC*, pp. 526, 557), which led to the misleading statement in *Anonimalle*, pp. 132–3, that the clergy made their grant in parliament. For taxes granted in convocation between 1348 and 1378 see J. R. L. Highfield, 'The Relations between the Church and the English Crown', pp. 221–50, and for 1379–81 see A. K. McHardy, *The Church in London 1375–1392* (London Record Soc., XIII, 1977), pp. ix–xv.

[47] Above, p. 94, and *Councils & Synods II*, pp. 824, 947.

[48] W. Wake, *State of the Church*, appendix, p. 14, and D. Wilkins, *Concilia*, II, pp. 40–1. Also see 'Annales de Oseneia' in *Annales Monastici* (RS), IV, p. 286 (Stubbs, *Select Charters*, p. 423, and noted in E. Barker, *Dominican Order and Convocation*, p. 62).

ecclesiastical assemblies.[49] The principle of consent gave a voice to the lower clergy, and it is important to remember, not only that the taxation of clerical income was as important to the crown in monetary terms as the taxation of lay goods, but also that, as shown by the 1291 assessment, the income of the lower clergy, that is, the income from individual parish churches and parochial benefices (tithes, oblations and glebe lands) was not far short of double the income from temporalities (the manors and lay tenements belonging mainly to prelates and religious institutions).[50] In 1256 the proctors of the beneficed clergy of the archdeaconry of Lincoln and the proctors of the diocese of Coventry and Lichfield had drawn up detailed political complaints with the welfare of the whole community of the realm in mind; in 1296 or 1297 the proctors of the clergy presented a written statement to the bishops against granting a subsidy to the king; after the death of Archbishop Winchelsey and the accession of Archbishop Reynolds in 1313 the lower clergy were without a leader among the prelates and they defended their interests and their point of view with vigour; and in 1356 the clergy of the Canterbury province once again argued against granting a subsidy, ignoring the advice of the prelates.[51] The parochial clergy through their proctors had some political muscle.

Who, then, were the proctors of the lesser clergy?[52] The electing of proctors to represent corporations or communities in courts of law had become, in the words of Gaines Post, an 'almost indispensable procedure'.[53] It seems unlikely, *prima facie*, that the proctors elected to represent cathedral chapters and diocesan clergy in clerical assemblies and in parliament saw themselves as proctors with a difference. We need to know more about the men elected and their powers before we can effectively distinguish them from other kinds of proctors. But it is, of course, clear that, unlike the proctors of absent individuals summoned to parliament, they are above the suspicion, well founded or

[49] See especially Lunt, 'Consent of lower clergy to taxation', pp. 117–69, and H. S. Deighton, 'Clerical taxation by consent, 1279–1301', *EHR*, LXVIII (1953), pp. 161–92.
[50] See the table in Stubbs, *Const. Hist.*, II, p. 580. For the totals of lay and clerical taxes for the period 1294–1313 see J. H. Denton, *Robert Winchelsey and the Crown* (Cambridge, 1980), pp. 297–301.
[51] *Councils & Synods II*, pp. 506–9, 1156–7; J. H. Denton, 'The "communitas cleri" in the early fourteenth century', *BIHR*, LI (1978), pp. 72–8; and M. V. Clarke. *Representation and Consent*, pp. 24–5, and see pp. 166–8.
[52] For what follows I am most grateful for the guidance and assistance of John P. Dooley.
[53] G. Post, *Studies in Medieval Legal Thought*, p. 61.

not,[54] of doing little more than present excuses for absence. One important source is a list of proctors sent to the Carlisle parliament of 1307,[55] for this provides more concentrated evidence than the extant parliamentary proxies in the Public Record Office (classification SC10). It is immediately apparent from a study of the proctors in this list that representation in parliament was more complicated than the writs of summons alone might lead us to believe. We are looking for one proctor from each cathedral chapter and two from each diocese. Since the list appears to be a complete record of received proxies, the absence of many representatives from the Welsh dioceses (excepting St Asaph) is noteworthy, as also are the absences from the diocese of Coventry and Lichfield (though Bishop Walter Langton was there) and from the diocese of Canterbury (no doubt because of the suspension from office of the archbishop of Canterbury). From each of the other dioceses there was virtually full representation. Some cathedral chapters sent more than one proctor (two from Worcester, Lincoln, Salisbury, Hereford and St Asaph, and three from Norwich); but we can assume that the intention often was for only one proctor to act, as implied by the use in proxies of the terms *in solidum* and *coniunctim et divisim*.[56] Similarly, there were four proctors from the dioceses of Carlisle and Winchester and two from one of the two archdeaconries of the diocese of Hereford. It was certainly, however, the common practice to send, as requested, only two proctors from each diocese. The habit of sending

---

[54] Excuses for absence could be sent without the naming of proctors: PRO, Parliamentary Proxies, SC10/2/58 and 72 (abbot of St Augustine's Canterbury in 1309 and bishop of Llandaff in 1310), and *Register J. de Halton*, ed. W. N. Thompson (CYS, 1913), II, p. 233 (prior of Carlisle in 1316), and see *Rot. Parl.*, I, p. 190 (abbot of Combe in 1307). But this was no doubt frowned upon; and exemptions from attendance granted to individual prelates were very often qualified by the requirement of sending proctors: see Roskell, 'Attendance of the lords', pp. 202–3.

[55] *Rot. Parl.*, I, pp. 189–91 and *Parl. Writs*, I, ii, pp. 183–8. See Roskell, 'Attendance of the lords', p. 161 n. 1. For the proxies from PRO SC10 relating to the diocese of Carlisle during the episcopate of Halton (1292–1324) see *Reg. Halton* (CYS), II, pp. 231–5 (and for proxies in this register see I, pp. 241, 314–15, II, pp. 97–8, 225). PRO C270/35/17 is the proxy of the clergy of the archdeaconry of Salop for the parliament of 27 April 1309.

[56] For examples see *Councils & Synods II*, pp. 1253–4, 1289, 1294–5, 1303–5 and *Reg. Halton* (CYS), II, pp. 231–2. See D. E. Queller, *The Office of Ambassador in the Middle Ages* (Princeton, 1967), pp. 56–7. One obvious reason for appointing a number of proctors was to ensure that someone would be able to act; there is an indication in the list for the Carlisle parliament that some proctors would not themselves be able to attend, for the archdeacon of Surrey appointed a proctor while he had himself been appointed as a co-proctor by his bishop.

proctors from an archdeaconry rather than a diocese (especially in dioceses which had only two archdeaconries, like Worcester, Chichester, Winchester and Hereford) is interesting, for it was stated in the *Modus* that the diocesan clergy were represented by two proctors from each archdeaconry rather than from each diocese, which amounted to an enlargement of the representation of the parochial clergy from the actual 42 to 120 and more.[57]

A confusing factor is the frequency with which a proctor served in many capacities. Seven separate proxies survive, for example, appoint-the bishop of St David's, each of the four archdeacons of the diocese, ing Master David Fraunceys to act at the York parliament of 1322 for the cathedral chapter and the clergy of the diocese. While this is per-haps an extreme case, there are others. Master Hugh of Swaffham was nominated for the Carlisle parliament of 1307 by the archdeacon of Norwich, the prior of Norwich (with two others), the chapter of Norwich (with two others) and the clergy of the archdeaconries of Norwich and Norfolk, and Walter of Lugwardine was appointed by the bishop of Hereford, the chapter of Hereford (with one other), the archdeacons of Hereford and Salop and (with one other) the clergy of the archdeaconry of Salop.[58] The complication is increased when one considers that some of the nominated proctors were royal clerks, a practice which is not likely to have been adopted by the clergy for clerical assemblies when they met separately from parliament. Master William Pickering, for example, was summoned to Carlisle as a royal councillor and as archdeacon of Nottingham, and he was also appointed as a proctor by the archbishop of York to act for him in the case con-cerning Tickhill, alias Blyth, which was being claimed as a royal free

[57] See M. V. Clarke, *Representation and Consent*, pp. 327–9, 374, and J. S. Roskell, 'Consideration of *Modus*', *BJRUL*, L (1967–8), pp. 419–22. The figure exceeds 120, since the *Modus* includes also deaneries, by which must have been meant not rural deaneries but rather the deaneries or groups of parishes which were outside the normal diocesan and archidiaconal organisation—as were those of the abbeys of Evesham, St Albans and Glastonbury, and those of the royal free chapels of Shrewsbury, Derby, Stafford, Penkridge, Wolverhampton, Tettenhall, Bridgnorth, St Oswald's Gloucester, Wimborne Minster and St Martin-le-Grand London (see J. H. Denton, *English Royal Free Chapels 1100–1300* (Manchester, 1970), especially pp. 17, 114, and J. Sayers, 'Monastic archdeacons' in *Church and Government in the Middle Ages: Essays presented to C. R. Cheney*, ed. C. N. L. Brooke *et al.* (Cambridge, 1976), pp. 181–5, 201–2).

[58] J. S. Roskell, 'Consideration of *Modus*', p. 419 n. 1, and *Rot. Parl.*, I, pp. 190–1.

chapel.[59] But it is worthy of particular note that the intermingling of proctors for the Carlisle parliament is found especially in relation to the bishops, the archdeacons, the priors or deans and the cathedral chapters. It is not so notable with the proctors of absent abbots. Nor is it so notable with the proctors of the parochial clergy. A majority of the proctors of the secular clergy appointed in only one capacity were proctors of the parish clergy; and the parish clergy of eleven dioceses, out of sixteen represented, nominated at least one man who served in no other capacity. It appears, from the evidence for 1307, that it was often local clergymen who were sent to parliament from the dioceses and that many of them could represent the interests of the parish clergy with relatively little danger of conflicting allegiances.

By the end of the reign of Edward I knights and burgesses had been summoned 'with sufficient regularity to suggest that their presence was coming to be regarded as so desirable as to be indispensable'.[60] The same must certainly be said of the lower clergy. The period from the last part of Edward I's reign through to 1340 witnessed the attempt by the crown to bring the clergy and the laity of the realm into one assembly. This was one of the first major experiments in the history of the English parliament, and an initial examination of the details of the experiment was made by Maude Clarke.[61] The aims and intentions of the king's government in relation to the clergy are reflected in the unmistakable doctrine of the *Modus* that the community of the realm must include the clergy: the clergy were deemed to be, in Clarke's words, 'an integral and permanent part of parliament', in which there must be a 'joint and harmonious co-operation of all the orders of the realm'.[62] Although the clergy continued after the 1330s to respond to the summons to parliament and although most of the clerical assemblies can be perfectly aptly described as the king's convocations of clergy, in which the ecclesiastical hierarchy followed the lead of the king and

[59] See G. P. Cuttino, 'King's clerks and the community of the realm', *Speculum*, XXIX (1954), p. 404 n. 74, and *Parl. Writs*, I, ii, pp. 182, 186; and William Pickering was appointed proctor (with one other) by the clergy of the York diocese for the parliament at Northampton in October 1307 (PRO SC10/1/30). Warin Martyn, appointed as proctor at the Carlisle parliament by the bishop of St David's and by the archdeacon of St David's, was a knight for other examples of laymen sent as proctors of the clergy see A. K. McHardy, 'Representation of the lower clergy', p. 107 n. 65.

[60] McKisack, *Borough Representation*, p. 23.

[61] M. V. Clarke, *Representation and Consent*, especially pp. 128–50.

[62] *Ibid.*, pp. 153–4, and see J. S. Roskell, 'Consideration of *Modus*', pp. 441–2.

his council, it is none the less of far-reaching significance that the crown failed to bring securely into parliament what we may perhaps term the 'clerical commons'. One of the obstacles in the way of the crown was the division of the English church into two distinct provinces, with the archbishops of Canterbury and York jealously guarding their own jurisdictions.[63] But the fundamental obstacle was the traditional and continuing belief of the clergy, especially the lower clergy, in their essentially independent status.

The emergence of a distinctly lay commons in parliament was directly related to the successful withdrawal of the clergy into convocation for the most important aspects of their preparing of petitions and their granting of taxation. In 1397 it was considered that the proceedings in parliament required the assent of the clergy as a whole and Sir Thomas Percy was appointed proctor of the clergy at the request of the commons; but the clergy themselves regarded the proceedings of parliament as frequently outside their competence.[64] Animosity between the laity and the clergy was a recurring feature of the fourteenth century and it is reflected in the development of the two related but distinct institutions. Times of crisis, as in 1371,[65] produce evidence of anti-clericalism, and the suspicion of the laity was often that churchmen were reluctant to share the burden of the defence of the realm. Also, parliament became a forum for complaints against the church. Part of the complaint of the 'poor men of England' in 1305, regarded by some as perhaps the earliest example of a commons' petition, was against the practices of the ecclesiastical judges.[66] A petition of 1320 in the name of the 'communitas regni' complained that the prelates were taking cognisance of cases belonging to the crown and the royal dignity.[67] In 1371 the commons petitioned that the chief offices of state

[63] For example, the archbishop of Canterbury and his suffragans agreed to attend parliament in April 1309 only after the archbishop of York, who was carrying his cross erect in the southern province, had been sent away from London: *The Historical Works of Gervase of Canterbury*, ed. W. Stubbs, II (RS, 1880), pp. 322–3. For the dispute in general see especially A. Hamilton Thompson, *The Dispute with Canterbury* (York Minster Historical Tracts, X, 1927) and M. V. Clarke, *Representation and Consent*, pp. 140–50, 152.

[64] See references in Pollard, *Evolution of Parliament*, pp. 199–200, 208, and see *Reg. Gandavo* (CYS), p. 418. The memorandum about the appointment of Percy is translated in *EHD IV: 1327–1485*, p. 453.

[65] See M. V. Clarke, *Representation and Consent*, pp. 30–1.

[66] *Memo. de Parl.*, pp. lxxiv, 305, and Rayner, ' "Commune petition" ', p. 550.

[67] *Rot. Parl.*, I, pp. 375–6, cited in W. R. Jones, 'Bishops and the two laws', *Speculum*, XLI (1966), p. 226.

should be held by 'laymen of the realm who can answer for their mis-deeds in the king's courts'.[68] The complaints drawn up at the Carlisle parliament of 1307 against papal exactions appear to have come from prelates and clergy as well as from earls and barons, and they were in some measure reiterations of the clergy's own petitions to the pope in 1297; but anti-papal petitions in parliament during the fourteenth century became petitions of the commons, against which the prelates objected.[69] We should be in no doubt that the failure of the crown to make the community of the realm in parliament a community of laity and clergy is a story of success for the highly organised English church. But can the clergy have foreseen the dangers? 'In course of time,' in the words of Pollard, 'the side which rejected the union for the sake of independence fell into a state of subjection.'[70]

[68] *Rot. Parl.*, II, p. 304, cited in Tout, *Chapters*, III, p. 266.
[69] *Councils & Synods II*, pp. 1182–5, 1232–6, and Pollard, *Evolution of Parliament*, pp. 203–4.
[70] *Ibid.*, p. 194; and see Stubbs, *Const. Hist.*, II, pp. 204–5, and III, p. 462.

A. L. BROWN

5

Parliament,
c. 1377–1422

BY THE EARLY 1370S parliament was a well established institution, the great political assembly of the English, with important rights and a developed procedure. During the following forty years or so, primarily because of discontent with taxation and the repeated failure of kings and councillors to provide military success and 'good', acceptable government, parliament was the scene of great political events. Many well known incidents took place there, involving kings, lords and commons, ranging from points of procedure to sustained criticism of government, the appointment of committees and councils to achieve better government and state trials. At the same time, and no doubt partly in consequence of these events, the institution itself and interest in it grew markedly, not at odds with what had gone before but to such an extent that the period stands out. It is with this growth that this chapter is primarily concerned, and only secondarily with the incidents which have been much discussed and disputed. It sets out first to define parliament—for example, how often and for how long it met, who were its members, and how it did its business—and how these changed. Then, against this background, it seeks to establish contemporary attitudes in parliament, the assumptions and expectations about government and society, attitudes which help to place the incidents in perspective.

Any study is circumscribed by the evidence, and the principal evidence here is the rolls of parliament. These are bulkier than ever

before and more informative, but they follow a stereotyped and res-
trictive pattern, recording the opening formalities, the speech explaining the cause of the summons and the business the king wished done,
the appointment of receivers and triers of private petitions, the terms
of any grant of taxes, some of the issues raised and the cases heard
(sometimes at great length), and the 'common' petitions with the king's
answers. It is striking how convention-bound the clerk of the parliament was in writing the roll; there is, for example, little record of
discussions of matters of policy such as are found among the frag-
mentary agenda and papers of great councils, occasionally with the
record of individual opinions.[1] Surprisingly, perhaps, this affects our
knowledge of the lords more than of the commons, because the latter
put their point of view in writing or through a spokesman and it is
often recorded, while the former normally spoke their opinions in the
king's presence and these are unrecorded. The historian must search
the formal statements and documents on the rolls for snippets of information to reconstruct the life of parliament. Chronicles often mention parliament but generally too briefly to be of much additional help;
the exception is the *Anonimalle Chronicle*, which contains a long and
detailed account of some of the proceedings during the Good Parliament
of 1376.[2] This opens a door into the commons and lords and is a constant
reminder of what the rolls do not tell us.

If we were to take 1371 as a starting point, there were fifty parliaments during the period, almost one a year, excluding the parliament
summoned in Richard II's name to meet in September 1399,[3] but including Henry IV's last parliament in 1413, for which no record
survives. Statutes of 1330 and 1362 laid down that there must be at
least one parliament each year, but they were never observed. There
was no regularity of summons whatsoever. For example, there were
three parliaments within ten months in 1382 but none at all between
1373 and 1376 or between 1407 and 1410. Save in exceptional circumstances the king summoned parliament when he wished; in practice—
ignoring the rhetorical reasons often given at the opening of sessions—

---

[1] Most of the very miscellaneous collection of great council records are printed
in *Proc. P.C.*
[2] *Anonimalle*, pp. 79–94.
[3] The status of the assembly which met in September 1399 and saw Richard II
deposed and Henry IV become king has been much—overmuch—discussed. See
B. Wilkinson, 'The deposition of Richard II', *EHR*, LIV (1939), and in Fryde and
Miller, I, pp. 329–53, with references to other articles.

the timing was most often determined by his need for a new grant of taxes, occasionally by some great matter of state such as the treason trials of 1388. Annual parliaments had been a subject's ideal since the beginning of the century but the expressed reason changed significantly. At first it was to provide a remedy for delays in the courts and to secure answers to private petitions, but such reasoning, reflecting an older view of parliament, died out in the later fourteenth century. A commons' petition of 1376 seems to show a new attitude. It asked for annual parliaments 'to correct errors and faults in the realm', and, because the background was a period of over two years without a parliament and then sustained criticism of misgovernment and corruption in the Good Parliament of 1376, the petition probably meant annual parliaments to remedy misgovernment.[4] This is certainly what parliaments often did during this period. The king's reply, however, was (typically) merely that the statutes should be observed, and the request was not repeated. This interpretation conforms with a change that had been taking place in parliament as a whole. It had long been the great assembly in England, as the Ordinances of 1311, for example, show clearly, but by the 1370s it was a much changed assembly. For one thing the commons, not the baronage, now represented the 'community' and the business of parliament was much more 'political': the discussion of the king's affairs, the grant of taxation necessary to sustain them, and the remedy of the grievances of the kingdom rather than of individuals. The attitudes and attributes of the classic English parliament were already being formed within an older structure.

There were no rules about the time of the year that parliament met, though sessions in the summer, the time of campaign and harvest, were rare. This was the reason given for delaying Richard II's first parliament, in 1377, until October.[5] The favoured months were October, November and January, but a number of sessions were held after Easter. More often than not parliament was summoned to meet on a Monday but often, as Professor Roskell has shown, there was a postponement because insufficient lords and commons had arrived.[6] Westminster Palace was the normal place of meeting: forty-two of the fifty parliaments met there, and suspicion was justifiably aroused by a summons

---

[4] *Rot. Parl.*, II, p. 355. There is a lucid account of these requests in Edwards, ' "Justice" '.

[5] *Rot. Parl.*, III, p. 3.

[6] Roskell, 'Attendance of the lords'.

elsewhere. For example, Thomas Walsingham comments on the motives for the summons to Gloucester in 1378 and Northampton in 1380.[7] At Westminster the opening session of all members was held in the Painted Chamber, though in 1399, significantly, it was in Westminster Hall, presumably to accommodate the many other gentlemen and commons said to have been present at the usurper Henry IV's first parliament.[8] The lords met in the White Chamber, also within the Palace, as they appear to have done since early in the century, while the commons, who had been moved about, began to meet regularly in the refectory of Westminster Abbey from 1397.[9] The lords' meeting place was the same until the nineteenth century, the commons' until their move to St Stephen's Chapel about 1550, and the term 'house' begins to be applied to these 'chambers'. The *Anonimalle Chronicle*, for example, speaks of the commons coming 'al huse de parlement' in 1376—that is, to the lords in the White Chamber, and there are other such references, though the terms 'house of commons' and 'house of lords' were not yet in use.[10]

The length of session varied widely, from a little over a week in 1415 at the time of the Agincourt campaign to twenty-three weeks in 1406. The overall average and the average number of weeks of session a year was between five and six. Both figures were significantly higher than in the past. Figures before 1350 are incomplete, but one- or two-week sessions were probably normal, while in the twenty years before 1371 the average session was about three weeks and the yearly average about two weeks. The *Anonimalle* chronicler drew attention to the fact that the Good Parliament of 1376 lasted a full ten weeks, longer than any previous parliament, but there were even longer ones in the reigns of Richard II and Henry IV. This is an indication of how parliament was changing, and a rough guide to the parliaments which were most 'difficult' from the king's point of view is provided by those which lasted more than five weeks—almost all those between 1376 and 1382, between 1385 and 1390, and all those of Henry IV save the last. Henry

[7] T. Walsingham, *Historia Anglicana*, ed. H. T. Riley, I (RS, 1863), pp. 380, 449.

[8] *Rot. Parl.*, III, p. 415.

[9] I. M. Cooper, 'The meeting-places of parliaments in the ancient palace of Westminster', *Journal of the British Archaeological Association*, 3rd ser., III (1939), pp. 97–138; Powell and Wallis, *House of Lords*; Edwards, *Commons*, pp. 25–7. Edwards, *Second Century of Parliament*, reviews his earlier contributions on this and many other topics.

[10] Chrimes, *Eng. Const. Ideas*, pp. 126–7, and see below, p. 182.

V's parliaments were briefer, but the averages rise during Henry VI's reign, only to fall again in the Yorkist and Tudor reigns. Any assessment of the medieval parliament must take into account these considerable variations in the length, and therefore the character, of sessions.

Membership by the 1370s was largely regularised in its classic form. The king himself was expected to be present because it was his parliament, though if that was impossible, say, because of illness or campaign, a lieutenant could hold it in his name.[11] This happened in five of Henry V's parliaments. The lords spiritual and temporal (the terms came into regular use at the end of the fourteenth century) were summoned individually.[12] The lords spiritual were all the twenty-one English and Welsh archbishops and bishops and an almost standard list of heads of religious houses, normally twenty-five abbots, all but two Benedictine, the Benedictine prior of Coventry and the prior of the Hospitallers. The bishops were present by virtue of their status or office, though the old story was sometimes heard, for example from Archbishop William Courtenay in 1388, that they did so because they held by barony.[13] The list of abbots and priors was the residue of a longer list for earlier parliaments and had become more or less finalised in the 1360s.[14]

The summons of the lords temporal is a more complicated subject because their status was changing and they were evidently self-conscious about it. Dukes, marquises, earls and barons were normally summoned to parliament if they were of age and able to attend, but summons was not a matter of legal right; a lord might be deliberately omitted and lords not known to have been summoned were occasionally present. The three highest grades formed almost a group apart; 'earl' was of course an ancient title, but the first English duke (Edward of

[11] According to the chronicler Henry Knighton the absence of the king became an issue in 1386. Richard II withdrew to Eltham because his officers were under attack in parliament, and a delegation of lords had to remind him that by 'ancient statute' he must hold parliament once a year and that members might return home if the king failed to attend within forty days without good reason; *Chronicon Henrici Knighton*, ed. J. R. Lumby, II (RS, 1895), p. 217.

[12] Powell and Wallis, *House of Lords*, is a quarry of information on this and all matters relating to the lords. Chrimes, *Eng. Const. Ideas*, pp. 101–4, lists the sanctioning clauses of statutes from 1377, and these show the terminology for the lords becoming firm in this period.

[13] *Rot. Parl.*, III, p. 236. The same story was sometimes told of the lay lords. For representation of the lower clergy see above, pp. 103–5.

[14] Powell and Wallis, *House of Lords*, and D. Knowles, *The Religious Orders in England*, II (Cambridge, 1955), pp. 299–308.

Woodstock) had been created only in 1337, and the first marquis was Richard II's favourite, Robert de Vere, earl of Oxford, who was created marquis of Dublin in 1385. The creation of new titles is itself a sign of status-consciousness. The holders bore territorial titles but these had now little meaning; they might have to be endowed with land—even (without shame) with money—to maintain their status, and the succession to the titles was coming to be restricted to heirs male, that is, to be held in tail male rather than in fee.[15] The title 'baron' was being transformed in the same way, and largely because of parliament. In 1300 baronies were a matter of tenure but their number was uncertain and summons to parliament was 'haphazard', with the names and numbers of barons varying widely. Repeated summons slowly led to uniformity and to the evolution of a definable group of barons whose titles by the mid-fifteenth century were to be matters of hereditary status, not tenure. Increased definition combined with failure of heirs had inevitably led to a decrease in the number of barons as defined by summons to parliament, and on a number of occasions Edward III had deliberately reinforced the grade. The last occasion was in 1371, and it is interesting that three of the 'new' barons were not summoned to any further parliament thereafter, something quite usual in the past but never to happen again.[16] Edward's choice was restricted by the convention that 'new' barons should hold lands, perhaps acquired by marriage, which had been held by a man summoned to parliament in the past, a reflection of the old tradition that barony was a matter of tenure and no doubt of fear that the grade would be diluted. In 1387 Richard II took the unprecedented step of 'preferring' by patent John Beauchamp of Holt, steward of his household, 'to be oone of the peers and barons of our realm of England, willing that the said John and the heirs male of his body issuing shall possess the estate of baron, and shall be called lords Beauchamp and barons of Kidderminster'.[17] The reference to Kidderminster may have been in deference to the concept of ancient baronies but the rest of the wording reflects the new ideas of status and honour. Beauchamp was a leading loyalist and his preferment was a political act in a time of particular tension. Six months later he was convicted in parliament, without benefit of trial by his

[15] McFarlane, *Nobility*, especially pp. 272–5, and Powell and Wallis, *House of Lords*.

[16] Powell and Wallis, *House of Lords*, pp. 368–70.

[17] *Dignity of a Peer*, V, p. 81; Powell and Wallis, *House of Lords*, p. 402.

peers, and executed. He had no male heirs and the title became extinct. Richard's ill repute probably attached to this method of preferment, as it did to the title of marquis, but after half a century what he had done in 1387 began to be done often, and the new status of the baron was virtually complete.[18]

The new status of the lay lords was accompanied by a new concern with the signs of rank. The first recorded dispute about precedence led the king and his council in March 1405 to resolve that the earl of Warwick should sit above the earl marshal and Lord Grey of Codnor above Lord Beaumont in parliaments and councils, and disputes of this kind became common in the reign of Henry VI.[19] This implies a regular order of seating in the lords, and there is some evidence that the seating arrangements were very similar to those in the well known drawing of parliament in 1523; indeed, they had probably been *in general* the same since at least early in the fourteenth century. Dress also became important. The new creations in 1385 and 1397 were invested with ceremony in parliament—there is mention of coronets, caps and appropriate gowns—and this seems to be an early stage in the evolution of the traditional scarlet peers' robes with their varying bands of white fur to distinguish the grades. Froissart's account of Henry IV's coronation procession in 1399 mentions the lords' scarlet robes with bands of fur: three for dukes and earls, two for barons. (By the mid-fifteenth century the dukes had advanced to four.) The legislation of 1390 about the giving of liveries and contemporary rules about good manners and precedence illustrate the same point.[20] Another curious example of this concern with status is the practice in the late fourteenth century of designating new barons as 'bannerets'. For example, lists of councillors or committees in parliament often distinguish 'barons' from 'bannerets'. Presumably the 'old' barons wished to preserve their seniority, and this may have been one reason why John Beauchamp was made a 'baron' in 1387.[21] The distinction dies out in the early

[18] See below, pp. 155–8, for creations in the reign of Henry VI and a continuation of this theme by Professor Myers.

[19] *Proc. P.C.*, II, pp. 104–5; see below, p. 155.

[20] J. Froissart, *Oeuvres*, ed. Kervyn de Lettenhove (Brussels, 1867–77), XVI, p. 206; McFarlane, *Nobility*, pp. 122–3. Powell and Wallis, *House of Lords*, give many references to dress, and see below, p. 159.

[21] Powell and Wallis, *House of Lords*, p. 403. 'Banneret' had been a term used at the beginning of the fourteenth century merely for a knight particularly experienced in war and entitled to a banner rather than a pennon, and to higher wages.

fifteenth century probably because precedence made it unnecessary. These signs and symbols of 'nobility', a word newly applied in the fifteenth century to the men just described, and concern about dress, cognisances and so on suggest a self-consciousness among the lords which would surely have resisted any claim by the commons in parliament, if it had been made, to a share of the lords' traditional place in government.

Concern about rank and status and symbols was not confined to the peers. The grades which by the sixteenth century were classified as the lesser nobility—knight, esquire and gentleman—were also being ordered at this time. Indeed, *gentils* now becomes a common parliamentary word. These were men who according to a statute of 1445 should be the county members of parliament and who were concerned to be distinguished from borough members and from their inferiors in the counties.[22] The same sort of concern goes down through society to those who wished, as in 1381, to be rid of the taint of villeinage. Events in parliament must be seen against this background of hierarchy and concern about status. It is also worth remarking that here is a structure, formed about this period, which in fundamentals survived through early modern times and in many respects into the nineteenth century.

The lords were nominally a body of about a hundred, with the number of lords spiritual almost constant at forty-six to forty-eight and the number of lords temporal summoned varying considerably because of new creations, extinctions, minorities and service abroad. In this period, until 1400, the lay lords summoned were normally in a slight majority, but thereafter the reverse was true, for Henry IV was wary of new creations and the French war reduced the number of lay peers summoned to some of Henry V's parliaments to less than twenty. Actual attendance was another matter. Professor Roskell has shown that it is likely that often less than half those summoned actually attended.[23] There were exceptions, for example in 1397 and 1399, when concern on their part or pressure from above brought more lords to a parliament, but normally only a few abbots and priors, only a moderate number of barons, a reasonably good number of bishops, and a good number of dukes and earls attended. The lords in session must commonly have been a body of only forty or so peers, with the great

[22] McFarlane, *Nobility*, p. 122; *Statutes*, II, p. 342.
[23] Roskell, 'Attendance of the lords'.

officers present *ex officio* if they were not peers, and up to thirteen judges and lawyers summoned by name but probably present only when their professional advice was required.[24] These forty peers were much the same men who were summoned to great councils, assemblies specially summoned by writs under the privy seal, meeting more often than parliaments, discussing matters of state but no longer with power to tax or enact statutes. Many peers had also some experience at the (continual) council, some were regular attenders, and some were members of the governing circle on which the king relied.[25] Dukes and earls were the most powerful men in the kingdom, men whose rank made them military commanders, ambassadors, courtiers and 'politicians', and who were evidently conscious of the obligations of their rank. Bishops were often administrators or lawyers who had served and perhaps were still serving as royal ministers or councillors. Some barons were courtiers or councillors but the majority were rather substantial county men, of varying wealth, barons by heredity, who showed little interest in serving in central government and who were distinguished only by status from the wealthier county gentlemen. Abbots and priors were monks who had become the heads of important religious houses, but few took much part in national affairs. The lords who attended parliament regularly were therefore predominantly powerful and experienced men who were accustomed to meeting together to discuss matters of state. They were always much involved in affairs. They were the men among whom the bitter personal enmities of this period at times flourished. They were the men who must have 'mattered' most in parliament.

The commons, in contrast, was a body nominally of more than 250 members and much less coherent. Sheriffs were ordered to have two knights chosen from each of thirty-seven counties (Cheshire and Durham not being represented) and two citizens or burgesses from

[24] Numbers varied from seven or eight to thirteen, including normally all the judges of the two benches, perhaps the chief baron of the exchequer, and a few serjeants and civil lawyers. It was a group of professional advisers rather than councillors.

[25] The great council and the council are discussed in T. F. T. Plucknett, 'The place of the council in the fifteenth century', *TRHS*, 4th ser., I (1918), pp. 157–89, and A. L. Brown, 'The king's councillors in fifteenth-century England', *TRHS*, 5th ser., XIX (1969), pp. 96–118, and the governing circle in A. L. Brown, 'The reign of Henry IV: the establishment of the Lancastrian régime', in *Fifteenth-century England, 1399–1509*, ed. S. B. Chrimes, C. D. Ross and R. A. Griffiths (Manchester, 1972), pp. 1–28.

each city or borough in those counties, in practice from eighty or so towns which by tradition had come to be represented.[26] This meant a house of seventy-four county and about 180 town members, including the fourteen representatives of the Cinque Ports. It is impossible to say how many actually attended but it is probable that the great majority did so, if only because there is so much evidence of increasing interest in representation.[27] For example, the number of towns represented had declined during the first half of the fourteenth century but began to rise—at the towns' own request—in the 1350s and continued to do so through the fifteenth and sixteenth centuries. There was a significant though not dramatic rise in the amount of previous experience and re-election of county members in the last two decades of the fourteenth century.[28] Professor Roskell has shown that in the parliament of 1422 almost a quarter of the borough members were not strictly residents and that local gentlemen, officials and lawyers were already 'invading' the borough seats; this proportion was to increase considerably in the following half-century.[29] The medieval volumes in the *History of Parliament* series will in due course give more precise evidence on all these issues, but there is a time scale which seems to recur again and again in the history of parliament. Features well known in Tudor parliaments can already be traced clearly in parliaments of the mid-fifteenth century, and there are indications that their origins go back even into the fourteenth century, with evidence of a quickening pace towards its close. This time scale applies clearly to interest and inter-ference in county elections. Although quite a number of contentious county elections from the reign of Henry VI have been documented in recent years, the only one known from this earlier period occurred in Rutland in 1404, when the sheriff was found to have made a false return.[30] Curiously, however, more of the general complaints and

[26] The fundamental books on the membership of the commons are Roskell, *Commons in 1422*, and McKisack, *Borough Representation*.

[27] Pollard, *Evolution of Parliament*, pp. 316–20, 387–429, argued that borough members were poor attenders because writs for the expenses of many were not enrolled in chancery, but this is now discounted.

[28] Numbers of borough members rose in the second half of the fourteenth century, apparently fell back a little in the reign of Henry IV and rose again in that of Henry VI. McKisack, *Borough Representation*, pp. 27–30, 44–5, and below, pp. 165, 191–2. N. B. Lewis, 'Re-election to parliament in the reign of Richard II', *EHR*, XLVIII (1933), pp. 372–3, prints tables of re-election of members from the late thirteenth to the late fourteenth centuries.

[29] Roskell, *Commons in 1422*, p. 49.

[30] *Rot. Parl.*, III, p. 530. See below, pp. 161–2.

legislation about elections come from this earlier period. Hitherto, no code of electoral practice had ever been laid down: the presumption was that the sheriff would conduct the election in the county court, the mind of the county would somehow be declared, and county 'knights' would be chosen. In 1372 an ordinance, apparently made on the king's initiative, barred sheriffs and lawyers with business in the king's courts from election.[31] In 1376 the commons themselves petitioned that the county knights be chosen 'by common election of the better people (*les meillours gentz*) in the counties' and not be returned by sheriffs alone without proper election.[32] The complaint was about sheriffs and presumably about 'lesser' people interfering, but the king's answer was merely that election should be 'by common assent of all the county [court]', that is, by the traditional method. In the Long Parliament of 1406 the subject of county elections was again aired and the first statute regulating them was passed.[33] Elections were to be proclaimed in full county court and freely and impartially conducted by all those present, and to prevent fraud by the sheriff the result was to be returned in an indenture sealed by all the electors (although in practice only some of them did so). Penalties for breach of this statute were added by further statutes of 1410 and 1413, and the latter added that county members and those who elected them, 'knights, esquires, and others', must have been resident in that county on the date of the writ of summons.[34] These were preliminaries to the famous statute of 1430 which restricted the electorate to the forty-shilling freeholders because, it was said, disturbances were being caused by the claims of lesser people to participate in elections. This statute determined the county franchise until 1832. County elections were the main object of concern, but return by indenture was *in practice* extended by the writs of summons to boroughs, and the statute of 1413 and the residence qualification did apply to boroughs, though the borough franchise was not defined by statute until 1832. It seems impossible not to conclude that from the later fourteenth century there was growing interest in county elections, more irregularity, and growing concern about this.

[31] *Ibid.*, II, p. 310. This refers to 'knights and the more substantial serjeants' who should be returned as 'knights in parliament'. 'Knight of the shire' had become a technical term. The writs for the Coventry parliament of 1404 forbade the election of all lawyers.

[32] *Ibid.*, II, p. 355.

[33] *Ibid.*, III, pp. 588, 601; *Statutes*, II, p. 156.

[34] *Statutes*, II, pp. 162, 170.

John of Gaunt, Richard II and Henry IV were all accused of interfering in elections in order to 'pack' parliament, and though it is not clear that they did so it is significant that the charge was made.[35]

A proper assessment of the status and careers of the county and borough members must await Professor Roskell's volume in the *History of Parliament* series. However, much work has already been done.[36] The county members were almost invariably landed knights, esquires, or at least gentlemen resident in the county they represented, as the statutes of 1413 and 1445 required. Many had experience in county office as sheriffs, escheators, justices of the peace, tax collectors, or the like. Many had military experience; it is notable, for example, that almost half the county members in the parliament of 1422 had served for a time in France under Henry V.[37] They were county men with very much the same outlook as the lay lords to whom they were often linked by ties of family and service as officers, councillors or retainers. Sometimes, certainly in Lancashire, probably in Yorkshire, and in other counties too, lords determined, or had a strong voice in, elections, but even then there is no reason to doubt that the county members represented the community of their counties as they can be shown to have done in the mid-fifteenth, sixteenth or eighteenth centuries. There was no reason for conflict between the interest or outlook of the titled nobility and the gentry, who were later to be called the lesser nobility. The burgess member, however, was of lower status even when he was a gentleman. The typical burgess was still a prosperous merchant or trader who had served as an official in the normally close corporation of his town and perhaps as a royal customs collector or deputy to the chief butler of the realm; but increasingly he might be a lawyer or a royal officer or a member of a county family anxious for a seat in parliament. We can still only speculate why this latter group wanted a seat. It is unlikely often to have been for direct gain; it must surely have been a matter of the prestige and connections it brought, and thus further testimony to the place of parliament in the kingdom.

Membership of parliament must have fostered a sense of community between the county knights and the burgesses, but there is a great deal

[35] *Chron. Angliae*, p. 112; T. Walsingham, *Historia Anglicana* (RS), II, p. 161, and *Rot. Parl.*, III, pp. 235, 420; *Eulogium Historiarum*, ed. F. S. Haydon, III (RS, 1858), p. 402.

[36] *A Bibliography of English History to 1485*, ed. E. B. Graves (Oxford, 1975), pp. 522–4.

[37] Roskell, *Commons in 1422*, p. 94.

of evidence of social division between them. For example, the regulations about county elections were different and more demanding than those for boroughs; the long account of the Good Parliament in the *Anonimalle Chronicle* reports the action of knights but scarcely mentions burgesses; and no burgess became speaker for the commons in parliament during the middle ages. The county knights were gentlemen; for example, in 1397 they as a body took an oath by acclamation and by raising their right hands to maintain the judgements as the lords spiritual and temporal had done individually, but the burgesses are not mentioned.[38] The burgesses were merchants who could give advice about trade and about loans: for example, in 1372 they met separately, after the knights had been sent home, to grant a special tax for the defence of the sea.[39] An assembly of merchants met in 1382 to discuss loans for a campaign, but in 1401 over 200 county gentlemen were summoned by name to a great council, apparently to discuss war and how it could be sustained.[40] There is even the slight possibility that in the commons' chamber the knights sat while the burgesses stood.[41]

When parliament met in this period, proceedings followed a pattern already established. At Westminster the lords and the others summoned by name probably assembled with the great officers in the Painted Chamber, within the Palace proper, while the commoners gathered in Westminster Hall, often only to hear an adjournment proclaimed because so many from both houses had failed to arrive.[42] When proceedings began the lords were probably checked against the list of summons while the names of the commons were read out from the sheriffs' returns,[43] and the latter were led through to *stand* at the bar

---

[38] *Rot. Parl.*, III, p. 356.

[39] *Ibid.*, II, p. 310.

[40] *Ibid.*, III, p. 122; *Proc. P.C.*, I, pp. 155–64.

[41] H. G. Richardson, 'The commons and medieval politics', *TRHS*, 4th ser., XXVIII (1946), p. 38.

[42] In 1381 and 1383 the lords and the chancellor, the treasurer and other officials waited in vain for others to arrive; *Rot. Parl.*, III, pp. 144, 149. Adjournments were proclaimed in Westminster Hall in 1373 and 1376; *ibid.*, II, pp. 316, 321.

[43] There are a number of references to calling members by name, for example, *ibid.*, III, pp. 184, 229. Attendance lists of the lords were being kept by the mid-fifteenth century, and copies of lists said to be of those present on 20 October and 24 November 1402 survive in College of Arms MS 2H 13, ff. 384v–5, but the figure of ninety lords said to be present is suspiciously high. Cf. W. H. Dunham, ' "The Books of the Parliament" and "The Old Record", 1396–1504', *Speculum*, LI (1976), pp. 697–8.

of the house, where the king sat in state surrounded by the lords *seated* in order in their robes.[44] An address was then given, often part sermon and replete with scriptural quotations, part practical explanation of the state of the kingdom and the reasons for the summons, and almost invariably by the chancellor. In most cases the essence was that the king was faced with difficulties and required taxes. Lords and commons were told to meet separately to discuss these matters, their 'charge', to consider how government could be improved and to present their grievances. Finally the names of panels of receivers and triers of private petitions were read out by the clerk of the parliament, chancery clerks to receive, peers and judges to 'try' them, one panel for English, Irish, Welsh and Scottish petitions, another for all overseas petitions, and a few days were given for the petitions to be presented. The announcement was made in parliament, but probably anyone could hand in petitions. This was an ancient but now relatively unimportant part of parliament. Edward I had been inundated with petitions of all kinds during his parliaments, but now, when petitions could be presented to the king, the council or the chancellor at any time, only a small number of grievances which could not be remedied elsewhere seem to have come to the receivers.[45] In the late fourteenth century sometimes more than fifty triers were appointed, and possibly all the lords present were assigned to one or other panel. In the early fifteenth century the panels were smaller and more conciliar. It is noticeable that it is the bishops, dukes and earls who figure most on these panels and the abbots least, the pattern that has been suggested for the attendance of the lords in parliament. The commons, of course, were not included at all.

On the second day the separate sessions of the lords and the commons normally began, probably from 8 or 9 a.m. until the mid-day meal.[46] Sometimes the 'charge' was further explained by a minister or councillor, separately or in joint session, and in the course of the parliament the commons would come before the king and the lords from time to time and there would be a good deal of coming and going of ministers and groups of lords and commoners. One relatively well documented form of communication was 'intercommuning', groups of lords or

[44] *Rot. Parl.*, III, p. 184
[45] Above, pp. 49–50.
[46] *Rot. Parl.*, II, pp. 321, 361, and III, pp. 33, 338.

commoners going to the other house or meeting in a third place.[47] This was common in the late fourteenth century, most often in the form of a group of lords chosen by the commons sent down to the commons' chamber to advise on the preparation of an answer to the 'charge'. It was used by the commons to strengthen their hand in criticising the conduct of government and at times was understandably disliked by the king. It is last recorded in 1407, but the use of delegations between the houses certainly continued. The official record, however, affords only glimpses of the 'inner' history of parliaments and virtually nothing of the personalities involved.

The character of the two houses must have been quite different, because the membership and business were so different. The king himself was often present with the lords, though this could be an embarrassment and in 1407 Henry IV agreed that in future the lords should be free to discuss the state of the realm and its reform without him.[48] Their first business must have been the 'charge' given both houses and this probably led to days of discussion of the kind that is occasionally documented in great councils. The parallel is probably a good one: the lords assembled were sometimes referred to as the 'great council', and the presence of the great officers, the judges and many peers with experience of the council and high office must have made the discussions wide-ranging, informed and practical. On some issues the lords were asked to give their opinions one by one.[49] In most parliaments a grant of taxation had to be agreed with the commons, and this was probably the origin of intercommuning. Although the commons were the formal grantors of taxation by the 1390s, the experience of the lords was probably often, and on some occasions certainly, called upon to guide the commons.[50] Petitions, both private petitions referred there by the

[47] Edwards, *Commons*, assembles the evidence. A particularly interesting example of (an otherwise unrecorded) 'communing' between lords and commons about a wide range of issues on 31 October 1399 is a memorandum printed from a formulary copy in H. G. Richardson and G. O. Sayles, 'Parliamentary documents from formularies', *BIHR*, XI (1934), pp. 157–8.

[48] *Rot. Parl.*, III, p. 611. It is not known how the lords conducted their business or whether there was already a chairman other than the king or his lieutenant. The duke of York, the senior lay peer present, presided at trials in 1388 in the absence of the king, but this was a special case. There is plentiful evidence of the chancellor, who was to become the lords' speaker, acting as the king's mouthpiece in parliament, but this was to preserve the king's dignity, not to act as chairman.

[49] *Ibid.*, III, pp. 136–7.

[50] For example, *ibid.*, III, pp. 89–90.

triers and common petitions sent up from the commons, were read before the lords and advice was offered to the king on how they should
be answered. Probably in practice some of the more active members,
in effect the council, considered them first. On a number of occasions
this business could not be completed before the end of parliament and
had to be committed to a group of lords.[51] The triers of private petitions,
peers and judges, must have held their separate meetings. The lords
also sat as a court, hearing appeals alleging error in the court of king's
bench and cases which seemed appropriate only to parliament such
as great inheritance suits seeking revocation of earlier confiscations,
cases of treason in the field, and sometimes state trials conducted in
several forms.[52] Judgements in parliament of course belonged entirely
to the king and the lords. The impression the lords give is one of a
relatively small body, akin to a large council or a great council, performing the functions both of a council where the lords exercised their right
to counsel the king and of a court, the high court, where administrative
and judicial decisions were made. It was both an assembly of the great,
where feuds might erupt, and a hard-working council.

The commons meanwhile met in separate session. The *Anonimalle
Chronicle* describes the scene in the chapter house of Westminster
Abbey in 1376. The members came in, sat down, and at once took an
oath to speak openly but to keep their proceedings confidential, a
significant act of community for such a large body from all over the
country. Then members, always knights, went forward one by one,
apparently without formality, to a lectern in the middle of the floor,
rapped on it for quiet and addressed the house freely and forcefully
about the charge. Debate went on for some days before the commons
came before John of Gaunt, the king's representative, and the lords and
through their speaker began to express their views about misgovernment. Over a period of weeks separate sessions, joint sessions and

[51] *Ibid.*, II, p. 304 (commons petitions), and III, p. 256 (private petitions). The
most famous example was the committee of lay lords and knights appointed in
1398 and given extended powers by forging the parliament roll; J. G. Edwards,
'The parliamentary committee of 1398', *EHR*, XL (1925), and in Fryde and Miller,
I, pp. 316–28.
[52] This period witnessed important developments in state trials in parliament,
in particular the first impeachment there in 1376, the first appeal there in 1388,
and the growth of attainders, subjects too technical to discuss here. Among many
studies see four articles by T. F. T. Plucknett in *TRHS*, 4th ser., XXIV (1942), and
5th ser., I–III (1951–3), G. Lambrick ,'The impeachment of the abbot of Abingdon
in 1368', *EHR*, LXXXII (1967), pp. 250–76, and Bellamy, *Treason*.

sessions with an intercommuning group of lords were held, accusations of corruption and misgovernment were made and pressed home, some of the accused were tried, suggestions for better government were put forward, and a short-term victory was achieved. This was admittedly an exceptional parliament, but blunt speaking took place in many parliaments in this period in an atmosphere which must have been not unlike 1376. There is a different impression of the commons in the poem *Mum and the Sothsegger* which describes, or rather caricatures, a parliament in the late 1390s.[53] It tells of members who slept and said little, others who talked freely but to no purpose; some who stammered and mumbled, some who became tied up in words, some who had taken bribes, some who had been lobbied by the council, some who sought their own advantage, and so on. The poet is moralising about the evils of his time and is not to be taken literally, or as speaking of all members. No doubt both he and the chronicler each presents a facet of the truth.

In practice the business of the commons was to grant taxes and to represent the grievances of the community, verbally and in writing, and often the latter extended to giving advice about government; indeed, the king sometimes pressed them to give advice. The basis of their strength in this period was their right to assent to all taxes, a right which in practice was already recognised but which was so new that the commons themselves still cautiously asked for it to be confirmed on several occasions.[54] By the end of the fourteenth century this phase had passed, and the commons' primacy in matters of taxation began to be formally recognised. Until the 1390s taxes were granted by lords and commons, thereafter by the commons with the assent of the lords, and in 1407 this formula was acknowledged by Henry IV. In an effort to persuade the commons to act quickly Henry had asked the lords how much taxation was necessary and had their answer given to a commons' delegation. The commons were 'greatly disturbed' at this attack on their 'liberties', and the king hastened to calm the situation. Both houses, he said, might discuss taxes, but no report should be made until they were agreed on the tax to be *granted* by the commons and *assented* to by the lords, and then only in the accustomed manner by the mouth of the commons' speaker.[55] Grants were made on the last day of parlia-

---

[53] *Mum and the Sothsegger*, ed. M. Day and R. Steele (Early English Text Soc., orig. ser., 199, 1936), pp. 24–6 (modernised extract in *EHD, IV, 1327–1485*, pp. 453–4).
[54] *Rot. Parl.*, II, pp. 308, 365–6.
[55] *Ibid.*, III, p. 611.

ment normally in the form of an 'indented schedule'. One part must have been presented to the king and the other retained, presumably by the commons' clerk, as security that the king observed the precise terms of the grant.[56] The commons sometimes—in this period often— went a good deal further than controlling the grant of taxes; they often laid down how taxes were to be spent, and on occasion were given an account of how they had been spent. This subject is, however, better considered later with the wider question of the commons' part in government.

The second major duty of the commons was to represent the grievances of the community. This might be done in writing or by word of mouth. The most frequent was the written petition. At the end of the roll of most parliaments there is a section of 'petitions des communes'; in 1376 there were 140, but twenty or thirty was a more usual figure. These petitions, or bills as they were also called, sometimes led to the making of statutes—hence our terminology of legislation. They must be distinguished from the petitions about private matters handed in to the receivers, whose names were announced on the first day of parliament. These private (*singuleres*) petitions were 'tried' by panels of lords and judges, and those which could only or could best be decided in parliament were referred to the king and the lords. Common (*communes*) petitions, that is, petitions about common matters, were quite different.[57] They were presented in the name of the parliamentary commons—who represented the communities—to the king personally or the clerk of the parliament and were then considered by the lords before the king gave his answer to them, customarily on the last day of the session. These were *common* petitions but often their connection with the parliamentary commons was only nominal, for many were drafted by communities, groups, even by individuals. This is sometimes clear because the original petitioners are named in the

[56] There are many references to these *cedules* and one at least, in 1373, was sealed; *ibid.*, II, p. 316.

[57] The pioneer work on common petitions is Gray, *Influence of the Commons*, a much criticised but still useful source book. Rayner, ' "Commune petitions" ', Myers, 'Parliamentary petitions in the fifteenth century', and *id.*, 'Some observations on the procedure of the commons in dealing with bills in the Lancastrian period', *Univ. of Toronto Law Journal*, III (1939), pp. 51–73, have greatly clarified the issues. Professor Myers also discusses the matter below, pp. 167–80, and of necessity he considers the late fourteenth as well as the fifteenth century for the purpose. However, the circumstances pertaining at this earlier time need to be established here within their own context.

badly edited texts forwarded in the commons' name and there are occasional references to the practice. For example, the ordinance of 1372 banning lawyers with cases before the courts from serving as county representatives states that it was made because these lawyers were presenting petitions on behalf of their clients 'in name of the commons', and in 1394 two chaplains were accused of presenting a bill 'in the names of the commons', though it was the abuse of the common petition for private purposes that was wrong, not the preparation of common petitions outside the commons in parliament.[58] The implication of these cases, of the lack of a uniform phraseology in petitions, of careless editing and repetitious, even (over several parliaments) of contradictory, requests, is that the procedure for considering petitions in the commons was undeveloped. Admittedly we know almost nothing about this procedure, but it would be wrong to think in terms of 'readings' or even of the commons necessarily approving all these petitions formally.[59] Their contents are very varied. Some concern a town, a county or a group of counties, a group of people, the entire kingdom. Typical subjects are the abuse of purveyance, defects in the law, courts which exceed their jurisdiction, livery and maintenance, farms of shires, the term of office of sheriffs, weights and measures, disobedient villeins, trade regulation, and many more. Some were certainly drafted outside the commons but some certainly were not, some were no doubt generalised complaints arising from members' particular complaints, some in all probability arose out of the general debates such as those in 1376 we happen to know from the *Anonimalle Chronicle*. Sometimes a group of petitions about, say, the threat of Welshmen in England, the extortions of courts, or about foreign trade, suggest that this was an issue that had stirred the assembled commons, and chroniclers occasionally refer to a great 'issue' in a particular parliament. The great majority of statutes were based on such petitions and concerned these kinds of topic.

While it is important to emphasise that these were common petitions because they concerned common issues and that procedure in the

---

[58] *Rot. Parl.*, II, p. 310, and III, p. 321.

[59] It is not even clear in what form common petitions were presented. Until 1423 they were enrolled on the parliament roll in one schedule with the king's answer after each petition, and Gray considered that they must also have been presented in one schedule. This may have been true earlier, but there is some evidence that by this period they were presented individually; if this is true, it is likely to have led to a change in procedure and probably to closer scrutiny.

commons was probably rudimentary—even 'primitive' by later standards, so Professor Myers remarks elsewhere—there are, none the less,
clear signs that by the early fifteenth century things were changing.
The commons themselves were becoming aware of their status as
petitioners. In 1401 they asked that answers be given to 'their' petitions
before they made their grant of taxation (that is, instead of *after* the
grant and on the last day of the session, as was traditional), but
Henry IV refused to change.[60] More important, in 1414 they asked
that no statute or law made as a result of any request by their speaker
or by written petition should differ in any particular from it without
the commons' assent. Henry V's answer was merely that no enactment
should be made *contrary* to their request.[61] This petition was seem-
ingly a reaction to events in the previous parliament, not a general
'constitutional' claim, but its preamble is surprising. The commons, it
claimed, had always been part of parliament, both as assentors and
petitioners, with the right of assent to every statute and law. This was
quite untrue, but it is the making of the claim that is significant, and
the wording of statutes shows that the commons' claim was not utterly
wild. In the earlier fourteenth century statutes were normally said to
be made with the assent of the lords; by the later part of the century
often with the assent of lords and commons; and in the early fifteenth
century the phrase 'by advice and assent of the lords spiritual and
temporal at the instance and/or request of the commons' became more
or less standard.[62] More significant still, because it was a matter of
more than terminology, is the growth in the number of petitions from
individuals, sometimes important individuals such as John, duke of
Bedford, and Bishop (later Cardinal) Henry Beaufort, and from groups
to the commons, asking them to present their petition to the king. The
earliest come from Richard II's reign, although there are very few of
them; they become more common in Henry IV's reign and numerous
in Henry V's.[63] This must be a recognition of the growing status of the
parliamentary commons as petitioners. Moreover late in Henry V's reign
it became common for these private petitions to be endorsed in the

---

[60] *Rot. Parl.*, III, p. 458.
[61] *Ibid.*, IV, p. 22. Gray, *Influence of the Commons*, pp. 260–87, and Chrimes,
Eng. Const. Ideas, pp. 159–64, disproved the older view that this incident gave the
commons the right to assent to all legislation.
[62] Chrimes, *Eng. Const. Ideas*, pp. 101–4, lists the enacting clauses of statutes
from 1377. See also Roskell, *Speakers*, p. 158.
[63] Rayner, ' "Commune petitions" ', pp. 213–15, and below, pp. 168–9.

commons 'soit baille as seignurs', the phrase which became traditional on 'private bills' forwarded by the commons to the lords. It is also significant that, on occasion at least, petitions to the lords were sent to the commons for approval. The assent of the two houses was becoming more than a matter of words. The implication of all this evidence must be that in the early fifteenth century the principle of commons' assent to all legislation was acceptable though not always fully practised, that a conventional terminology for enacting statutes and for endorsing private bills was growing up, and hence that a conventional procedure for handling and even approving such bills and perhaps all petitions was probably also developing. By the mid-fifteenth century, as Pilkington's case of 1455 was to show, legislative procedure was considerably formalised, to the extent that the clerk of the rolls of parliament could give evidence in court about it.[64] It seems reasonable to deduce a progress going back to this earlier period.

The same is probably true of other aspects of parliamentary procedure, but little is known about them. The striking exception is the speakership of the commons. Its early history is admittedly poorly documented, but Professor Roskell's careful study has established beyond reasonable doubt that the office developed rapidly from early in this period.[65] There is no evidence that it existed at all before 1376; the commons had apparently addressed the king and the lords during the course of parliament through delegations of a dozen or so members, one of whom acted as spokesman for the occasion. In 1376, however, the same spokesman, Sir Peter de la Mare, acted throughout the parliament, and the unusually sustained criticism during that parliament, the courage of Sir Peter (for which he was imprisoned), and the evidence that the office rapidly became formalised over the succeeding twenty-five years, make it likely that he was indeed the first 'speaker'. There was probably a speaker in every parliament thereafter; indeed, his identity is known in six of the next seven parliaments, and, after a gap, the list is almost complete after 1397. His 'protest' on taking office quickly becomes stereotyped. In 1376 Sir Peter was not chosen until the commons had debated for a number of days and required a spokesman to 'speak' for them, but in 1384 they were instructed on the first day to choose their speaker, and this was normal from the reign of Henry IV. The fact of having been chosen probably gave him some

[64] See below, p. 148.
[65] Roskell, *Speakers.*

authority within the commons, and there is a little evidence of this. Some speakers, such as Sir Arnald Savage in 1401 and 1404 and Sir John Tiptoft in 1406, played prominent, outspoken parts in parliament; in February 1404 two archbishops, a bishop, an abbot, Prince Henry, a duke, an earl, a baron and Speaker Savage sealed a letter to the community of the kingdom of France; and petitions begin to be addressed to the speaker and the commons.[66] It is therefore likely that by the early fifteenth century the speaker had some measure of control over business.

The parliamentary procedure that became classic evolved over a long period, but there are indications that the time scale mentioned several times in this chapter applies here also. By the later sixteenth century the procedure was well developed and documented; increasingly its features have been recognised in the mid-fifteenth century; and, although the process did not begin in the half-century before 1422, it appears that it had developed significantly in this earlier period.

A much more difficult subject is the role in government and the attitudes of the several parts of parliament. It is almost impossible to discuss them without 'whig' undertones, without anticipating later ideas and terms, and informed contemporaries give little help because they saw parliament in a very practical way. They recognised its importance as the great assembly of the realm and they knew how it functioned, but while they understood certain customs and assumptions about government, they indulged in little constitutional or political thinking, and even when they did it was extremely traditional. For example, Thomas Hoccleve, a privy-seal clerk, presented Henry V with an English *Regement of Princes* he had compiled, but it contains only traditional generalisations of a moral nature, and the same is true of other tracts for kings.[67] In the mid-fifteenth century Chief Justice Fortescue wrote in more precise and legal terms, but while he laid weight on the rights of the three estates and the restraints on the king's freedom of action he rarely even used the word 'parliament'. Literature in general, even so-called political poems, is equally silent or general. When contemporaries wrote or spoke about government it was in such terms as that

---

[66] H. G. Richardson and G. O. Sayles, 'Parliamentary documents from formularies', pp. 161–2.

[67] T. Hoccleve, *The Regement of Princes*, ed. F. J. Furnivall (Early English Text Soc., extra ser., 72, 1892–7); *Four English Political Tracts of the Later Middle Ages*, ed. J.-P. Genet (CS, 4th ser., XVIII, 1977).

the king should be valiant and just, preferring poor men's causes, taking counsel from great and wise men, avoiding flatterers, and so on. There was also a range of customs derived from the past, for example from Magna Carta, that time of 'great nobility and wise discretion'.[68] Kings ruled by nature and by right and had great prerogatives, though they were not above the law and had often been restrained and occasionally deposed. Taxes and laws had long required consent, and now this meant the consent of parliament to all taxes on the laity and to all statutes. Kings had a duty to take counsel, and lords had a right and duty to give it. No man should lose his life or liberty or property save by 'due process' of law. Within a loose framework of ideas such as these 'political' conflicts were fought out. In practice new customs were created and precedents established which much later became powerful political weapons, but practice was not matched by theory.

Within this framework parliament had an important and increasing place. It represented all in the kingdom. In 1365 Chief Justice Thorpe had declared that the law held that everyone knew at once what parliament has decided 'because parliament represents the body of all the realm'; more significantly, there are frequent references during this period, for the first time, to the three estates in parliament, and the rolls of Henry V's parliaments commonly refer to the lords spiritual and temporal and the knights and burgesses coming to parliament on behalf of all the community of the realm.[69] It was the proper place to establish the form of government during the minorities of 1377 and 1422 and to affirm the deposition and usurpation before the three estates in 1399. On several occasions—for example, in 1383 and 1386—a great council of magnates felt that a decision about war and government during the king's absence on expedition required a parliament.[70] Parliament was the highest court in the kingdom, the highest council, the sole source of statutes and lay taxation.

Within parliament the estates had differing roles. The king and the lords, the original members, were the most important: the commons, the more recent, was growing considerably in power and therefore demands more attention. Parliament was the king's institution; he summoned it and normally held the initiative there; he was the ruler and governor; he was treated with respect and by convention deferred

[68] *Rot. Parl.*, III, p. 15.
[69] Chrimes, *Eng. Const. Ideas*, pp. 352, 116–26.
[70] *Rot. Parl.*, III, pp. 144, 215.

to, though sometimes he was given blunt advice; he often refused requests; he could dissolve parliament; but he summoned parliament to obtain advice and support and therefore, by and large, he conciliated it. The advice that counted most was that of the lords. In 1427 the ambitions of Humphrey, duke of Gloucester, were to lead to an unusually explicit statement of the pre-eminent role of the lords: the royal authority to govern belonged during the king's incapacity to the lords spiritual and temporal in parliament or in great council or to those lords chosen to serve on the continual council.[71] In 1422 as in 1377 it had been the lords who had determined how government during the minority would be conducted. In normal times it was their advice that counted most. It was the lords, or at least the more active among them, who were frequently consulted in great councils about matters of state, and normally without representatives of the commons. The same was true in parliament. On a number of occasions the commons disclaimed the role of counsellors, and when they asked for the advice of the lords, for example through intercommuning, and spoke of their own simplicity, they were being more than merely polite.[72]

In 1399 Archbishop Arundel gave a contemporary view of the role of the commons. They had disclaimed being party to judgements in parliament unless they were shown them by the king as a matter of grace. Arundel, on the king's behalf, agreed. Judgements, he said, belonged to the king and the lords, the commons were rather 'petitioners and demanders', but in making statutes, granting taxes and in matters touching the 'common profit of the realm' the king specially wished their advice and assent.[73] This was a fair statement. The commons' particular duty was to bring forward complaints for the king and the lords to remedy, but in this period 'the common profit of the realm' took on an extended meaning, sometimes to the embarrassment of the king. In 1414 the commons claimed to be 'as well assentirs as peticioners' in the making of statutes, and this was almost true in practice. It was, however, in matters of taxation that their power was greatest. By the 1370s their right to assent to all lay taxes was accepted, and this was no formality. Kings and ministers had to struggle to persuade

[71] *Proc. P.C.*, III, p. 233.
[72] See below, pp. 137–9.
[73] *Rot. Parl.*, III, p. 427.

the commons to grant taxes throughout the 1370s, the 1380s and the reign of Henry IV.[74] For example, in 1406 the commons held out from March until 22 December, in spite of reassurances, before making a grant on severe conditions. Sometimes requests for taxes were refused or modified, for example in 1376, 1378, 1381, 1382 and 1383. In 1400 Henry IV was reluctant even to ask parliament and prevailed on the lords in a great council to help him as individuals. Even Henry V in the last years of his victorious reign had to accept that the commons would not always grant taxes. On several occasions in the 1380s the commons insisted on breaks of a few days or weeks in the levy of customs duties to assert their right to refuse them. The king was able to take the financial sting out of this, however, by forbidding exports during the breaks.[75]

The determination of the commons is impressive, although more often than not the king did obtain his taxes—indeed, very large sums, including the first grants of the customs duties for the term of the king's life in 1398 and 1415.[76] It was accepted that subjects had a duty to assist the king in time of need,[77] and in practice it must have been difficult to refuse support for policies recommended by the king and the lords who had often discussed them earlier in great councils. The commons, however, *often* made their grants of taxes on conditions— that the money was spent only on war, sometimes on specified campaigns, occasionally that the grant would lapse if peace was made, and on a number of occasions on condition that the money was received and paid out by specially appointed treasurers of wars and not by exchequer officials along with the other revenues. How well these

[74] 'Incidents' were numerous in these parliaments and no attempt will be made to document them all. The best source of reference to them is still Stubbs, *Const. Hist.* Several incidents have been added or redated since he wrote; see in particular J. J. N. Palmer, 'The parliament of 1385 and the constitutional crisis of 1386', *Speculum*, XLVJ (1971), pp. 477–90, and his *England, France and Christendom. 1377—99* (London, 1972), pp. 237–8, for a suggested redating to 1388 of a petition in *Chronicon Henrici Knighton*, ed. J. R. Lumby (RS); and A. L. Brown, 'The commons and the council in the reign of Henry IV', *EHR*, LXXIX (1964), and in Fryde and Miller, II pp. 31–60, for the parliament of 1401.

[75] *Rot. Parl.*, III, pp. 104, 144, 204. J. J. N. Palmer, 'The parliament of 1385', p. 487.

[76] *Rot. Parl.*, III, p. 368, IV, pp. 63–4.

[77] Harriss, *King, Parliament and Public Finance*, discusses fourteenth-century attitudes to taxation, and see also his remarks above, pp. 40–3.

conditions were observed is another matter.[78] On a number of occasions the commons themselves sought to find out how taxes had been spent. For example, in Richard II's first parliament they asked that an account be given to the peers and a year later they asked that they themselves be told, a novelty reluctantly conceded as a matter of grace on condition that it should not be held a precedent.[79] On several occasions in the 1380s accounts were conceded, even volunteered. In 1406 Henry IV is reported to have said that kings did not render accounts but in practice he even allowed the commons to nominate six of their own members to assist in such an audit.[80] The period is full of such incidents and there can be no doubt that the commons fought with determination to minimise taxation and ensure that it was properly spent. Ministers became accustomed to persuading suspicious commoners by giving them more information about royal finance. One by-product was apparently the preparation of more royal 'balance sheets' than at any other time in the middle ages.

These incidents used to be seen in very 'constitutional' terms, but the background to them was not fundamentally politics or any premature constitutionalism so much as a period of heavy military expediture and taxation, often to little apparent advantage. The major French war had resumed in 1369 and continued with its related campaigns and fleets through the 1370s and most of the 1380s. Henry IV had to face rebellion and threats from overseas for more than half his reign. In neither period was there much success or glory; indeed England itself was under threat. Henry V resumed the French war on a grand scale and significantly for a few years after Agincourt when it was successful and popular he obtained taxes with little difficulty in brief parliaments. War was very expensive. Even in peacetime garrisons such as Calais and Berwick were costly, and from the 1380s there were always paid wardens on the Scottish March.[81] An indication of the cost of a cam-

---

[78] There are a number of files of documents relating to treasurers of wars among the Exchequer Accounts in the Public Record Office which could form the basis of a study of their work. Formal requirements such as the assent of the 'great council' for payments laid down in 1404 were observed, at least on paper, and most payments were evidently for military expenses, but a painstaking 'audit' would be necessary to reach a firm conclusion.

[79] *Rot. Parl.*, III, pp. 17, 35–6.

[80] *Eulogium Historiarum*, ed. F. S. Haydon (RS), III, p. 409; *Rot. Parl.*, III, p. 577.

[81] R. L. Storey, 'The wardens of the Marches of England towards Scotland, 1377–1489', *EHR*, LXXII (1957), pp. 593–615.

paign is given by the estimate in 1382 that a French expedition would cost £60,000 for 3,000 men-at-arms and 3,000 archers for six months, that is almost the entire yield of two tenths and two fifteenths.[82] No wonder that the commons looked for cheaper solutions. It was circumstances like these, the consequential shortage of cash and royal debts, particularly for the household, and the inevitable complaints about misgovernment and injustice, that soured this period and brought about the impressive determination of the commons to seek better value for their money and better government generally. Perhaps they also explain why the commons' determination seems to rise and fall during and after this period.

This determination on a number of occasions went far beyond taxation and expenditure into sensitive areas of the king's liberty. In the Good Parliament of 1376, for example, the commons declared that they were as willing as any in the past to aid the king with their lives and goods, and always would be, but it was obviously true that if the king had had loyal councillors and good officers around him he would have been rich and would have had no great need of taxes, particularly bearing in mind the profits won during the war.[83] After demonstrating the villainies of those around him, assuming that punishment would follow, the commons then turned to the future and asked that a new chancellor and treasurer be appointed and that the king assign three bishops, three earls and three barons to be of his council, men who would not hesitate to speak the truth and act profitably, and in particular that wardships and marriages should not be granted away without the advice of the council.[84] There was no suggestion that commoners should be nominated as officers or councillors nor that the commons in parliament should have any hand in the nomination—even the lords are said to have disclaimed any share in the choice of councillors.[85] What the commons were seeking was better, more economical government: 'good and abundant government', as they phrased it on a number of occasions

[82] *Rot. Parl.*, III, p. 123. The weight of taxation in the decade before 1381 is discussed in C. Oman, *The Great Revolt of 1381*, 2nd edn., ed. E. B. Fryde (London, 1969), pp. xii–xviii; and J. J. N. Palmer, *England, France and Christendom*. considers the expenses of the war and the crises in parliaments of the late 1370s and early 1380s. Holmes, *Good Parliament*, gives an excellent account of the military and diplomatic background to the parliament of 1376.

[83] *Rot. Parl.*, II, p. 323.

[84] *Anonimalle*, p. 91. The parliament roll gives an account of this incident which differs in detail but not in spirit from the chronicle account.

[85] *Ibid.*, p. 91.

in the Long Parliament of 1406. This is typical of the commons' requests throughout the period; they varied in detail but the same themes recur. There were a number of requests for a reduction of expenditure on the royal household and for enquiries into its administration. These were understandable, because the household was the largest continuous single item of expenditure and its debts affected a great many people, but Richard II in particular was sensitive about interference in what he considered to be his own domestic affairs.[86] Another common theme was that the king should not make grants that diminished his revenues or that they should be made only with the approval of his council or even that there should be a resumption of grants made in the past.[87] The request in 1376 that wardships and marriages should not be granted away was of this kind. Again this was understandable: why should taxes be voted when the king was not safeguarding the revenues he already possessed? In normal times he should be able to 'live of his own'. There was a naivety in all these demands. Kings were expected to be both economical and generous; they had to support the royal family and reward their supporters; and there was in fact no great pool of lands and revenues which could have made taxation unnecessary. H. G. Richardson likened the commons' attitude to that of 'modern ratepayers' associations' and though this is too extreme it has a certain truth.[88] The commons were inclined to hammer away at half-truths such as restraining royal generosity or the removal of household servants, particularly foreigners. These were some of the political myths of the age, but they were no less potent for being myths.

Another frequent request was for the appointment of councillors. The ideal was a substantial council, a balanced selection of the various grades of peers, as in 1376, together with a clear promise in parliament that the councillors would do their duty and that the king would take their advice—particularly when he wished to grant away any of his resources. This was asked for in 1376, in Richard II's reign, and in 1401, 1404, 1406 and probably on other occasions in Henry IV's reign. The

[86] Tout, *Chapters*, IV, and A. Rogers, 'Henry IV, the commons and taxation', *Mediaeval Studies*, XXXI (1969), pp. 44–70, discuss household finance before and after 1399.

[87] B. P. Wolffe, *The Royal Demesne in English History* (London, 1971), and 'Acts of Resumption in Lancastrian parliaments, 1399–1456', *EHR*, LXXIII (1958), and in Fryde and Miller, II, pp. 61–91, and A. L. Brown, 'Commons and council', pp. 48–9.

[88] H. G. Richardson, 'Commons and medieval politics', p. 28.

last group of incidents are particularly interesting because they can be set against the records of who actually attended the council, and they show clearly the limited and practical character of the ideas and objectives.[89] The commons never suggest that they should have any hand in appointing the councillors; they do not ask that men of their own status be appointed—indeed, there was a common feeling that such men could not withstand the pressures on a councillor. They did not seek to make the councillors 'responsible' to them—that would have been a notion quite foreign to the time—though they might criticise them if they failed. Often it was not even *new* councillors that they sought. What the commons wished was for the king to appoint a strong council, 'charge' the members openly in parliament to do their duty, bind them by oaths, ideally pay them to attend, and himself promise to take their advice. The commons could then report this to their communities, and so, it was hoped, better, more economical government would result. In principle this was obvious and sensible, better than a charter or a set of ordinances for ensuring that the right decisions were taken day by day. In normal times the council worked closely with the king in governing; when he was a child or abroad it was reinforced and given greater authority; a stronger council was surely the way to bring about 'good and abundant government' when things were going wrong. It is not surprising that the council was again and again the keystone of schemes for better government during the later middle ages. In practice these schemes had limited success. In 1380, for example, the commons, apparently disillusioned after almost three years of continual councils, asked for the councillors to be discharged and no more appointed.[90] However, the schemes were soon revived again. The most impressive feature of these proposals and criticisms is indeed not their content but the frequency and determination with which they were made.

Some historians, reacting against Stubbs's extreme 'whig' view of the commons, have questioned whether they could have acted without the support, indeed the direction, of groups among the lords. These doubts are fewer now that the aims of the commons are better understood. The relations of members of the lords and commons were clearly close but complex. Contacts between them outside parliament were many and intimate but within a status-conscious social structure. In parlia-

[89] A. L. Brown, 'Commons and council'.
[90] *Rot. Parl.*, III, p. 73.

ment the lords as a body were often more sympathetic to royal plans and problems because many lords were involved with them as individuals and had been consulted about them in advance. The lords, however, probably often agreed with the commons' criticisms. Their opinions are generally less well known than those of the commons, but, for example, in 1385 and 1406 it is known—from non-parliamentary sources— that the lords shared the commons' ideals,[91] and the two houses clearly discussed together the important issues raised in parliament much more than is recorded.[92] There also seems no doubt that members of the commons on occasion spoke with great bluntness. Sir Peter de la Mare, speaker for the commons in 1376, is the most obvious example. Doubts, but probably unjustifiable ones, have been cast on his independence because he was the earl of March's steward, but the same cannot be true of Sir Arnald Savage, speaker in 1401 and 1404, or Sir John Tiptoft, speaker in 1406. In 1404 Savage was so blunt—and, incidentally, asked that lords should speak their minds openly—that the king is said to have withdrawn from parliament for five or six days.[93] Yet both Savage and Tiptoft were royal servants, and Savage was already a councillor, whilst Tiptoft became one and treasurer of the royal household before the close of parliament.[94] Loyal criticism was apparently acceptable, at least to Henry IV. It was after all, the duty of the commons to represent the grievances of the community, as they were often told to do at the opening of parliament. This was less the role of the lords, which was more to give counsel. The commons were chary of giving counsel, though some of the well known examples of this involved special pleading. In 1383, for example, the speaker declared that the proposed royal campaign in France or any other great campaign was a matter for consideration by the lords, not the commons, but he went on to 'advise' a less expensive campaign and greater attention to the Scottish March. This, he said, was 'advice', not 'counsel', to which Richard II replied that he saw little difference between the

[91] See 'The advice of the lords concerning the good government of the king and the realm' (redated to 1385 by J. J. N. Palmer, 'The parliament of 1385') in *Proc. P.C.*, I, pp. 84–6, and the views of 'the lords spiritual and temporal assembled in this present parliament' of 1406, in *ibid.*, I, pp. 283–7.

[92] The most impressive example of the range of these discussions is a list of items of 31 October 1399; see above, n. 47.

[93] C. M. Fraser, 'Some Durham documents relating to the Hilary parliament of 1404', *BIHR*, XXXIV (1961), p. 198.

[94] Roskell, *Speakers*, and *id.*, 'Sir Arnald Savage of Bobbing', *Archaeologia Cantiana*, LXX (1956), pp. 68–83.

words.[95] The commons were probably being careful, as they had been before, to avoid assuming responsibility for a campaign and therefore for paying for it. They were again cautious about giving counsel regarding peace with France in 1384 and 1394, claiming that they were not counsellors and that the issues were too high and difficult for them.[96] In practice the commons did express opinions on many matters of state—on campaigns and on papal provisions, for example—but such issues were apparently often considered in parliament only by the lords, and this was certainly so in great councils. The commons had a conventional and probably often sincere desire not to meddle in matters of state but at the same time a practical concern with matters that touched them closely, particularly those that touched their pockets! Deep-seated reverence for status and their material power gave the lords an unquestioned superior role. Ideas were, however, beginning to change slowly, for example it was not unusual for the king to refer to the views of the three estates in diplomatic correspondence, and the treaty of Troyes in 1420 required the ratification of the prelates and clergy, the nobles and magnates, and the commons, and this was given in parliament.[97]

In the final analysis it must be admitted that little is known about the inner and personal history of individual parliaments; the parliament rolls are too brief and formal to make this possible, and the chronicles give only snatches, sometimes prejudiced snatches, of information. Whilst it has been possible to generalise about the fifty parliaments, the composite picture is certainly too institutional. Nevertheless the significance of the period in the long-term history of parliament seems clear. Parliament's development had already gone far by the beginning of the 1370s, and in the following half-century it continued along the same lines. But the pace quickened. Procedure hardened markedly, classic parliamentary rights began to be recognised, the importance of the commons increased significantly, interest in election and elections grew, and again and again parliament was the great national assembly and high court where major issues were aired and decided, sometimes in scenes of high drama. The immediate reason for these developments was that this was an era of failure and disappointment down to 1415, leading to longer sessions, haggling over

[95] *Rot. Parl.*, III, pp. 145–6.
[96] *Ibid.*, III, pp. 170, 315.
[97] Chrimes, *Eng. Const. Ideas*, pp. 118–19.

taxation, blunt criticism and on occasion to bitter personal hostility involving the king and some of the lords. Wider changes such as the increasing role of laymen in all levels of government and the increasingly precise social divisions among the greater and lesser nobility— both of which are particularly apparent at this time—must have had their influence but they were not unique to the period. Political ideas had apparently little influence; ideas and attitudes—and misconceptions—were traditional. This is not surprising—even the revolution in the seventeenth century caught parliamentarians intellectually unprepared and looking to the past, sometimes to this period, for justification —but it is worth stressing because 'whig' views have been so influential. What happened in this period was permanently important; it marked a significant stage in the evolution of the classic English parliament and the strong precedents that were set made its continuance if not inevitable at least more likely. Succeeding periods were very different. Sometimes parliaments seem pacific and compliant, and impeachment, for example, was used only once in the entire fifteenth and sixteenth centuries. On the other hand, the 'invasion' of the borough seats by gentlemen and lawyers and the hardening of procedure and parliamentary rights continued. For explanation one must surely look to the combination of deference and desire for good leadership with outspokenness about matters of immediate practical concern, a combination which is so very evident in this period.

A. R. MYERS

6

Parliament, 1422–1509

PARLIAMENTS HAD ORIGINATED in the thirteenth century as especially important sessions of the king's council. 'The king had his court in his council in his parliaments,' Fleta had said at the end of that century; the essential element was that the king was taking advice or action with the aid of his leading tenants and officials. Traces of this wider meaning still survived in our period; in 1429 an assembly of lords only could be called a parliament in the council minutes, and the same name is applied to a meeting of lords of the council in 1436.[1] And though by the fifteenth century parliament had developed from an occasion into an institution, from an enlarged meeting of the king's council into a particular kind of king's council, with unique composition and powers, it was still predominantly the king's assembly, to assist him in the work of government. It was he who summoned, prorogued and dissolved parliaments, and determined their agenda, if he were a grown man and in possession of his faculties. Parliament was so much a royal assembly that in 1422, when the king was not yet a year old, the archbishop of Canterbury opened parliament in his name; and in 1423

---

[1] *Proc. P.C.*, III, p. 324, IV, p. 352. The usage may have been encouraged by the summoning during this century of great councils which included some of the same personnel as a parliament, and by the habit of the king's council of meeting in the parliament chamber when parliament was not in session (e.g. *Proc. P.C.*, IV, p. 213, V, pp. 6, 7–10, 276–7; PRO, Council and Privy Seal Records, E28/73/75, E28/84/1, E28/86/2. I owe these references to Dr B. P. Wolffe).

it was thought desirable to enhance the authority of parliament with the presence of the baby king, even though he had to be seated in his mother's lap.[2] The last king of our period, Henry VII, could not only summon parliament at his will and determine its agenda but even in his first, when he was only newly and weakly seated on the throne, he instigated a petition to confirm his title and presented the bills for enactment with his own hand.[3] Moreover he secured the passage of a bill of attainder against his foes, because he wished it, even though many of the members of the commons were against it.[4] Eleven years later he delivered into parliament a bill of trade with his own hand.[5] And throughout this century the king retained a real power to grant, refuse or alter petitions. Bishop Stubbs thought that Henry V's answer to the commons petition of 1414 had been an undertaking that 'the acts when finally drawn up should correspond exactly with the petitions'.[6] Subsequent work has shown, however, that the king granted a great deal less than this—nothing more, in fact, than a promise not to enact anything that was contrary to the petitions of the commons.[7]

It might seem that this view of the relationship between king and commons was invalidated by the events of the parliament of 1449–50. Then, as usual, the chancellor, John Stafford, archbishop of Canterbury, declared on behalf of the king the business of the session; but the government's intentions were frustrated by a revolt of the commons. The government was weak and discredited by the recent defeats in France and by the murder with impunity during the parliamentary session of one of the king's chief councillors, Adam Moleyns, bishop of Chichester.[8] The king's chief minister, William de la Pole, duke of Suffolk, asked parliament for a vote of confidence, but the reply of the commons was to impeach him.[9] Yet Henry VI, even in his beleaguered position, was able to take the proceedings away from parliament, stop the impeachment and make his own decree 'by his owne advis, and

[2] R. Fabyan, *The New Chronicles of England and France*, ed. H. Ellis (London, 1811), p. 593.
[3] *Rot. Parl.*, VI, pp. 268, 288.
[4] *The Plumpton Correspondence*, ed. T. Stapleton (CS, old ser., IV, 1839), p. 49.
[5] Pollard, *Evolution of Parliament*, p. 264.
[6] Stubbs, *Const. Hist.*, III, p. 269; see above, p. 128.
[7] See K. Pickthorn, *Early Tudor Government: Henry VII* (Cambridge, 1934), p. 125; Gray, *Influence of the Commons*, pp. 169–70; and especially Chrimes, *English Constitutional Ideas*, pp. 159–64.
[8] *William Gregory's Chronicle of London*, ed. J. Gairdner (CS, new ser., XVII, 1876), pp. 189, 194.
[9] *Rot. Parl.*, V, p. 176.

not reportyng hym to th'advis of lordes, nor by wey of jugement, for he is not in place of jugement'. Admittedly the verdict of five years' banishment was very unpopular, and Viscount Beaumont, though his title was a creation of Henry VI, declared on behalf of the lords that the decree did not proceed from their advice and counsel;[10] it is also true that royal authority was dramatically challenged by the murder of Suffolk on his way to exile.[11] But for the longer-term history of parliament it is probably of more importance that even Henry VI could block an established procedure of parliament which was supported by the commons and at least many of the lords. Impeachment was such a subversion of the original purpose of parliament that it was never likely to be used when the government was strong, and after 1450 it was not to be tried again until 1621. In normal times the king regarded it as part of his undoubted prerogative to appoint his ministers and councillors and keep them in office as long as he chose. Parliamentary definition and approval for the appointment and functions of councillors was an exceptional feature of government during the minority of Henry VI, who got rid of it as soon as he came of age in 1437.[12]

Under the Yorkists and Henry VII the king's dominance over parliament revived, and the king could look to it to aid his purposes. In the parliament of 1478 no one ventured to say a word when the king accused his brother Clarence of treason.[13] Henry VII never once found it necessary to veto a bill;[14] it is unlikely that it would have reached the stage of presentation if he had disapproved of it. 'Every one of Henry's acts, whatever its nominal origin, must have begun with the royal tolerance at the very least, and some of the proposals made by the commons were certainly made because it was known that they would be welcome to the king.'[15] Edward IV summoned only one parliament, lasting five weeks, in the last five years of his reign, and Henry VII held only one, lasting nine weeks, during the last twelve years of his. There is no evidence that anyone objected to this infrequency; men were thankful if the king did not demand taxes,[16] and as for private

[10] *Ibid.*, V, p. 183.
[11] *Three Fifteenth-Century Chronicles*, ed. J. Gairdner (CS, new ser., XXVIII, 1880), p. 99.
[12] *Proc. P.C.*, V, p. xxii.
[13] 'Historiae Croylandensis Continuatio', in *Rerum Anglicarum Scriptores*, ed. W. Fulman (Oxford, 1684), p. 562.
[14] J. Gairdner, *Henry VII* (London, 1892), p. 212.
[15] K. Pickthorn, *Early Tudor Government: Henry VII*, p. 130.
[16] *The Paston Letters, 1422–1509*, ed. J. Gairdner, III (Edinburgh, 1910), p. 82.

petitions, these could be presented to the chancellor or to the king's council without all the trouble and expense of a parliament.

Nevertheless, even if parliaments could be infrequent, especially under Edward IV or Henry VII, parliament was now more than an occasion. It was a universally recognised part of the machinery of government, with definite powers, composition and procedure, all of which became more clearly specified during the period 1422–1509. It is true that parliament was more limited in power than it later became. Before the Reformation it could not interfere in matters that clearly concerned the church authorities. In a case heard in 1506 in the law courts the question was whether the king could be made a parson by act of parliament. A serjeant-at-law argued: 'It seems that the king cannot be called parson by act of parliament, for no temporal act can . . . make a temporal man have spiritual jurisdiction.' The chief justice of common pleas, Sir Thomas Frowicke, summing up at the end of the case, agreed. 'I have never seen that any temporal man could be parson without the agreement of the Supreme Head. . . . Thus a temporal act, without the assent of the Supreme Head, cannot make the king a parson.'[17] Until the Reformation Parliament did so in 1536, no parliament had presumed to abolish the rights of jurisdiction of a whole category of courts, such as those of the Marcher lordships. Men still appealed to laws other than statute law. Richard, duke of York argued in 1460 that the oath of loyalty taken by the lords to Henry VI was invalid in the face of God's law and commandment;[18] next year his son Edward was to claim the throne by God's law, the law of nature and man's law.[19] In 1467 Robert Stillington, bishop of Bath and Wells, as chancellor, told the lords and commons that justice was founded on the law of God, the law of nature and positive law.[20] This is of especial significance, for the king's chief lieutenant in parliament, a man who was moreover now one of the king's principal lawyers and official keeper of the king's conscience, was telling parliament, which made enactments that altered 'positive law', that there were grounds for justice other than the system of law on which parliament legislated. Sir John Fortescue, who had been chief justice of the king's bench, went so far in his *De Natura Legis Naturae* as to say that an unjust statute

[17] *YB 21 Henry VII*, plea 1 (p. 2), quoted by C. H. McIlwain, *The High Court of Parliament and its Supremacy* (New Haven, 1910), pp. 277–8.
[18] *Rot. Parl.*, V, p. 377.
[19] *Ibid.*, V, p. 464.
[20] *Ibid.*, V, p. 622.

could be disregarded, and that a statute could not enact any rule other than natural law or custom.[21]

However, the same Fortescue could hold that the distinction between the French and English monarchies lay in the fact that the king of France could rule his people by such laws as he made himself and set upon them taxes without their assent, whereas the king of England could not rule his people 'bi other lawes than such as thai assenten unto'.[22] He makes it clear elsewhere that parliament was the institution which made the laws and levied the taxes: 'in regno namque Angliae reges sine trium statuum regni illius consensu leges non condunt nec subsidia imponunt subditis suis'.[23] There had been a real and important development since the early fourteenth century in both spheres. In that earlier period it had not been clear whether the judges were justified in modifying or even setting aside the mandate of a statute if it conflicted with a rule of common law. Now the position had been clarified. By about 1350 statutes had become distinguished from ordinances;[24] from this time ordinances, usually proclaimed by the king and his council, were sometimes turned later into statutes if it was felt that the enactment needed greater authority or permanence, as, for example, with the Statute of Labourers of 1351 or the Statute of the Staple in 1354. The distinction is neatly illustrated by a petition of 1414 in which the commons petitioned for the authority of parliament to be given to the king to make with his council an ordinance that would regulate coinage matters until the next parliament, when the provisions might be re-enacted as a statute to endure in perpetuity.[25] It also became clearer during our period that acts of parliament bound all the king's subjects in England; in 1441 it was still possible for a serjeant-at-law to argue, though without receiving the court's approval, that someone who possessed a charter of exemption from taxation was not bound by a grant made in parliament, whereas in 1463 another

[21] Chrimes, *Eng. Const. Ideas*, p. 201.

[22] J. Fortescue, *The Governance of England*, ed. C. Plummer (Oxford, 1926), p. 109.

[23] J. Fortescue, 'De Natura Legis Naturae', in *The Works of Sir John Fortescue*, ed. Lord Clermont (London, 1869), I, p. xvi.

[24] Tout, *Chapters*, III, p. 182.

[25] *Rot. Parl.*, IV, p. 35b. There seem to be no grounds for the view of Gray that in the fifteenth century the distinction between statute and ordinance became blurred once more (Chrimes, *Eng. Const. Ideas*, pp. 275–7).

serjeant argued, with the approval of the court, that by such a record as an act of parliament every Englishman was bound.[26]

By the fifteenth century it had become certain that statute law was superior to common law, even if the judges did not like what the statute-makers had done to the rules of common law. No one, so the judges held in 1492, could prescribe against statute; and in 1505 the judges maintained that statute not only broke the custom of the realm but also the custom of an administrative department such as the exchequer.[27] By the fifteenth century it had been ruled that statute could override the law merchant.[28] As for canon law, whereas in the fifteenth century, as we have seen, it seemed inconceivable that a layman could be granted rights of spiritual jurisdiction by an act of parliament, or thereby usurp the powers of the pope, parliament could and did pass acts which, from the standpoint of high churchmen, trespassed on the church's jurisdiction, as in benefit of clergy, sanctuary and heresy. Parliament also resisted in 1428 the determined attempt of Pope Martin V to secure, by pressure on Henry Chichele, archbishop of Canterbury, the repeal of the Statutes of Provisors and Praemunire, which the pope regarded as flagrant violations of the rights of the papacy.[29]

As for taxation, parliamentary control was now firmly established in principle. In practice the king, if he were strong enough, could evade this control to some extent by asking for benevolences, as Edward IV and Henry VII both did. But the very fiction that benevolences were supposed to be voluntary gifts by loving subjects to help their liege lord in his financial plight was in itself a testimony to parliamentary control of taxation. That control may have been somewhat weakened by the growing tendency in the fifteenth century to grant the customs duties for life, instead of only for a year or so, as had been the practice in the fourteenth century. Late in 1415, in the euphoric aftermath of Agincourt, the commons granted the customs duties to Henry V for life,[30] Henry VI had to wait until 1453 before being granted a similar boon,[31] but Edward IV was given the privilege after

---

[26] Chrimes, *Eng. Const. Ideas*, pp. 78, 269.
[27] *Ibid.*, p. 284, quoting *YB 1 Henry VII*, Mich., plea 4.
[28] Chrimes, *Eng. Const. Ideas*, p. 289.
[29] *Rot. Parl.*, IV, p. 322.
[30] *Ibid.*, IV, p. 64.
[31] *Ibid.*, V, p. 229.

only four years of rule, in 1465.[32] Richard III was conceded the customs for life in 1484 in his first (and only) parliament;[33] and this precedent was followed in Henry VII's first parliament,[34] 'for the defence of this youre said realme and in especiall for the saufeguard and keeping of the see'. But if parliamentary control was weakened by this tendency it was not destroyed. The great and varied efforts by strong kings like Edward IV and Henry VII to increase their revenues from non-parliamentary sources are a testimony to their respect for tradition and for present feeling for parliamentary control of taxes.

Moreover they felt it necessary to observe the tradition that the king was entitled to ask his subjects for aid only in case of national need, especially for the defence of the realm. It was therefore politic to limit the demand for a subsidy to preparation for war, and then only if it could be plausibly represented as defensive—if not for defence against invasion, then against attacks on the king's rights. Just as the chancellor, Henry Beaufort, bishop of Winchester, had asked parliament for financial aid in 1414 because the king intended to exert himself 'for the recovery of the inheritance and right of his crown which had been long withheld',[35] so in 1472 John Alcock, bishop of Rochester, announced that the king intended to prosecute the war in France for the purpose of recovering all the 'oold enheritaunce of the corone and reame of France and the duchies of Normandie, Gascoigne, and Guyan, and for the defense of this his realme of England'.[36] It is true that occasionally the king might make a profit from such a parliamentary subsidy, as Henry VII did from the grants of 1491 for the war in France, and from the grant of 1497 for the war in Scotland. But this was only because both campaigns were brief and the king had the benefit of a benevolence and a forced loan. Moreover this was generally regarded as sharp practice, and it was a piece of luck that the campaigns turned out to be short. The experience of the Lancastrian kings had been that when war was begun in earnest, especially in France, the expenditure quickly became uncontrollable, and that in spite of loans the king became more and more dependent on parliament. For tradition was now too clear for the king to appeal for aid to other kinds of assembly, as Edward I and Edward III had obtained authority for customs dues

[32] *Ibid.*, V, p. 508.
[33] *Ibid.*, VI, p. 238.
[34] *Ibid.*, VI, p. 268.
[35] *Ibid.*, IV, p. 34.
[36] *Ibid.*, VI, p. 122.

from assemblies of merchants. It is true that back in 1400 the lords
spiritual and temporal, meeting in council, had granted aid to the king
to meet the menace of a Scottish attack; but this was specifically stated
to be to avoid the need to summon a parliament, and the aid was
limited to the resources of the persons present at the council.[37] The
principle of parliamentary control of taxation was thus doubly
recognised.

During the fifteenth century the manner in which that control was
exercised became more defined. In 1407 it had been recognised that the
commons could deliberate by themselves on the state of the realm and
the necessary remedies, and that, as Professor Brown noted earlier, the
lords could discuss the same subject without the king's presence, and
that any resulting grant should be announced by the speaker of the
commons.[38] This did not prevent the lords from subsequently over-
riding the terms on which the commons had made their grant. In 1426
the duke of Bedford declared in the Leicester parliament that, on the
advice of the judges and others learned in the law, the subsidy granted
in 1425 by the commons on certain conditions would be levied without those provisos.[39] By the middle of the century the procedure had
hardened. In a case heard in 1455 in the exchequer chamber the defen-
dant, John Pilkington, imprisoned for abduction, had challenged the
validity of an act of parliament ordering his appearance before the lords
to answer the charges against him; so Thomas Kirkby, clerk of the rolls
of parliament, was called in to explain what was needed to ensure
the validity of an act of parliament. He assumed that the consent of
king, lords and commons was necessary for the passage of a bill. He
said that if the lords wished to alter a bill from the commons, and if
the change was in harmony with the proposal of the commons the
bill would not be sent back to them. But if the lords were to make an
amendment which extended the scope of the bill it would be sent back
to the commons with their endorsement. Thus if the commons, he said,
were to make a grant for two years, and the lords wished to increase
it to four, the latter must endorse the bill with the words: 'Les seigneurs
sont assentus a durer pour quatre ans'. If the commons did not agree
to this the bill would not be enacted.[40] This description is supported

[37] *Proc. P.C.*, I, p. 104.
[38] *Rot. Parl.*, III, p. 611. See above, p. 123.
[39] *Ibid.*, IV, p. 301.
[40] *YB 33 Henry VI*, Pasch., plea 8, printed in Chrimes, *Eng. Const. Ideas*, pp.
361–2.

by all that we know of contemporary practice. In 1482 in the abbot of Waltham's case counsel argued that the commons alone could make a valid grant, but it is unlikely that this was more than a counsel's argument.[41]

For the whole trend of fifteenth-century development was for the necessary participation of king, lords and commons in parliamentary acts. Few contemporary comments on this phenomenon have come down to us; but some informed commentators attributed it to the origins of parliament as the king's high court. In the draft of the sermon which the chancellor, John Russell, bishop of Lincoln, prepared for the intended parliament of Edward V in 1483 he said, 'See the passynge of every act made in a parliament, and alle is oo thynge, that that the Romaynes did in ther tyme, and that that we do nowe in thys the kynges most hyghe and souerayne courte.' In the second draft of his sermon, prepared for the parliament of Richard III which met in the following year, he was more explicit: 'In thys grete body of Englonde we have many diuerse membres vndre oone hede. Howe be hyt they may alle be reduced to iij chyef and principalle, whyche make thys hyghe and grete courte at thys tyme, that ys to seye the lordes spiritualle, the lordes temporalle, and the commens.'[42] Not surprisingly, it was the lawyers who carried the analogy furthest.

> The parliament is the king's court and the highest court he has [said Chief Baron Fray in 1441]. By his authority and his writ, parties are to be called into his court to respond; so are the lords by his writ called to come to his parliament, and likewise knights and burgesses, to be elected by his writ. And attainders and forfeitures which are adjudged in the same parliament are revenues of this court, and so are the fifteenths by this grant of revenues.

Other judges regarded acts of parliament as judgements of the court.[43]

This view of parliament influenced some developments of the period. Those who attended a royal court by the king's command had been under his protection since Anglo-Saxon days; safeguards for members

---

[41] *YB 21 Edward IV*, Mich., plea 6. For the view that it might have been a valid opinion in law see Pollard, *Evolution of Parliament*, p. 328, and Chrimes, *Eng. Const. Ideas*, pp. 154–5.

[42] Chrimes, *Eng. Const. Ideas*, p. 187.

[43] *YB 19 Henry VI*, Pasch., plea 1. See T. F. T. Plucknett, 'The Lancastrian constitution', in *Tudor Studies*, ed. R. W. Seton-Watson (London, 1924), pp. 161–81, and Chrimes, *Eng. Const. Ideas*, p. 74.

and their servants on their way to and from parliament were made, first by royal command and then by statute. In 1404 Richard Chedder, a member's servant, had been attacked and maimed by one John Savage; the commons petitioned that the murder of a member or his servant should be counted as treason, maiming should mean the loss of a hand for the assailant, and assault should be punishable by imprisonment. This the king refused, granting only that John Savage should be attainted by fine and double damages unless he presented himself for trial.[44] In 1433 the rule of double damages was enacted by statute.[45] Then anyone attending the king's courts had a right of immunity from arrest. There had been examples in 1290 and 1315 of royal protection for this privilege being applied to attendance in parliament; in 1429, 1475 and 1478 there were cases of royal support for the claim. In the first instance the king vetoed the arrest of a member's servant, and in the second and third he stopped the arrest of two members of the commons.[46] It is true that this privilege could be nullified by the influence of the powerful; in 1453 no less a person than the speaker of the commons, Thomas Thorpe, who was also a baron of the exchequer, was imprisoned in the Fleet for non-payment of a fine for trespass committed in seizing some goods of the duke of York. This was an act of revenge by the duke for Thorpe's opposition to him; but when the commons sent a deputation to the king and lords for the release of their speaker, and the lords in consequence consulted the judges, the latter replied:

> they ought not to aunswere to that question, for it hath not be used afore tyme that the justicez shuld in eny wyse determine the privelegge of this high court of parlement; for it is so high and so mighty in his nature that it may make lawe, and that that is lawe it may make noo lawe; and the determinacion and knowlegge of that privelegge belongeth to the lordes of the parlement, and not to the justices.[47]

Thorpe was less fortunate than Thomas Yong or Young, member for Bristol, who had been imprisoned in 1451 because he had proposed that the duke of York should be declared heir to the throne, but was released in 1456 when the duke was in control of the government.[48]

[44] *Rot. Parl.*, III, p. 542.
[45] *Statutes*, II, p. 286.
[46] *Rot. Parl.*, IV, pp. 357–8, VI, pp. 160–1, 191–2.
[47] *Ibid.*, V, pp. 239–40.
[48] *Ibid.*, V, p. 337.

The proceedings in the case of Thomas Thorpe may have been consulted when a more weighty issue arose, that of the succession to the throne. In 1460, after the battle of Northampton, the duke claimed the throne, the claim was referred to the lords of parliament, and they turned to the justices for advice. The reply which the justices gave was very like that of the judges in 1454: the matter was so high that it was above the law 'and passed ther lernyng, wherfor they durst not enter in to eny communicacion therof, for it perteyned to the lordes of the kyng's blode, and thapparage of this his lond to have communicacion and medle in such maters'. The lords had already admitted their duty to consider the petition 'in asmuche as every person high and lowe, suyng to this high court of parlement, of ryght must be herd'. They had to combine their function of judges in this high court, so clearly confirmed in 1399,[49] with their function of the king's principal councillors 'and also that the kyng myght understond that the said lordes diden their true and feithfull devoire and acquitaille in the said mater, desired all the lordes that every of theym shuld sey what he cowede sey in fortefiyng the kyngs title, and in defetyng of the clayme of the seid duc'.[50]

This important case clearly illustrates the dual aspect of parliament as the king's most solemn council and as his highest court. It could be used to strengthen and uphold the royal authority, but it could also be used by subjects to insist on the judicial hearing of requests and complaints. These could range from the demands of an individual, even of a duke of York claiming the crown, to the complaint of a group, even of the commons insisting on the trial and dismissal of the king's chosen ministers. A similar dual aspect is apparent in another concept which came into prominence in the fifteenth century, that of the estates of the realm. The king of England had for his own purposes summoned to parliaments as early as the thirteenth century individual bishops, abbots and barons, and representatives of shires and boroughs. For the latter he had insisted on full powers, so that whatever was decided in parliament (especially in matters of taxation) should be binding on all communities represented therein. This was to be of importance for the future of parliament as the nation's mouthpiece,[51] but on this theory it is difficult to explain why parliament could be deemed to

[49] *Ibid.*, III, p. 427.
[50] *Ibid.*, V, p. 376.
[51] Edwards, '*Plena potestas*'.

represent the whole realm, since some areas, such as Durham and Cheshire, sent no members.[52] As late as 1492 the knights of the shire for Lancashire could claim that their county was not to be deprived of its judicial privileges, because it had not consented to it.[53] It would seem that of more importance was the development of the theory that parliament represented the estates of the realm. This was part of a very widespread movement of thought in Western Europe: 'on the continent of Europe, west of Russia and the Balkans, the five centuries before 1789 might well be called "the Age of the Estates", the great link between the age of feudalism and the modern world'.[54]

In England the use of the word 'estate' to describe an order of society or a section of parliament seems only to begin in the fourteenth century. Yet by 1397 the notion of estates of parliament was used by the chancellor himself in open parliament.[55] Its application to the English parliament was furthered by the deposition of Richard II. The estate of an anointed king was so awe-inspiring, especially after a century in which it had been consciously enhanced,[56] that his deposition had to be justified and legitimised in every possible way. If a list of his enormities was to be publicly read, his abdication accepted and his deposition pronounced, by whom were all these proceedings to be solemnised? The parliament summoned in Richard's name had in law ceased to exist the moment he abdicated; but if the gathering could be declared to be an assembly of all the estates of the land (as Henry of Lancaster described it when he had been seated on the throne) and if it could be described as such by the spokesman of the deputation appointed to announce to Richard his deposition,[57] then the proceedings might have the justification of representing the people of England.

After this important occasion the concept was applied not only to parliament as a whole but to its constituent elements. By 1407 the commons described those whom they represented as an estate,[58] and by 1410 the speaker of the commons could describe the knights and

[52] Chrimes, *Eng. Const. Ideas*, p. 80 n. 2.
[53] *Rot. Parl.*, VI, pp. 456–7.
[54] A. R. Myers, *Parliaments and Estates in Europe to 1789* (London, 1975), p. 9, and see pp. 165–76 for a select bibliography of the literature on this vast subject.
[55] *Rot. Parl.*, III, p. 347.
[56] See, *inter alia*, P. E. Schramm, *A History of the English Coronation* (Oxford, 1937), pp. 74–87.
[57] *Rot. Parl.*, III, pp. 417–24.
[58] *Ibid.*, III, p. 611.

burgesses themselves as one of the estates of parliament.[59] In the previous year the king himself had told the pope that statutes or ordinances previously made could not be revoked or changed without the assent of the estates of the realm in parliament.[60] This was reiterated by Henry V in 1419 when he told the pope that the Statute of Provisors could not be repealed without the consent of the three estates.[61] The treaty of Troyes of 1420 provided that the treaty must be ratified by the three estates of each realm; and in the subsequent act of the English parliament the three estates were defined as the prelates, the magnates and the commons. Thereafter the expression 'the three estates of the realm in this present parliament assembled' became a commonplace in the prorogations throughout the century.[62] In 1467 the chancellor, Bishop Stillington, explained that justice depended on three estates, the lords spiritual, the lords temporal and the commons, under the royal estate of the king.[63] This is significant, coming as it did from the spokesman of the king; but the most important declaration was that of Richard III to his parliament of 1484. This declaration began by affirming the legitimacy of Richard III, the bastardy of Edward IV's sons, and the hereditary right of Richard III, which was therefore justly grounded on the laws of God, nature and the realm. However, the people at large might not understand this. So the declaration recalled

howe that the courte of parliament is of suche authorite, and the people of this lande of suche nature and disposicion, as experience teacheth, that manifestacion and declaracion of any trueth or right made by the thre estates of this reame assembled in parliament, and by auctorite of the same, maketh, before all other thynges, moost feith and certaynte, and, quietyng mens myndes, remoeveth the occasion of all doubtes and sedicious langage. Therfore, at the request and by assent of the thre estates of this reame, that is to say, the lordes spirituelx and temporelx, and commens of this lande assembled in this present parliament, by auctorite of the same, bee it pronounced, decreed, and declared that oure said soveraigne lorde the kyng was and is veray and undoubted kyng of this reame of England.[64]

[59] *Ibid.*, III p. 623.
[60] E. F. Jacob, 'Some English documents of the Conciliar movement', *BJRUL*, XV (1931), p. 379.
[61] *Foedera*, IV, part iii, p. 137; J. H. Wylie and W. T. Waugh, *The Reign of Henry V*, III (Cambridge, 1929), p. 171.
[62] *Rot. Parl.*, IV, p. 120, V, pp. 67, 172, 213, 270, VI, pp. 39, 424, 426, 444.
[63] *Ibid.*, V, pp. 622–3.
[64] *Ibid.*, VI, pp. 241–2.

This is a specially striking example of the way in which the older notion of parliament had had grafted on to it the idea of a national assembly, acting on behalf of the three estates, combining with the king to provide an authority of parliament which would otherwise have been lacking. During the fifteenth century this formula of approval for statutes had gradually been adopted. The first occurrence of an act of parliament by the assent of the lords spiritual and temporal, and at the instance of the commons, had been in 1402; thereafter, with only a few exceptions, it became normal practice, until the reign of Richard III, when the formula became 'by advice and assent of the lords spiritual and temporal and of the commons'. This was followed by the phrase 'and by authority of parliament', which first occurred in 1433 and became normal from 1444.[65] The commons might not be judges in parliament, but they had become part of the legislative authority because of their representative character. Edward IV gave royal acknowledgement of the idea of national representation when he began his speech to his first parliament with the words 'James Strangways and ye that be commyn for the common of this my lond'.[66] He would doubtless have been startled to find his grandson using this idea in the Reformation Parliament for such great changes in the government of the church; but the developments of the fifteenth century in the legislative authority of parliament and in its representative character as an assembly of three estates had opened the possibility of such a use of the institution. As noted earlier, in 1463 a serjeant-at-law could argue in the court of common pleas, and the judge could accept, that an act of parliament was the highest record in the law, for by such a record every man was bound, since every man was party to it.[67]

Just as the legislative authority of parliament gained more precision during this period, so did the composition and powers of the lords of parliament. During the century the rules about the summons of lords to parliament became more precise. Professor Brown has already pointed out that as late as the reign of Edward III the list of those who were summoned as barons varied considerably.[68] After the accession of Richard II only four men had been summoned to parliament whose ancestors had not been summoned in the first half of the century; and

[65] Chrimes, *Eng. Const. Ideas*, p. 105.
[66] *Rot. Parl.*, V, p. 487.
[67] Chrimes, *Eng. Const. Ideas*, p. 78; see above, pp. 144–6.
[68] See above, pp. 113–17, for his discussion of the composition of the lords in this earlier period.

after Philip Despenser's elevation in 1388 no new baron was summoned for nearly forty years. The list of bishops and abbots was already stereotyped, and the limited number of members with personal summons could not be increased without resentment from the temporal lords and even some of the spiritual ones. Now that the composition was becoming so constant, there was an increased sense of cohesion. 'The term "banneret" as a note of distinction between two kinds of lords of parliament is not official use after 1399. From 1425 *chivaler* was appended in the lists not as hitherto to a few but to all the names.'[69] On the other hand, disputes about precedence became keener. The altercation between the earl of Warwick and the earl Marshal in 1405 was renewed in 1425.[70] In the next parliament (1426) there was also a dispute between Lords Hastings and Talbot.[71] Lords had begun to worry about when their ancestor first received a summons, whether attendance had been continuous since then, and whether they were heirs to parliamentary lordships. In 1429 Richard Neville was summoned as earl of Salisbury in right of his wife;[72] and in 1433 John Arundel claimed the earldom of Arundel and a seat in parliament by an extremely distant connection with the previous earl.[73]

Professor Brown has already shown that many themes remarked upon in relation to parliament later on can be traced back at least as early as the period with which he was dealing, and here a further case in point can be noted. Now that parliamentary lordship was so restricted and so valued, the king determined to assert his ancient right to summon a man if he wished. Richard II had tried to do this when he had summoned John Beauchamp, the steward of his household, to parliament in 1387, after creating him by letters patent Lord Beauchamp and baron of Kidderminster.[74] But Beauchamp was appealed in parliament in 1388 by the king's foes and beheaded. Without supposing this to be directly a case of cause and effect, it was a setback to the king's attempt to restore his freedom of action in relation to the composition of parliament. Equally so was the undoing after Richard's deposition of his lavish creation of dukedoms for his supporters in 1397, and any early attempt of the Lancastrians to follow his example would probably

[69] Powell and Wallis, *House of Lords*, p. 437.
[70] See above, p. 115. *Rot. Parl.*, IV, pp. 267–72, for its renewal.
[71] *Ibid.*, IV, p. 312.
[72] *Proc. P.C.*, III, pp. 324–6.
[73] *Rot. Parl.*, IV, pp. 441–3.
[74] See above, p. 114.

have met with resistance. However, the government could not be expected to forego indefinitely the right to reward its supporters, and probably the council of the minority of Henry VI, dominated by lords spiritual and temporal, was able to do what a king might have found it difficult to initiate after the memory of Richard II. Yet even such a council found it prudent to take action in parliament 'by the advice and assent of the lords', and so, in 1432, the young king,

> in the presence of the three estates of the parliament . . . by the advice and assent of . . . the duke of Gloucester . . . , the bishop of Winchester . . . and the other lords spiritual and temporal in the said parliament, erected, promoted, and created the said John [Cornwall] a baron indigenous of his realm of England and conferred, gave, granted and assigned to him the name, style, title and honour of baron of Fanhope, willing . . . that he have, hold and possess his seat and place in the parliaments and councils of the king among the other barons of the realm of England.[75]

But the creation was a precedent, and in 1441 the king, who had been declared of age in 1437, issued a patent which announced that

> by the advice of our council we have . . . created our beloved and trusty knight, Ralph Boteler, our chamberlain, to be baron of Sudeley in the county of Gloucester . . . and have invested, adorned, and ennobled him with the pre-eminencies, dignities . . . pertaining to . . . the status of a baron of our realm of England, both in sitting in our parliaments and councils and everywhere else, and wish him to be called a noble of our realm; to have and to hold the name . . . to himself and the heirs male of his body lawfully begotten in perpetuity.[76]

This was to be an important landmark in the history of the lords of parliament. Limitation to heirs male marks the divergence of the dignity of a baron from the tenure of land, which would descend by ordinary rules of inheritance, that is to say, in the absence of heirs male, to heirs general or co-parceners. From this time onwards there were to be two kinds of lords of parliament: the increasing number who, like Lord Sudeley, were peers created by royal patent in tail male; and the remainder, ever diminished by extinction, who were peers by prescription, as heirs of estates whose holders had been summoned in the fourteenth or the thirteenth century. The fall of the duke of Gloucester

---

[75] *Rot. Parl.*, IV, pp. 400–1.
[76] *Dignity of a Peer*, V, p. 239; *Cal. Patent Rolls 1441–6* (HMSO, 1908), p. 51.

in 1447 was followed by the creation of four other lords temporal by patent in tail male. In 1461 the creation of Lord Herbert of Herbert showed the abandonment, under the influence of the new procedure, of the tradition that a barony must necessarily be based on the tenure of a large estate with a recognisable *caput*. It took time for the principles of these new creations to have full effect; and as late as 1477 when George Neville was deprived of his dukedom of Bedford, it was thought sufficient formal reason to say that he had inadequate lands to support his dignity.[77] But by 1497, when Lord Willoughby de Broke claimed the barony of Latimer, the old notion that lords came to parliament in respect of the baronies they held was replaced by the modern theory that they held their seats by virtue of a king's writ to themselves or their ancestors.[78] By the reign of Henry VIII the older principle that the possession of land justified the privilege of a summons to parliament had become insufficient. Mr Wimbish had married the daughter and heiress of Gilbert, baron Tailboys of Kime, and earlier precedents would have entitled him to a summons in right of his wife; but he had no heir, and so the king himself ruled that he should not be summoned.[79]

There was another significant aspect to the creation of Sir Ralph Boteler as Baron Sudeley. He was declared to be ennobled and to be called a noble of the realm. This may have been due to French influence, but, in any event, it was a novelty for an English official document. It implied that the lords were conceived to be not merely individual members of a parliamentary group but a noble order or estate. This idea was further expressed in the following year, 1442, when the duke of Gloucester's second wife, Eleanor Cobham, was tried for witchcraft against the king. Though she was condemned by a church court, the commons petitioned that in cases of indictment for treason or felony peeresses should be tried by such judges as peers of the realm would have had in such cases.[80] This would have made no sense if the lords of parliament had simply been viewed in the old way as king's councillors or judges of a high court; but it did cohere if the lords were now regarded as an established estate or order, whose nobility extended to

---

[77] *Rot. Parl.*, VI, p. 173.
[78] Powell and Wallis, *House of Lords*, p. 537, and appendix A, pp. 583–91.
[79] Pike, *House of Lords*, p. 107.
[80] *Rot. Parl.*, V, p. 56.

their wives, and to which additions were made sparingly under precise rules.

This growing exclusiveness and precision had contrary effects. On the one hand, lords knew that if they and their forefathers had received a summons to parliament it would be extremely hard for the crown to deprive them of their seat. This tended to make some of them careless of attendance, especially if, as in the drift towards civil war in the 1450s and the sharp reversals of fortune from 1459 to 1461, it might be politic not to be involved in current disputes.[81] On the other hand, if they did attend it was important to be recorded as having been present. A claim in 1427 by Reginald West for a summons to parliament not only stressed that his ancestor, Roger, lord de la Ware, had been summoned by writ in 1299 but that Roger's successors had attended continuously since then.[82] In the case of those peers who were too important to be excluded for non-attendance, it would nevertheless be useful to show the king that they were supporting him by their attendance.

This may have been a factor in the compilation of presence lists increasingly from the reign of Henry IV. In an early seventeenth-century manuscript in the College of Arms, MS 2H 13, discovered by Professor W. H. Dunham in 1953,[83] there are presence lists and reports of debates of fifteenth-century parliaments.[84] At the latest by the reign of Henry VI attendances were evidently being recorded in 'books of the parliament'. On f. 387a of MS 2H 13 we read:

Memorandum that in the bokes of the parliament kept by the clerkes of the parliament in the tyme of our late souereigne lord King Henry the vjth. yt doth appere that the lord of Saint Jones [the Prior of St John of Jerusalem] was plased above all the Barons of the Realme, and next hym did syt the Lord Grey Ruthyn, then the Lord Grey of Codnor, the Lord Clynton, and the Lord Awdeley, and so in order folouinge dyd syt all the rest of the barons of the reaulme as well as soche dayes and tymes when the said late king was present in the parlement

---

[81] Roskell, 'Attendance of the lords', especially pp. 189–96; though attendance was good in October 1460 and November 1461 (pp. 195–6).

[82] G. E. Cokayne, *Complete Peerage*, new edn., IV (London, 1916), p. 153 n.b.

[83] W. H. Dunham, ' "The Books of the Parliament" and "The Old Record", 1396–1504', *Speculum*, LI (1976), pp. 694–712.

[84] See R. Virgoe, 'A list of members of the parliament of February 1449', *BIHR*, XXXIV (1961), pp. 200–10, and A. R. Myers, 'A parliamentary debate of the mid-fifteenth century', *BJRUL*, XXII (1938), pp. 388–404, which contains a presence list of lords.

amongest his nobles as at all other tymes duringe the said parlement. . . .
And in lyke wyse yt dothe appere in the parlements holden in the tyme
of our late soueraigne lordes dayes king Edward the iiijth. that the said
lordes before mencyoned did syt and were placed in the parlement
accordingly.

As such importance was now attached to correct precedence, it was
natural to have uniforms which would outwardly show degrees of
rank. As has been seen, these did not have to be invented in this
period;[85] there is now even pictorial evidence. In 1446 King's College,
Cambridge, was granted a charter confirming its privileges. In the initial
letter, a capital H, is a picture of the kneeling commons presenting
the petition, the seated king granting it, and the lords standing by as
witnesses of it. Cardinals Beaufort and Kemp are present in their
cardinal hats, four or five bishops in their mitres, all on the right side
of the throne. Two temporal lords on the left of the throne, dressed
in scarlet robes with four bars of white fur, probably depict the royal
dukes, Gloucester and York. Behind them is a row of four lords, of
whom two visibly have three bars, the earls. Behind these are four
more, the two visible with two bars, the barons. The rear is brought up
by two judges in robes and coifs, the one in front, Sir John Fortescue,
wearing a belt because he was a knight.[86] This scheme was standard
by Tudor days.[87]

The growing exclusiveness of the lords meant that they could insist
all the more on their role as principal councillors of the king. They
had been given a special opportunity to assert this role when Henry V
died, leaving an heir not yet a year old and hence with the prospect of
a long minority. Humphrey, duke of Gloucester took his stand on the
late king's will and on his own nearness in blood to the king; but the
lords of the council (an archbishop, seven bishops, two dukes, three
earls, nine barons) insisted that the government of the minority must
be settled by parliament, which meant in practice the lords of parliament.[88] The appointment of Gloucester as protector, the definition of
his powers, the nomination of the council, and the statement of its

---

[85] See above, p. 115, for Froissart's reference to peers' differentiated robes in his
account of the coronation procession of Henry IV in 1399.

[86] Powell and Wallis, *House of Lords*, p. 477 and plate XIV.

[87] See *ibid.*, plate XVIII (procession roll for the parliament of 1512) and plate
XXII (Tudor drawings of parliament robes).

[88] J. S. Roskell, 'The office and dignity of protector of England', *EHR*, LXVIII
(1953), especially pp. 196–8.

functions, were all authorised by the lords in the parliament of 1422. The participation of the commons was limited to approval of these measures and the addition of an article to the terms of appointment for the council.[89] The council nominated in parliament was composed either of lords, spiritual and temporal, or of men who were later summoned as lords. In 1427 it was stated by the chancellor in the Star Chamber, on behalf of the council, that during the king's minority the execution of his authority 'belongeth unto the lordes spirituall and temporell of his londe, at suche tyme as thei be assembled in parlement or in grete consaille; and ellus, hem not being so assembled, unto lords chosen and named to be of his continuall conseill'.[90] By 1426 the continual council was composed entirely of lords spiritual and temporal;[91] and the council appointed by Henry VI when he reached his majority in 1437 was not much less aristocratic.[92] It is true that for another generation traces lingered of the originally equal membership of lords and officials in the upper house. The Fane fragment of the 1461 lords' journal mentions that bills were referred to mixed committees of lords, judges and expert officials.[93] In the reign of Henry VII the judges were frequently consulted in council on the legality of procedures in parliament, and in the first years of Henry VIII's reign the judges, the attorney- and solicitor-general, the serjeants-at-law and masters in chancery were regular members of committees for considering bills.[94] But by that time there was a clear distinction between the lords, as full members of parliament, and officials who acted simply as advisers in a subordinate capacity.

In 1484 Bishop Russell, as chancellor, could attribute important executive functions to the king's court and council in parliament. 'Thydyr be broughte all maters of weight, peax and warre with outward londes, confederacions, liques, and alliances, receyuynge and sendynge of embassades and messages, brekynge of treux, prises yn the see, routtes and riottes, and vnlaufulle assemblies, oppressions, extorsions, contemptes and abusions of the lawe, many moo surfettes then

---

[89] *Rot. Parl.*, IV, pp. 174–6.
[90] *Proc. P.C.*, III, p. 238; *Rot. Parl.*, V, p. 408.
[91] *Proc. P.C.*, III, p. 213.
[92] *Ibid.*, VI, p. 312.
[93] *The Fane Fragment of the 1461 Lords' Journal*, ed. W. H. Dunham (New Haven, 1935), pp. 19, 25.
[94] Pollard, *Evolution of Parliament*, pp. 293–4.

can well be nombred.'[95] Henry VII, for all his inexperience in 1485, knew which group was the most important for the prevention of 'routs and riots, unlawful assemblies, and abuse of laws'. On 19 November 1485 all the lords spiritual and temporal took a solemn oath in the parliament chamber before the king against misprision of felony, retainder, livery, maintenance, riot and favouring of riots.[96] As for legislation, the position of the lords was slowly strengthened in this century, in the language of the statutes. In the reign of Richard II statutes had normally been made with the assent of the lords, and sometimes with the assent of the commons too. During the reign of Henry IV it became normal to record the advice as well as the assent of the lords. With the accession of the infant Henry VI it became standard practice to make statutes by the advice and assent of the lords spiritual and temporal at the instance and/or request of the commons. By the reign of Edward IV it had become normal to enact by advice and assent of the lords spiritual and temporal and at the request of the commons, and by authority of parliament. From 1485 it became invariable to enact by advice and assent of the lords spiritual and temporal and of the commons and by authority of parliament.[97]

In practice the influence of the lords varied. During the minority of Henry VI they clearly dominated the government, and when he was grown up groups of lords could make difficulties. Both lords spiritual and lords temporal, however, were inclined to support the king on most occasions, except in times of great weakness for him and bitter dissension (as between 1459 and 1461).[98] Moreover the king was the apex of society and of patronage; unless he was very weak, like Henry VI, or ran counter to aristocratic feeling and interests, like Richard II, he need not fear opposition in parliament from temporal lords. It seems to have been the custom to ask for opinion individually in parliamentary sessions, so that a lord would need to be both strong and disaffected for him to express an opinion which he knew could be displeasing to the king.

There was in this period a certain increase in the privileges of the lords by the consent and initiative of the crown. In 1404 the commons had alleged that the sheriff of Rutland had acted improperly by return-

[95] Chrimes, *Eng. Const. Ideas*, p. 188.
[96] *Rot. Parl.*, VI, p. 288.
[97] Chrimes, *Eng. Const. Ideas*, pp. 101–4.
[98] Roskell, 'Attendance of the lords'.

ing William Ondeby instead of Thomas Thorp as member. The case was remitted by the lords in parliament, who exercised jurisdiction by deciding that the return should be amended in favour of Thorp, and by committing the sheriff to the Fleet prison until he should pay a fine at the king's pleasure.[99] In 1439, when the sheriff of Cambridgeshire failed to make a return, the commons were not even named; the matter was settled by the king and lords of parliament.[100] In the case of claims to freedom from arrest, for both members of the commons and their servants, in 1429 (Larke's case), 1475 (Hyde's case) and 1478 (Attwyll's case), it was the lords of parliament who acted as judges.[101] In 1453, when the commons appealed for the release of their speaker, Thomas Thorpe, and the duke of York opposed it the judges were asked for their comment. The lords spiritual and temporal took their reply to mean that they were the supreme arbiters with regard to privilege of parliament and its consequences. They decided that Thomas Thorpe must remain in prison; the commons accepted their ruling and elected another speaker.[102] It was confirmed in this century that parliament had the right and the duty to correct any error found in the common law courts, especially king's bench; and in 1485 they were decided by all the judges to be vested exclusively in the lords.[103]

For the lords their judgements on cases covering elections to the commons or freedom from arrest were confirmations of their role as judges in parliament. For the commons these cases were indications of their growing prestige. In the early days of parliament attendance had been regarded as a burden, but gradually during the fourteenth century attendance had become part of the accepted institutions of English society, and to be a knight of the shire was now regarded as an honour. It is significant that Chaucer's aspiring franklin, said to be a model among landed gentry, had often been a member for his shire. During the fifteenth century the speed of change quickened markedly. In 1413, as already noted, parliament had enacted that knights and burgesses must be resident on the day of issue of the writ of summons in the

---

[99] *Rot. Parl.*, III, p. 530. See above, p. 118, for mention of the Rutland case in the context of the proper conduct of parliamentary elections.
[100] *Rot. Parl.*, V, pp. 7–8.
[101] *Ibid.*, IV, pp. 357–8, VI, pp. 160, 191.
[102] *Ibid.*, V, pp. 239–40.
[103] W. S. Holdsworth, *A History of English Law*, I, 3rd edn. (London, 1922), p. 36, quoting *YB 1 Henry VII*, Pasch., plea 5.

shire or town which they sought to represent.[104] This implied that a growing number of men had been seeking to be members for shires and boroughs in which they did not dwell. So far as the boroughs were concerned the order was probably broken from the start. Already in the first parliament of Henry VI's reign over forty of the 188 burgesses were non-residents, but as yet there were few real 'carpetbaggers'; most of the non-residents lived near the borough they represented, and some were even entered on the roll of out-burgesses.[105] Thereafter the proportion of non-residents did increase rapidly.

The most important phase of the decline of the number of towns completely conforming to the statute of 1413 and returning two in-burgesses to parliament seems clearly to belong to the first half of Henry VI's reign: in 1422 the proportion of such boroughs wholly adhering to the statutory requirement of residence was 64%; twenty years later it was 39% and from then on until the end of Edward IV's reign or thereabouts the proportion moved up and down between 40% and 30%, standing (at 30%) as low in January 1449 as it was to stand in 1478. . . . Whereas in the parliament of 1422 there were just over four times as many boroughs electing two resident burgesses as there were returning two non-residents, in those parliaments of Edward IV's reign for which something like full returns have survived, there were four boroughs returning two 'outsiders' . . . to every three returning two of their own resident burgesses.[106]

This in itself would indicate that there was growing competition for seats in parliament; and that impression is confirmed by other indications. In 1422 only a handful of the members were royal officials or members of the royal household or seignorial administrators; by the middle of the century they were very numerous, and by 1478 they numbered 17 per cent of the whole house, as high a proportion as that of Elizabethan parliaments.[107] Lesser officials, such as lower exchequer clerks or yeomen of the crown, tried for borough seats. Higher officials, like the treasurer or controller of the household, or the under-treasurer of the exchequer, sought a county seat. It was very unusual when a treasurer of the household (Sir John Fogge) was returned as a burgess, for the city of Canterbury, in 1467.[108] But gentry who did not occupy

[104] *Statutes*, II, p. 170. See above, p. 119.
[105] Roskell, *Commons in 1422*, p. 49.
[106] *Ibid.*, p. 133.
[107] *Ibid.*, pp. 134–5.
[108] *Ibid.*, p. 134.

important government posts were only too thankful to accept a borough seat if they could not secure a shire one. Moreover lords greater than gentry were now mindful of the value of seats in the commons for their supporters. As K. B. McFarlane said, 'A baron . . . was dependent upon the goodwill, the confidence and the co-operation of his less rich but still substantial neighbours. . . . Politics were a joint-stock enterprise and he and his advisers had got to make them pay.'[109] A retainer in parliament might be of service to a lord; but the lord might also be of service to the constituency which agreed to let him have one of its seats. As John, viscount Beaumont wrote to the mayor and burgesses of Grimsby in 1459 when he asked for a seat there for his trusty servant, Ralph Chaundeler, 'And such as I may do for you I shall at all tymes the rather perfourme to my power as knoweth God which have you ever in keping.'[110] In the parliaments of Edward IV landed gentry made up at least two thirds of the members.[111] It was the mid-fifteenth century that saw the establishment of that preponderance of the gentry in the commons which was to be so important for English parliamentary development. The growing desire for a seat in parliament was shown in yet another way, the increase in this period of the practice of re-election. William Burley (d. 1458), twice speaker of the commons, heads the list, for he represented Shropshire nineteen times between 1417 and 1456;[112] but his record was closely followed by that of Robert Whitgreve (d. 1452), who was member for Stafford sixteen times and for Staffordshire another two. There were other cases of frequent re-election: William Soper (d. 1458 or 1459) and John Sheldwich (d. 1460) were each elected thirteen times for Southampton and Canterbury respectively; William Tresham (d. 1450) and John Stanney (d. 1496) were members for Northamptonshire and Chichester respectively on eleven occasions. Between 1439 and 1509 eighty men sat in six parliaments or more;[113] and it was by now a common occurrence for a man to sit in two or three parliaments.

The ease with which a noble might secure a seat for his retainer in

---

[109] K. B. McFarlane, 'Parliament and "bastard feudalism" ', *TRHS*, 4th ser., XXVI (1944), p. 73.
[110] McKisack, *Borough Representation*, p. 62.
[111] Roskell, *Commons in 1422*, pp. 129, 132.
[112] J. S. Roskell, 'William Burley of Broncroft, speaker for the commons in 1437 and 1445–6', *Trans. of the Shropshire Arch. Soc.*, LVI (1960), pp. 263–72.
[113] J. C. Wedgwood and A. D. Holt, *History of Parliament: Biographies of the Members of the Commons House, 1439–1509* (London, 1938), pp. 941, 782, 761, 871, 801, xxxviii.

parliament varied not only from one parliament to another but with the type of seat. County electorates were comparatively large, and knights of the shire had more prestige than burgesses (except citizens of London). County electorates could therefore rarely be openly coerced, though they might be influenced, manipulated or subtly browbeaten.[114] It was often easier to influence a borough election; but there were fewer boroughs to influence. Throughout the fourteenth century and the reigns of the first two Lancastrian kings the number of boroughs represented in parliament had slowly dwindled. 'Whereas Edward I summoned 322 representatives of cities and boroughs, Henry VI in 1445 summoned but 198.'[115] In view of the growing pressure for seats for royal nominees or seignorial retainers, it is not surprising that the king revived his right of summoning additional borough members. Between 1447 and 1453 Henry VI summoned representatives from five tiny places, pocket boroughs from the start, Wootton Bassett, Hindon, Westbury, Heytesbury, Gatton. Edward IV followed suit with Grantham, Ludlow and Much Wenlock.[116] In 1472 John Paston deemed that there would be no difficulty in the creation of another pocket borough, or else that his brother might be returned for an existing borough through the influence of the chamberlain, Lord Hastings.[117]

Yet another indication of the growing prestige of the commons was the appearance of contests for some parliamentary seats. It is true that here and there the old aversion to parliamentary representation lingered; as late as 1453 New Woodstock asked for exemption from parliamentary duties to be included in its charter.[118] Moreover some boroughs wished to be represented only if they could benefit from an influential patron; in that case there was unlikely to be a contest. On the other hand, the smooth language of the normal parliamentary return may conceal a disputed election,[119] and there is other evidence of a growing interest in borough elections.[120] The legislation of this

[114] K. B. McFarlane, 'Parliament and "bastard feudalism" ', p. 63. 'The work of the Commons in parliament was only the last stage in the long process by which opinion was shaped, transmitted and given voice. In that process the county court had a central place' (J. R. Maddicott, 'County community', p. 42).
[115] Pollard, *Evolution of Parliament*, p. 316.
[116] McKisack, *Borough Representation*, pp. 45–6.
[117] *Paston Letters*, ed. J. Gairdner, III, p. 55.
[118] McKisack, *Borough Representation*, p. 46.
[119] K. N. Houghton, 'A document concerning the parliamentary election at Shrewsbury in 1478', *Trans. of the Shropshire Arch. Soc.*, LVII (1961–4), pp. 162–5.
[120] K. N. Houghton, 'Theory and practice in borough elections to parliament during the later fifteenth century', *BIHR*, XXXIX (1966), pp. 130–40.

period, as of that preceding it, reflected the increasing interest in the composition of the commons. In contrast to the statute of 1406 which had declared that the franchise included not only all freeholders but all freemen present at the county court on the day of the election,[121] an act passed in 1430 restricted the county franchise to freeholders who had lands or tenements to the value of 40s a year above all charges.[122] In 1445 a statute insisted that county members must indeed be knights of the shire, or at least squires or gentlemen born in the shire who were qualified to become knights;[123] this meant that they must have land to the value of £20 a year. But in view of the competition for places such a stipulation was unnecessary. English society was hierarchical, close-knit and aristocratic. Great lords needed an affinity or connection to support them. As the commons increased in prestige and usefulness it became more desirable for a lord to have the support of some members of parliament among his affinity, and more effective for a member to have a powerful seignorial patron. Such a relationship must normally be based on influence and mutual advantage, not on command or coercion.

Not only did many knights have close connections with the aristocracy,[124] but many lawyers already occupied shire seats: there were, for example, no fewer than twenty lawyers among the seventy-four knights of the shire in the 1422 parliament.[125] And, since there were at least thirty-seven lawyers who were returned as burgesses in the same parliament, there were as many lawyers in the commons then as there were to be in the parliament of 1584. Not that this strong element of lawyers was a novelty. As has been seen, it had been even a matter for concern as early as 1372.[126] But lawyers could not be kept out; and in at least one important respect they may have contributed to the growing prestige of the commons. Their professional training made them competent in the drafting of petitions to the high court of parliament, as had also been noted in 1372. We lack for this period such inside information to illumine proceedings in the commons as is provided by the journals, diaries and reports from the age of Elizabeth I onwards.

[121] *Statutes*, II, p. 156. See above, pp. 118–20, for a discussion of elections in this earlier period.
[122] *Ibid.*, II, p. 243.
[123] *Ibid.*, II, p. 342.
[124] Roskell, *Commons in 1422*, pp. 68–79.
[125] *Ibid.*, p. 66.
[126] See above, p. 76.

We can, however, see the results, which are a considerable advance in parliamentary procedure during the fifteenth century in the commons.

A certain amount of progress had already been made. For example, at least from the time of the Good Parliament of 1376 the commons had had a president who was empowered to address the king and the lords on their behalf, the speaker. In that same parliament there had been at any rate a rudimentary sense of order in the commons' debates.[127] However, procedure for dealing with bills had remained relatively undeveloped. True, from Richard II's time petitions had become more formal and precise, with sophisticated preambles and stereotyped conclusions; by 1400 adjectives such as 'sage', 'noble', 'haut' and 'puissant' were being applied to a person to whom the petition was addressed; and petitioners had begun to describe themselves as 'humble', 'pover', 'obeissant'. At the end of the petition the suppliant would commend himself by his loyalty, humility or poverty, even though this might be a fiction, and pleaded for relief 'pur Dieu et en oeuvre de charitee'. The diplomatic of the petition was therefore—like that of the bills in chancery—assuming a fixed form. The body of the petition was now made with the care of a legal document; this was all the more necessary as it became more difficult to obtain an answer, in view of the number of other petitions and the amount of parliamentary business to be transacted.

In other respects, however, the procedure for bills was primitive, by the standards of the late fifteenth century. It was possible for bills on the same theme to be presented by different persons in the same parliament. The author or sponsor of a private petition might well be unaware of another petitioner on the same subject, and he had little time to find out. From the early days of parliament the names of receivers and triers of petitions were read out by the clerk of parliament, immediately after the opening sermon, and petitions dealt with by this procedure had to be handed in within a few days; this left little time to arrange concerted effort. But towards the end of the fourteenth century some petitioners began to seek the formal support of the commons. If the latter adopted the petition, then it would not go to the receivers and triers. This did not in itself ensure co-ordination; for a while the duplication could still occur. In 1402 and 1429 even common

[127] See above, pp. 124–5.

petitions duplicated each other's requests.[128] But even redundancy is not so difficult to explain as downright contradiction, an instance of which occurred in 1410. In that year the commons presented a petition for the revision in favour of the Lollards of the 1401 Statute *De Haeretico Comburendo*. Yet within a fortnight they came before the king and lords and begged that they might have back again a petition delivered by them in parliament concerning the statute recently made against the Lollards, and that nothing should be enacted thereon. The king agreed on condition that his action should not be treated as a precedent.[129] But further down on the same parliament roll is another petition in favour of persons arrested as suspected Lollards.[130] So far from being perturbed by these inconsistencies, the commons had asked in 1406, through their speaker, that if they should deliver anything in writing they could reclaim that document whenever it should please them during the same parliament to the intent that the matter contained in the said writing could be reformed and amended by them if need should arise.[131] If a fully developed procedure, such as Stubbs postulated, complete with three readings, had been established in the early fifteenth century, surely such confusion would not have occurred.

By the end of the reign of Henry VI, however, important strides had been taken towards systematising the treatment of bills. As the prestige of the commons grew those who wished to present private petitions evidently found it advantageous to present them to the commons for sponsorship rather than simply leaving them to take their chance, unsponsored, with the receivers and triers. Of 125 unenrolled petitions printed for the reign of Richard II only two were addressed to the commons, whereas under Henry VI sixty of the 150 printed in *Rotuli Parliamentorum* were addressed to the commons alone.[132] As for enrolled private petitions, none was presented in the name of the commons

---

[128] *Rot. Parl.*, III, pp. 506–7, 510, IV, pp. 349, 358.
[129] PRO, Rolls of Parl., C65/71 (*Rot. Parl.*, III, p. 623).
[130] *Rot. Parl.*, III, p. 626.
[131] PRO, C65/68 (*Rot. Parl.*, III, p. 568).
[132] In *Second Century of the English Parliament*, especially pp. 54–5, Edwards pointed out that in the fourteenth century common petitions could without impropriety be presented to the king by persons or groups other than the commons in parliament assembled, since common petitions did not possess their quality of commonness because they were presented by the commons as a body. This agrees well with my view ('Parliamentary petitions', part II) that the fifteenth century was the period when the sponsorship or at least the approval of the commons in parliament gradually became increasingly desirable and finally essential for the presentation of common petitions, the predecessors of 'public bills'.

in the reign of Richard II, but in the reign of Henry VI sixty of the 198 enrolled were so addressed. And not only was there a rapid increase in the number of petitions presented to the commons in the Lancastrian period but the petitions came from an extraordinary diversity of persons. Thus in a common petition of 1423 concerning disorders in Herefordshire the commons stated that several persons had submitted petitions on this subject to them in the present parliament.[133] In a single parliament, that of 1432, the petitioners ranged from the mayor and constables of the staple of Calais to the representatives of the county electors, the cloth merchants and the commons of the shires of Hereford and Cornwall.[134]

To cope effectively with a growing and diversified mass of petitions the commons had to improve their procedures. They cannot have been reading bills three times as early as 1397, as Bishop Stubbs thought,[135] for in 1416 they were still in the stage of faulty redrafting which would not have survived three readings. In that year a petition was presented on behalf of Alexander Meryng and began, in its enrolled form, 'Item priount les communes,' but the appeal remains in the form of a petition addressed to the commons: 'Please a vos tres sages discrecions . . . du prier a nostre tres soveraigne seigneur le roy et a toutz ses seigneurs temporelx et espirituales en cest present parlement.'[136] Another common petition of 1416 began, 'Please a les honurables et sages communes dycest present parlement considerer.' But already they were experimenting with a method which was to have a very important future in regularising procedure, that of leaving the wording of the petition as it was presented to them, and simply writing above it a sentence commending it to the lords. It was apparently in 1394 that this method had first been tried; above the text of a petition from John Banberye of Bristol, addressed to the commons, was written: 'Soit parle aux seigneurs.'[137] During the reign of Henry IV superscriptions increased in number but were not yet frequent. They were very diverse in form, such as 'soit prie as roy', 'soit baille as roy', 'sue a

---

[133] PRO, C65/85 (*Rot. Parl.*, IV, p. 254).
[134] *Rot. Parl.*, IV, pp. 401–10.
[135] Stubbs, *Const. Hist.*, III, p. 480.
[136] PRO, C65/77 (*Rot. Parl.*, IV, p. 73).
[137] PRO, Ancient Petitions, SC8/4758. SC8/4569 is a copy of this but addressed to the king and lords. Evidently in this case appeal to the commons was more effective.

roy', 'soit parle a roy par les seigneurs'.[138] In the reign of Henry V more petitions were formally sponsored and the previous diversity was gradually replaced by uniformity. In the last two parliaments of the reign the superscription came to be 'soit baille as seigneurs'.[139] Not only was this form of superscription employed for private petitions; it was found useful for common petitions too, for it must have been a useful confirmation of those that the commons had discussed and approved. Above the text of three of the four surviving petitions of the 1423 parliament are written the words 'soit baille as seigneurs'; and the same is true of all the extant petitions of 1425.[140]

This development represents more than the addition of a few words. It implies that the commons had evolved a regular procedure for scrutinising bills; and the increasing number of petitions on which the superscription is found probably means that confidence in their advocacy was growing. The commons' increasing share in the process of legislation is reflected in another way. Soon they were expressing their assent in writing to bills sent down to them by the lords. It is likely that the very act of seeking their consent was new; historically the commons had been petitioners in parliament, seeking approval for their requests. The first extant instance of a written assent by the commons to a bill sent down to them by the lords is an undated bill of the reign of Henry V, which has the superscription: 'Les communes ount donez lour assent.'[141] The next instance occurs in 1429, when such an assent was written on two common petitions. One of them shows by its wording that it was introduced in the lords and then sent down to the commons.[142] The confidence of the commons is shown in the proviso they made that their amendments were incorporated in the

---

[138] Soit prie a Roy—PRO, SC8/1086, /5609; Soit parle a Roy—PRO, SC8/1090; Sue a Roy—PRO, SC8/1120, /6030; Soit parle a Roy par les seigneurs—PRO, SC8/1078, /6251 (*Rot. Parl.*, III, pp. 514 (twice), 518, 515 (twice), 488, 489). An unprinted petition of this period has 'Soit baille a Roy' (PRO, SC8/6917).

[139] PRO, SC8/1157, /1160, /6459, /1161, /1168–70, /6236, /6097, /1173, /1176 (*Rot. Parl.*, IV, pp. 130, 141, 143 (nos. 22 and 23), 159 (nos. 5 and 6), 160 (nos. 7–9), 162, 164).

[140] 1423 parliament: PRO, Chancery, Parl. and Council Proceedings, C49/15/10–12 (*Rot. Parl.*, IV, pp. 258–9). 1425 parliament, in order of enrolment: PRO, SC8/1192; C49/16/5; SC8/6716, /1193, /1194, /1196, /1195; C49/16/6; SC8/1197, /1198; C49/16/7–10 (*Rot. Parl.*, IV, pp. 289–94).

[141] PRO, SC8/7489 (*Rot. Parl.*, IV, p. 91).

[142] PRO, C49/19/18 (*Rot. Parl.*, IV, p. 355).

bill.[143] The other petition began, 'Item priount les communes'; either the compilers of the petition had worded it in that form before it was sent down to the commons, to make it sound impressive, or else the commons changed the wording before returning the bill to the lords. The superscription was 'A cest bille les communes sount assentuz.'[144] The opening words of the petition are a warning to us that other petitions which appear to emanate from the commons may in fact be bills sent down to them by the lords. As for private petitions, apart from the isolated case in the reign of Henry V, already mentioned, this form of assent began to be used in the 1430s. In 1431 this kind of superscription appeared for the first time on two private petitions.[145] In 1432 the formula appears on a private petition for the first time as 'A ceste bille les communes ount donne lour assent,'[146] the words in which it was within a few years to be stereotyped. Almost at the same time the acts of parliament began to acknowledge in their wording the participation of the commons, in a more emphatic way. From 1433 the words 'and by authority of parliament' began to be added sometimes to the older formula 'by advice and assent of the lords spiritual and temporal and at the request of the commons'. From 1452 the phrase 'at the request of the commons' started sometimes to be exchanged for 'by assent of the commons'; and from the beginning of the reign of Henry VII the enacting formula came to be invariably 'by advice and assent of the lords spiritual and temporal and of the commons, and by authority of parliament'.[147] By 1489 the judges had ruled that an act of parliament without the consent of the commons was invalid.[148]

As the commons gained in prestige for sponsoring bills, and as the necessity of their assent to legislation was increasingly assumed, it became more worth while for interested parties to take trouble to secure their support. Closely knit communities like towns used their burgesses in this way. Thus in the accounts of the town bailiffs of Shrewsbury for 1408–9 the town's burgesses at the parliament of Gloucester in

[143] An appended schedule was inscribed 'les communes sount assentuz a la bille a cest cedule annexe, par issent qe les forsprises en cest cedule comprisez soient affermes come parcell de la bille' (C49/19/17).

[144] PRO, C49/19/21 (*Rot. Parl.*, IV, p. 357).

[145] PRO, SC8/1235, /1260 (*Rot. Parl.*, IV, pp. 370, 397).

[146] PRO, SC8/1268 (*Rot. Parl.*, IV, p. 415).

[147] Chrimes, *Eng. Const. Ideas*, pp. 103–4.

[148] A. F. Pollard, *The Reign of Henry VII from Contemporary Sources*, II (London, 1914), p. 19, quoting from *YB 4 Henry VII*, p. 18.

1407, John Scryven and Thomas Pryde, were paid 53s 4d for going 'versus regem pro pardonacione subsidii habenda'.[149] The petition (which was unsuccessful) was enrolled among the common petitions of 1407.[150] In 1425 William Weggewode, burgess for Cambridge, was paid £4 'by command of the mayor and bailiffs for the confirmation of the king's charter'.[151] John Hoord, MP for Shrewsbury in the parliament of 1472, was recompensed for his labour in resisting a bill for the payment of murage in that parliament.[152] In 1482 the citizens of Exeter presented a petition in parliament for the curtailment of the privileges of the Exeter Tailors' Guild; and a payment of £3 19s 8d was made to one of the burgess members for Exeter, John Attwyll, 'pro negociis civitatis tempore parliamenti pro annullacione carte scissorum'.[153] There seems to be only one recorded expression of remorse at such payments, and then only in a man's will made less than three weeks before he died. In the will of Nicholas Stathum, made on 15 July 1472 and proved on 5 August 1472, he wrote:

> Item, I resceiued x s of [   ] Bemont, a worshipfull squier of the west countre by the handes of Page in the last parleament. I did nothing therefore, and if I did yet it is agenst my conscience, for somoche as I was one of the parleament and shuld be indifferent in euery mater in the parleament. I wil he haue it ageyne.[154]

As in practice it grew more necessary to secure sponsorship for bills, it became more desirable to make the petition as foolproof in content and as attractive in form as could be contrived. This would cost money, but it would be worth while, to give the petition a better chance. In 1452–3 the Pewterers' Company of London paid 5s to 'a clerk of the Chauncery . . . for his rewarde in laboryng to serche for statuts and othir thyngs to thentent to labor to the parlement for a charter for

---

[149] *HMC, Fifteenth Rep.* (1899), appendix, part X, p. 27. See also *ibid.*, p. 30: 'Sol pro uno pixide empto ad imponendum [*sic*] cartam ville pro conductu ejusdem ad parliamentum, vid', *sub anno* 1483–4.

[150] *Rot. Parl.*, III, pp. 618–19.

[151] C. H. Cooper, *Annals of Cambridge* (Cambridge, 1842), I, p. 173.

[152] McKisack, *Borough Representation*, pp. 138–9.

[153] *Ibid.*, p. 134. For a payment of 26s 8d from the mayor of Barnstaple to one of the burgesses in the parliament of 1478 'pro carta domini regis confirmanda' see S. Reynolds, 'The forged charters of Barnstaple', *EHR*, LXXXIV (1969), p. 709.

[154] 'Nicholas Stathum's will', ed. C. H. Willams, *BIHR*, III (1926), p. 49.

the Craft to haue serche thurgh England'.[155] In 1460–1 the company had a petition to parliament professionally drawn up; 4s was then 'payde for makynge of a byll to Cobbe for to pute yn the parlemente howse for the welle of all the ffelechype'.[156] In 1487–8 they made a big effort; 6s 8d was 'paide to masters Kyngesmyll and Englethorp gentilmen of the temple for correctyng our bill and to be of our Counsell', 13s 4d was 'paide to John Pares Scrivener for drawyng and writyng of ij Supplicacions to the kyng and to my lord Chaunceller' and 2s 6d was 'paide for makyng of a Supplicacion for the Comon house'.[157] The bill, which sought parliamentary powers to suppress hawkers and pedlars, was evidently of sufficient importance to the company for it to be worth while bribing the speaker; one of the expenses of the petition read: 'paide for a garnysshe large vessell newe fascioned Counterfeit for Maister Speker of the parliament weiyng lxxxij *lb*, the *lb* iiijd. Summa, xxvijs iiijd'.[158] What the speaker was meant to do for this bill is not stated; but judging by later procedure he may already have had power to settle the priority of the reading of bills. The Elizabethan John Vowell, or Hooker, writing in 1571 of the parliamentary usages of his own day, remarks about the speaker that 'of the bills brought in, he hath the choice, which and when they shall be read, unless order be taken by the whole house in that behalf'.[159] This possibility becomes a likelihood when one reads that in 1487 the Pewterers' Company paid the clerk of the parliament to expedite the bill: 'Item paide to Thomas Bayne Clerke of the parliament house to spede our billes to be redde . . . vjs viijd.'[160] It also seems likely that there were other persons in parliament, in or out of the commons, who had to be bribed to help a bill forward. For example, there is in the accounts of the Cutlers' Company of London for 1461–2 an entry: 'Item paid in diuers expenses for suying of certyn matiers in the parlement for the wele and profite of the said Craft of Cotillers and in money gifen to dyuers persones for to shewe their gode willes and to be frendely and solicitours in the same matiers, £5 5s 8d.'[161]

---

[155] C. Welch, *History of the Worshipful Company of Pewterers of the City of London*, I (London, 1902), p. 18.
[156] *Ibid.*, p. 28.
[157] *Ibid.*, pp. 64–5.
[158] *Ibid.*, p. 65.
[159] British Library, MS Harley 1178, f. 22a.
[160] C. Welch, *Pewterers*, I, p. 64.
[161] C. Welch, *History of the Cutlers' Company of London*, I (London, 1916), p. 153.

Whether the speaker or the clerk of the parliament could perform extra services for a bill other than giving it priority, and what exactly well-wishers could do to help a bill, it is difficult to say. We know little about the procedures of the commons in this century in dealing with bills. There is some evidence that by the middle of the century the practice of reading a bill more than once had already been adopted by the lords. What appears to be one of the first recorded instances of it occurs in 1454, when a bill on behalf of Ralph, lord Cromwell seems to have been read three times before the lords.[162] It is true that these proceedings took place among the lords, not the commons; but since the custom of three readings was well established in both houses in the sixteenth century it is likely that, when at an earlier period there was a development in that direction among the lords, there would have been a similar trend among the commons as well. In 1461 the bill to alleviate the distress of the merchants and craftsmen of London was read on three successive days, 9, 10 and 11 December.[163] Then in 1495 the clerk's entry on the parliament roll, prefacing the royal assent, was 'cui bille trina vice lecte et clare intellecte'.[164]

The development of formal readings of bills must have hastened the definition of what was necessary to constitute formal approval. In the early centuries of the Germanic peoples there had been a presumption that unanimity was necessary for a valid decision, a view which powerfully affected trial by jury. Then under the influence of Roman and canon law the notion became diffused that perhaps a majority decision would suffice. This majority rule was sufficiently accepted by 1215 for the English barons to insist that the twenty-five barons who were to see to the enforcement of Magna Carta should proceed if necessary by a majority vote. We do not know how decisions were taken in the first century and a half of parliamentary development in England. Even the fullest account of parliamentary proceedings during that period, the *Anonimalle Chronicle*'s record of the Good Parliament of 1376, tells us nothing of how the commons reached their decisions. In the fifteenth century we begin to find a few references to majority votes in the commons. The burgesses for King's Lynn in the parliament of 1420 told their constituents that in that parliament two men, Roger Hunt and Richard Russell, had been nominated for the office of speaker, and

---

[162] *Rot. Parl.*, V, p. 264.
[163] *Fane Fragment*, ed. W. H. Dunham, pp. 19, 22, 25, 71.
[164] PRO, C65/128 (*Rot. Parl.*, VI, p. 492).

that the former had been elected by a majority of four votes.[165] As late
as 1441 Serjeant Markham denied that a grant of a fifteenth in parliament would necessarily bind everybody, but by 1476 majority decisions
were the established rule in the commons. In a lawsuit of that year
Justice Littlejohn pronounced from the bench, 'Sir, si en le parliament
si le greindre party des Chivallers des Counties assentent al feasans
dun act du parliament et le meindre part ne voil' my agreer a cel act,
uncore ce sera bon statute a durer en perpetuity.'[166]

The fifteenth century was also an important period in the development of procedure on amendments to bills. As legislation advanced in
precision and importance it was increasingly likely that the wording
of the original bill would not meet the wishes of all interested parties,
some of whom might wish the king to assent, if at all, only after
amendments had been made in their favour. During the 1430s and
1440s the financial position of the government became increasingly
precarious through a combination of imprudent royal generosity, bad
financial management of crown revenues and the mounting costs of
an unsuccessful war in France. Already by 1449 there was so much
discontent that the commons agitated repeatedly for an act of resumption. But as those who supported the government had benefited most
by royal grants they encouraged the king to resist, and the parliament
of 1449 was dissolved to avoid a surrender.[167] In 1450 the pressure
had become too great for such a manoeuvre to succeed. The commons
not only impeached Suffolk but presented a petition for the resumption
of all grants made since the beginning of the reign. At an early stage
fifteen clauses were added to it, exempting important persons and
interests such as the queen, the king's royal foundations of Eton and
King's Colleges, the provisions of the king's will, and so on.[168] The king

---

[165] Cited by McKisack, *Borough Representation*, p. 142, from King's Lynn, Municipal Archives, Gildhall Roll, 8–9 Henry V.

[166] *YB 19 Henry VI*, Pasch., plea 1, and *YB 15 Edward IV*, Mich., plea 2, quoted
by Chrimes, *Eng. Const. Ideas*, p. 137. Edwards, *Second Century of the English
Parliament*, p. 79, concluded a very interesting analysis of the commons' methods
of voting by saying, 'There can be little doubt, I think, that the methods used by
the Commons during our period was the method of voting by voices, which
continued to be their only method until about the middle of the sixteenth century,
when voting by division came in as a supplement to, but never as a substitute for,
voting by voices.' He went too far in saying 'their only method', though it was
probably the more usual one (that is, simultaneous shouts of 'Aye' and 'No').

[167] 'Bale's Chronicle', in *Six Town Chronicles*, ed. R. Flenley (Oxford, 1911),
p. 125, quoted by B. P. Wolffe in Fryde and Miller, II, p. 75.

[168] *Rot. Parl.*, V, pp. 183–6.

assented to this petition, with the reservation that he could add any provisos of exemption that he considered necessary, before the dissolution of parliament. In the event no fewer than 186 provisos of exemption were added.[169] Many of them were in favour of members of the royal household. From an exchequer document discovered by Dr B. P. Wolffe it is clear that 'a conference or committee of household men appears to have determined what each of their members should give up and what he should retain. . . . The form of the original petitions for exemptions submitted by some of the household men who appear in the list shows that before they submitted these petitions they had been told what they would be allowed to keep and what they must be resigned to losing.'[170]

In addition to provisos made with government backing and with royal sympathy, it was possible for the powerful to achieve such provisos without initial government aid though with the expenditure of more effort. In the parliament of 1453–4 the king's half-brother, Jasper, earl of Pembroke, introduced 'in domum inferiorem' a bill in which, along with all the demesne lands of the earldom of Pembroke, he asked for the priory of St Nicholas of Pembroke, in the hands of St Albans abbey. Bartholomew Halley, knight for Hertfordshire, wished to prevent the bill from going through as it was, but he was known as a friend of the abbot. He therefore approached John Skelton, member for Cumberland, at one time a squire in the service of Humphrey, duke of Gloucester, who had given the priory to St Albans in return for prayers. John Skelton was so indignant that the bill should endanger the repose of his former patron's soul that he opposed the bill publicly, and persevered in his speech to such effect that he secured a suitable exemption. In this form it went to the upper house ('ad domum superiorem'), and was accepted by the lords and the king.[171] This was not the end of the abbey's efforts to secure exemption from acts of resumption. In 1461 the commons asked for an act of resumption cancelling all alienation of royal lands by the Lancastrian kings. The commons' petition was approved by the lords and accepted by the king; but the latter added eighty-nine clauses of exemption saving the rights of persons and corporations whom he considered worthy of his favour

[169] *Ibid.*, V, pp. 186–99.
[170] B. P. Wolffe in Fryde and Miller, II, p. 79.
[171] *Registrum abbatiae Johannis Whethamstede*, ed. H. T. Riley, I (RS, 1872), pp. 92–4.

or clemency. The provisos did not include the abbey of St Albans in spite of the Yorkist sympathies of its abbot, John Whethamstede. This would have meant the loss of the abbey's priory at Pembroke. The abbot had not been able to attend parliament because of his infirmities, but he at once sent his archdeacon to Westminster to lobby for a regrant of the priory. It took five weeks' effort, with the intercession of the chancellor of England, to make the point.[172]

We rarely have as much information as this about the process of amendment, especially where the commons were concerned. Indeed, the only certain instance of an amendment by the commons in the first half of the century dates from 1429. In that year to an official bill concerning the misuse of judicial records was attached a schedule on which was noted: 'Les communes sount assentuz a la bille a cest cedule annexe parissint qe les forsprises en cest cedule comprisez soient affermez come parcelle de la bille.' The proviso follows and was incorporated in the enrolled form of the bill.[173] But, as in other aspects of commons development, the paucity of surviving evidence does not mean that no advance took place. By the middle of the century the participation of the commons in legislation was so well established that there was a clear rule about bills which they had amended. As was stated above,[174] evidence was given by the clerk of parliament in Pilkington's case in 1455 that if the commons had made amendments restricting the scope of bills, then those bills need not be sent back to them; but if they had made amendments extending the scope of bills they must be consulted again.

The provisos to the acts of resumption in 1450 are of interest for another development in parliamentary procedure. It is clear from the large number of exemptions added to the act of 1450 that the proposal caused intense anxiety among a great many influential people. It was worth straining every nerve, as the abbot of St Albans was later to do, to save valuable crown grants from being confiscated; and many provisos must have been presented in a very short time. For the promoter it was important to have a powerful backer. For the government it was essential to keep a sure record of which pleas for exemption had been granted and which had not. The first motive caused the petitioner

---

[172] *Ibid.*, I, pp. 416–18.
[173] PRO, C49/19/16, 17 (*Rot. Parl.*, IV, p. 354). See Gray, *Influence of the Commons*, p. 194.
[174] See above, p. 148.

to ensure, if possible, that a note should be written on the bill, usually in the bottom left-hand corner, to remind the lords of the identity of the backer. For example, we find 'per cardinalem'[175] or 'per dominum de Beaumond'; we even have 'per dominum regem' for household servants such as John Wodehous, yeoman of the crown, and John Brereley, sergeant at arms,[176] and for lords such as John, lord Dudley, John, viscount Beaumont, Ralph, lord Cromwell and seven other lords.[177] Sometimes the lords noted on the bill the result of their deliberations if it was more than a simple yes or no. They could not decide on the petition of the dean and canons of Westminster, and so they wrote on the bill, 'The lordes remitteth this unto the kinges highnesse.'[178] John, lord Stourton, treasurer of the king's household, put in his own bill and so convinced his fellow lords that they wrote, 'This bille is thought resonable by the lordes.'[179] The monks of Charterhouse had powerful advocates: 'This bille, consideryng the mater that is declared by my lord of Canterbury and the chief justice, is thought resonable.'[180] On a petition from a large group, all of whom had leased crown lands, the lords made a comment of general effect: they advised the king that, in future, lessees who would give the full value of the farm should be preferred to other men.[181]

The anxiety of the government led to a more permanent development. On nearly all the provisos that were granted the king was induced to write the royal sign manual, RH.[182] This useful idea was not continued in the next three acts of resumption, of 1451, 1453 and 1455,[183] but towards the end of the reign it was revived for a few bills in which the king took a special interest. Such were a proviso in 1460 in favour of the receiver-general of the duchy of Lancaster, or a bill which needed

---

[175] Per cardinalem—PRO, C49/56/5, 12, 13 (*Rot. Parl.*, V, pp. 193a, 192b (twice)); per dominum de Beaumond—C49/56/23 (*Rot. Parl.*, V, p. 191a).
[176] C49/56/6, 16 (*Rot. Parl.*, V, pp. 192b, 194a).
[177] C49/56/62, 50 (*Rot. Parl.*, V, pp. 191a, 189–90).
[178] C49/56/22 (*Rot. Parl.*, V, pp. 188–9).
[179] C49/56/3 (*Rot. Parl.*, V, p. 186b).
[180] C49/56/8 (*Rot. Parl.*, V, p. 186b). For a similar, but more verbose, comment in 1465 see a petition on behalf of the convent of Westminster Abbey, 'This provision is thought resonable and agreed by the lordes and passid hem': C49/56/60 (*Rot. Parl.*, V, pp. 522–3).
[181] C49/56/27 (*Rot. Parl.*, V, p. 187a).
[182] There are numerous provisos to the act of 1450 in files 54, 56, 58 of the Chancery, Parliament and Council Proceedings (C49), and other similar provisos are scattered throughout files 59 to 65.
[183] Fewer provisos are preserved for these acts of resumption in the series of Ancient Petitions (SC8) and of Chancery, Parliament and Council Proceedings.

explicit royal backing, an act to appoint Richard, duke of York to a special commission to repress disorder and rebellion.[184] Once the latter's son, Edward IV, was firmly in the saddle he took up the idea. An early instance in his reign occurred in 1464, when he wrote RE above a proviso to an act of resumption in favour of one of his French secretaries, Gervase le Vulre.[185] This was followed by several cases in 1465,[186] and at least one from 1467.[187] In the parliament of 1472–5 the practice became regular.[188] By this time the king was using this personal sign of approval for the usual kind of bills, not only provisos to acts of resumption. He may have felt after his victories in 1471 that he could emphasise his royal prerogative more decisively and symbolically. At any rate, from this time onwards it became the standard practice for the king to display his royal prerogative by inscribing at the top of approved bills his royal sign manual.

The practice illustrated the recovery by the Yorkist and early Tudor kings of initiative and control in legislation. In the Lancastrian period the weakness of the first and third kings and the preoccupations in France of Henry V gave the commons, for the first time in the history of parliament, the initiative in promoting legislation. 'In the second quarter of the fifteenth century almost every addition to the statute book originated in the commons.'[189] But the stronger and more determined Yorkist and early Tudor kings saw to it that important acts sprang from the royal initiative and will, whether they were openly presented as royal desires or concealed as bills emanating from the commons but in reality promoted there by the king's councillors. The initiative of the commons was thus a fleeting phase, not based on any permanent shift of social or political strength.

Nevertheless the fifteenth century had seen a permanent change in the process of legislation, for it was during this period that the consent of the commons to the passing of acts of parliament became essential. Just because of that development it became more desirable, from the king's standpoint, for important government bills to be presented to parliament in a text that was, in intention, the final one. Then it would

[184] C49/32/6, 4 (*Rot. Parl.*, V, pp. 382–4).
[185] PRO, SC8/1414 (*Rot. Parl.*, V, p. 530b).
[186] E.g. SC8/1417, /1418, /1419B (*Rot. Parl.*, V, pp. 541, 548b, 551b).
[187] SC8/1423 (*Rot. Parl.*, V, p. 613a).
[188] There are twenty-five such instances in the Ancient Petitions series alone, between SC8/1424 and SC8/1458.
[189] R. L. Storey, *The End of the House of Lancaster* (London, 1966), p. 12.

be harder for the commons to be so bold as to try to amend the bill by redrafting, by provisos or otherwise. It is perhaps significant that the first known instance when a bill was presented *formam actus in se continens* was in 1461, when Edward IV presented to parliament a bill for the attainder of Henry VI and his supporters. It was of vital importance to him that he should control from the outset the precise wording of this enactment. But such bills were submitted to the commons,[190] who thus became very familiar with the device. Their bills were also public bills, like the king's. Pollard and Chrimes were right to insist, against Gray, that the heading on the parliament rolls, 'communes petitions', means 'public petitions or bills', not 'petitions of the commons', and that there was no sharp cleavage between commons' bills and official bills.[191] So it was a natural development for the commons to follow suit, and by the reign of Henry VIII to begin to cast some of their bills in the form of acts. This eventually drove the king to limit himself to acceptance or rejection of their bills instead of amending them or otherwise moulding them to his liking before enactment.[192]

In this as in so many other ways the fifteenth century saw important developments in the history of parliament. No serious student of the institution would now endorse Bishop Stubbs's judgement that 'If the only object of Constitutional History were the investigation of the origin and powers of Parliament, the study of the subject might be suspended at the deposition of Richard II, to be resumed under the Tudors'.[193] It is clear that during the reigns of the Lancastrians and the Yorkists the commons had grown in prestige and power and had developed in cohesion and organisation. But they were not yet in a position to control the king if he was able and resolute, nor could they take the initiative if he bestirred himself, as Edward IV and Henry VII were to do. Some of the ways in which they dominated their parliaments have already been mentioned—their control of the summons,

---

[190] E.g. C49/29/12; *Rot. Parl.*, V, pp. 266–7, 380–2, VI, pp. 251, 270–3.

[191] A. F. Pollard, review of Gray, *Influence of the Commons*, in *History*, XVIII (1933), p. 262; Chrimes, *Eng. Const. Ideas*, pp. 239–45.

[192] Henry VII sometimes added provisos to bills when he gave his assent to them (*Rot. Parl.*, VI, pp. 182, 186–7, 460, 496). Elizabeth I did so on at least one occasion (Sir Simonds D'Ewes, *A Compleat Journal of the Votes, Speeches, and Debates, both of the House of Lords and House of Commons throughout the whole reign of Queen Elizabeth, of Glorious Memory*, ed. P. Bowes (London, 1693, p. 341), but she was the last monarch to do this.

[193] Stubbs, *Const. Hist.*, III, p. 2.

prorogation and dissolution of parliament, their influence on its agenda, their initiative in presenting bills, their power of creating new boroughs and influencing elections, their activity in getting councillors to sit in the commons and influence the conduct of business there. There was also the possibility of using the speaker to favour the king's aims.

In the early years of the century the speaker had usually been freely chosen by the commons, though at times the king rejected their choice.[194] Even then, however, the speaker was in most cases a man attached to the court. Sometimes he was an ordinary retainer, but more usually he held office under the crown, in the royal household or some administrative service or even in the king's council; during the minority of Henry VI he might be associated with one or more of the lords of the council.[195] But from the time of Henry VI's majority the government seems to have become more aware of the importance of the speaker to the king in the conduct of business in the commons. From the accession of Edward IV he was regularly paid a gratuity for his services to the crown in the exercise of his office. Thenceforward for many generations he was usually a lawyer experienced in working for the king.[196] To enhance the speaker's dignity Edward IV provided him with a royal serjeant-at-arms, to wait on him ceremonially and to lead him in processions.[197] The appointment of a royal servant like William Allington as speaker in the parliaments of 1472-5 and 1478 was meant by Edward IV to smooth the way for the approval by the commons of the king's business and wishes. Certainly in the first of these parliaments the commons voted the equivalent of nearly four subsidies—more than Edward had received in all the previous years of his reign[198]—in spite of the opposition to heavy taxation.[199] In the parliament of 1478 not only was no voice raised in favour of the king's brother, George, when Edward accused him of high treason but on behalf of the commons William Allington asked that Clarence's execution should be hastened.[200]

Henry VII was able to continue this tradition of influencing the commons through their speaker. In 1485 Thomas Betanson reported to

[194] Roskell, *Speakers*, pp. 68-70.
[195] *Ibid.*, p. 72.
[196] *Ibid.*, p. 342.
[197] *Ibid.*, p. 104.
[198] J. H. Ramsay, *Lancaster and York*, II (Oxford, 1892), p. 401.
[199] *Paston Letters*, ed. J. Gairdner, III, p. 82.
[200] See above, p. 143.

Sir Robert Plumpton that, though many members of the commons were against the bill of attainder condemning Richard III and his supporters at Bosworth Field, the bill had passed because 'yt was the King's pleasure'.[201] Doubtless the speaker used all his influence to see that the bill went through, in spite of the opposition, for the speaker in this parliament was Thomas Lovell. He himself had a strong vested interest in securing the condemnation of Richard III and his followers, and of the acts of Richard III, since he had incurred forfeiture of his estates for his support of Henry Tudor in the rising led by the marquis of Dorset in 1483. In the few months since Bosworth Henry VII had already made him treasurer of the chamber, chancellor of the exchequer, an esquire of the body and a member of the king's council.[202] That the speaker already directed proceedings in the commons is shown by the speech which Bishop Russell prepared for the intended parliament of Edward V. 'Yn the lower house,' declared the chancellor, 'alle ys directed by the speker.'[203] Yet the speaker was not simply the king's servant and supporter. He was bound to represent the commons, and in 1523 Sir Thomas More could dare to annoy Cardinal Wolsey by his sturdiness in doing so.[204]

This is significant of much else in the development of parliament by the early sixteenth century. It was still an occasional assembly. Government could proceed for months and even years without it, and the king's ministers expected to use parliament as an instrument of government when it did meet. Nevertheless within its proper sphere it had an increasingly assured position which could not be ignored or by-passed. The fifteenth century had seen a growing definition in the composition and powers of the lords. It is significant that in this period they began to be referred to as 'the higher house' or 'the upper house', just as the commons came to be thought of as 'the lower house' or 'the commons' house'; it shows an increasing awareness of the corporate identity and cohesion of each body.[205] During this period there was a growing awareness of the nature and supremacy of statutes and of the necessary role of both lords and commons in approving them. By the end of the fifteenth century judicial opinion had established that statutes could

---

[201] See above, p. 142.
[202] Roskell, *Speakers*, p. 298.
[203] Chrimes, *Eng. Const. Ideas*, p. 174.
[204] Roskell, *Speakers*, p. 328.
[205] Chrimes, *Eng. Const. Ideas*, pp. 126–30.

override rules of common law, that statutes were superior to ordinances, that statutes could bind all the king's domains and all the king's subjects, that statutes would be upheld even if they conflicted with royal pre-rogative, that statutes could override the law merchant and define the limits of canon law.[206] For the making of a valid statute the consent of the commons as well as the lords had become necessary, and the commons, it was now held, represented all the commons of the realm. Moreover no valid tax could be levied without the commons' grant and the lords' assent.

All this fell short of control of the government by parliament, and still further from control of government by the commons. But it did mean that the crown could not do without the co-operation of parlia-ment for the making of laws, the legalising of its actions and the levying of taxes, as all the Tudor monarchs were well aware. It is true that this did not in itself ensure an inevitable victory for parliament in the long run. A comparison with the numerous other contemporary parlia-ments in Latin Christendom will show that. Many of these assemblies, from Aragon to Poland, had powers as great as those of the English parliament, sometimes greater; yet between the sixteenth and eighteenth centuries some of these bodies were to wither, to be reduced to im-potence or to fall into abeyance. It is conceivable that if the early Stuart kings had been more skilful, and circumstances had been kinder to them, the English parliament might have shrunk into a mere docile instrument of royal authority and government as many continental assemblies of estates were to do, in Spain, France, Germany and Austria.[207] Professor Roskell has argued cogently that not until 1689 did parliament become indispensable to the ordinary conduct of govern-ment.[208] The events, forces and personalities of the sixteenth and seven-teenth centuries were crucial to the victory of the English parliament; but that does not mean that the developments of the fifteenth century were irrelevant or without significance. In particular they strengthened the foundations for the ultimate dominance of the commons in govern-ment. Their closer cohesion, their growing prestige, their improvements in procedure, their more assured share in legislation, their close co-operation with but not subservience to the lords, the increasing dignity of their speaker, all these factors contributed to the later victory

[206] *Ibid.*, pp. 269–89.
[207] A. R. Myers, *Parliaments and Estates*, especially ch. 4, pp. 97–143.
[208] Roskell, 'Perspectives', in Fryde and Miller, II, pp. 321–2.

of the commons.[209] Doubtless none of this would have been of any avail if the parliamentarians of the seventeenth century had been inadequate to the challenge of their time, and had not defeated, both in chambers of parliament and on battlefields, the repeated attempts of Stuart kings to establish autocratic government.[210] But without the progress achieved in the fifteenth century the ultimate success would undoubtedly have proved more difficult and perhaps impossible.

[209] For an analysis of the reasons for the relative success or failure of different monarchies and parliaments in their struggle for power see H. G. Koenigsberger, *Monarchies and Parliaments in Early Modern Europe* (London, 1975).

[210] For a recent discussion of why the system of 'mixed monarchy', which had lasted successfully from the fourteenth century to the seventeenth, broke down in the reign of Charles I see G. L. Harriss, 'Medieval doctrines in the debates on supply, 1610–1629', in *Faction and Parliament*, ed. Sharpe, pp. 73–103.

D. H. PENNINGTON

7

A Seventeenth-century Perspective

THIS TRIBUTE TO JOHN ROSKELL has brought together studies by six experts in the history of medieval parliaments. It is to that topic and period that he is devoting a lifetime of fruitful and unpretentious scholarship. But a good many historians whose main interest is in later centuries associate him first with a single lecture published in 1964, reprinted in 1970, and cited innumerable times in works on Tudor and Stuart as well as medieval government. 'Perspectives in English parliamentary history'[1]—a title often borrowed and adapted—showed how the true specialist can illuminate fields beyond his own. The 'great divide' in the history of parliament came, Roskell suggested, not under the Tudors or the early Stuarts or Cromwell but at the end of the seventeenth century, when at last 'the constitution of the *ancien régime* is now really at an end: not moribund but defunct'.[2] Only then was government by the crown without parliament impossible. This was not a reversion to Macaulayite notions of 1688 as the most glorious moment in the progress from Magna Carta to the Great Reform Bill. The sixteenth and seventeenth centuries were shown as a period, for parliament, of intermittent and often unsuccessful efforts to establish powers not fundamentally different from those it had sought in the middle ages. The overworked metaphor of the Tudors building on medieval

[1] See in list of abbreviations.
[2] Roskell, 'Perspectives', p. 322.

foundations was gently repudiated: if we have to think of an 'edifice' it is better not to make unreal distinctions between its parts.[3]

The essays in this book will interest those Tudor historians who believe that Pollard, Neale and Elton have in different ways underrated the continuing medievalism of the commons.[4] They throw even more light on the early Stuart parliaments that have become the subject of powerful revision. Writers who saw them mainly in terms of the drama ahead have been attacked by what can now be called a school of historians, if a loosely disciplined one, to whom the period seems less unified. Parliament, it is now suggested, still 'played little part in the government of England' and was more concerned with survival than with progress. The claims of the monarchy were new, the constitutional theories of parliament largely unchanged.[5] 'Whig historians,' Dr Harriss writes of the *fourteenth* century, 'have identified opposition to the crown with the cause of liberty and parliamentary democracy and have seen the commons as challenging the prerogative in the name of the representative principle.'[6] He could well have been referring to interpretations of the early *seventeenth* century. An unwhiggish view is put aptly by Professor Brown. Substitute for his dates those of 1604 to 1629 and his opening paragraph would still make a good introduction.[7] Jacobean parliaments had greater reason than any before them to avoid actions openly 'at odds' with precedent. Awareness of the past did not persuade them that they were marching triumphantly forward. It showed how much they had lost and were in danger of losing: medieval history was a weapon in a struggle to survive. In the often quoted words of Robert Phelips, England was the 'last monarchy in Christendom' where the 'original' constitution had not been overthrown. Benjamin

[3] *Ibid.*, p. 306.

[4] Pollard, *Evolution of Parliament*, pp. 160, 277, 325–6. J. E. Neale, *The Elizabethan House of Commons* (London, 1949), pp. 418–20. Of G. R. Elton's many arguments on this, the main points can be found in *Studies in Tudor and Stuart Politics and Government*, II (Cambridge, 1974), section 3. See also Roskell, 'Perspectives', pp. 303–7.

[5] Sharpe, in *Faction and Parliament*, ed. Sharpe, p. 25. This volume provides good examples of attacks on the 'traditional picture'. Others include C. Russell, *Parliaments and English Politics, 1621–1629* (Oxford, 1979); D. Hirst, *The Representation of the People? Voters and Voting in England under the Early Stuarts* (Cambridge, 1975); and the collection of essays on the Civil War in *Journal of Modern History*, XLIX (1978).

[6] Above, pp. 52–3.

[7] Above, p. 109.

Rudyard feared that the parliament of 1624 would be the last.[8] MPs agreed, for once, with James I when he announced that 'all novelties are dangerous'. It was, as they repeatedly tried to establish, the king whose doctrines of sovereignty and divine right were novel. Their aim was not a confrontation with the monarchy but a harmony that seemed to have existed, to some extent as recently as under Elizabeth I but certainly and more wholly at a remote and unspecified time. Despite James's misapprehensions his parliaments clearly believed some of their own assurances that mutual affection and co-operation would return.

In their conception of the past MPs combined a vague, almost utopian belief in an age of liberty, sometimes placed in Anglo-Saxon times, with a precise knowledge of precedent. To uphold their 'right and inheritance' a huge stock of historical references was built up. In the 1610 session alone, speeches recorded by the diarists include thirty-three different entries in the rolls of parliament and sixty-two statutes down to Henry VII.[9] Robert Bowyer, clerk of the parliaments, compiled his own lists of precedents. Among others William Hakewill, lawyer and constitutional historian, Noy, later the king's attorney-general, Sir Robert Cotton, whose library was a general meeting place, and the mighty Sir Edward Coke himself made their learning available—not always on the same side of the argument. An assiduous Jacobean MP must have sat through more lectures on the medieval constitution from his colleagues than ever modern undergraduates would tolerate from their tutors. But they were not much concerned with chronology. A statute of Edward III differed from one of Elizabeth mainly in raising more arguments about confirmation or revocation. Collectively the documents provided a record less of progress than of recurrent conflict. From it a largely static picture of the 'ancient constitution' had to be constructed.

Since parliament was fighting for survival, it ought logically to have been concerned above all to protect itself against unwanted dissolutions and to ensure that it would be regularly summoned. In this, precedent was unhelpful. Medieval parliaments, it appears, had little reason to worry. By the last quarter of the fourteenth century, so Professor Brown can assure us, 'parliament was a well established institution'. 'By the fifteenth century,' adds Professor Myers, 'it had developed from an

[8] *The Origins of the English Civil War*, ed. C. Russell (London, 1973), p. 102; id., *Parliaments and English Politics*, p. 56.

[9] E. R. Foster, *Proceedings in Parliament, 1610* (New Haven, 1966), pp. xxii, 288–91.

occasion into an institution.'[10] By the seventeenth it was in danger of developing into an expedient. The 'increasingly assured position' had already been shaken when Henry VII had one parliament in his last ten years. Between 1591 and 1601 there were two, for eleven weeks. Between 1611 and 1621 there was one. After the decade of intermittent parliaments in the 1620s, the 1630s showed that in times of peace, and quite possibly always, government without parliament had now become perfectly feasible. Parliaments were one of the options open to monarchs, with manifestly growing risks to set against their advantages. But ten years was very different from twenty or thirty : it left plenty of former MPs still young and active to whom a parliament was an obvious necessity.[11] Even in their most assertive periods, peers and MPs were reluctant to devise any guarantees of regular meetings. 'Annual parliaments had been a subject's ideal since the beginning of the [fourteenth] century,' says Professor Brown. Statutes providing for them might be ignored, but in practice one year was the average interval, and the habit of frequent summons was well established.[12] It was not among the precedents that appealed most strongly in later centuries either to taxpayers, for whom parliament meant above all subsidies, or even to the men who had sought or accepted election as MPs. However much they now 'derived pleasure rather than distress' from being elected,[13] parliament was still an episode. When it happened MPs were not anxious to stay at Westminster indefinitely. If they sought to control the adjournment of parliament it was not always because they wanted to prolong the sitting. One of the few proposals initiated by the commons in the Reformation Parliament was that they might be allowed to go home. In the 1620s, when James and Charles insisted loudly on the royal power to dissolve parliament whenever they chose, the opposition was concerned less with resisting the principle than with finishing the immediate business. The most dramatic act of defiance by the commons, in 1629, showed that they were not prepared to go much further than their medieval predecessors in self-preservation. Once the weeping Speaker Finch had been held down in his chair and a hasty version of Sir John Eliot's not very inspiring resolutions read, members went

[10] Above, pp. 109, 141.
[11] On the development of consecutive membership under Edward III see above, pp. 75–6, 82–3.
[12] Above, p. 111.
[13] Above, p. 72.

quietly away—for, it turned out, eleven years. In theory this was an adjournment; and in theory the house had asserted a claim to adjourn itself. In practice it was demonstrated that parliament had no permanent place in government, and might easily have none at all.

Of course, it could be claimed that defiance of royal commands was not the way to establish parliament as the king's partner in the administration of the state, and that his need for money would always compel him to ask respectfully for a subsidy. So it had been in, for instance, 1376;[14] and so at last it proved to be in 1640. But even if there had been greater assurance that parliament would be revived some day it could not have made plausible the assertions that it was the highest court in the land, and the only place where the king could exercise his fullest power. Parliament's law-making function had ceased to expand: it had become unpredictable. The spate of statutes in 1624 was an incident of politics and royal choice, not a piece of constitutional progress. The advantages brought by printing, easier communications, a smoothly working legal system, a paternal state, had not led to the development of any irresistible public demand for constant parliamentary government. Once a parliament was there, or had only recently been dissolved, it was easy to see reasons for upholding it. When memories of the excitements and conflicts faded only the most active and radical politicians remained indignant at its absence.

The failure to establish regular elections and sittings did not prevent one development that can be claimed as almost unreversed progress from the fourteenth century to the twentieth: more people participated, and sought to participate, as electors or as members, in the working of the parliamentary system. Here too delusions are tempting. The sporadic pressure in the 1290s to have knights of the shire chosen in full county court was not the beginning of a march towards those assertions in the 1640s that every Englishman should have a voice in choosing the government under which he lived. 'Representation' is a notion that produces even more fantasy and evasion than most aspects of political theory. Professor Holt sees a 'major snag' in the thirteenth-century supposition that magnates automatically represented their communities.[15] It was even less justifiable to speak, in the 1620s, of medieval kings having resort to 'their people assembled in parliament'.

[14] Above, p. 57.
[15] Above, p. 26. Robert Phelips, quoted in C. Russell, *Parliaments and English Politics*, p. 55.

Nevertheless the impact of elections and of events in parliament was on the whole greater in each century than in the previous one. The routine by which counties—not the most rational of units, but the ones most firmly linked to propertied society—sent commoners of high standing to parliament changed very little. Sheriffs did the same job with roughly the same amount of honesty all the time. The only significant reform was the statute of 1430 that replaced the *probiores*, the *meillours gentz* or just 'common assent' of the county court by the unforgettable 'forty-shilling freeholders'.[16] By the accidents of inflation, tenurial change and a little manipulation it became a franchise that facilitated an incalculable increase in the numbers of voters. Professor Holt has no reservations: in the reign of Henry III representation had 'nothing at all to do with consent'. It was the king who required the knights of the shire to appear; but they did not come as representatives of the community of the realm. Sometimes it was convenient to say that they acted 'on behalf of each and every man'; but this was for the benefit of the crown, not of the populace.[17] A century later the middle ages seem to have come closer to Stuart England. Professor Brown accepts that 'county members represented the community of their counties'; and, even earlier, Dr Harriss shows the knights in the 1330s as being required in the writs to present the 'grievances of their communities'. Dr Maddicott too is confident that at that time 'new law was created mainly . . . as a remedy for popular grievances, grievances which originated with a well-informed and demanding public opinion in the shires'. The common petition that could be the basis of a wide-ranging statute was part of a 'sudden expansion in the public role of parliament'. This was rooted in the misgovernment of Edward II, in whose deposition parliament played a part; and it made of parliament a meeting place for the concerns of the political nation. In 1340 'widespread protest against . . . taxation' and 'unprecedented unity, initiative and political vision' emerged.[18] The resemblances are inescapable.

Representation of the counties would make a neat, coherent story. What better constitution could the Tudors have inherited than one that sent from each shire two generally acclaimed members of the 'lesser nobility', the natural leaders and representatives of the community? But there were also the boroughs. Perhaps it is unjust to suggest that

[16] Above, pp. 119, 166.
[17] Above, pp. 21–2.
[18] Above, pp. 118–20, 61, 74, 54.

many medievalists are happier when discussing the orderly system of county government than when trying to make sense of the irrational assortment of places that had at first the misfortune and later the right of sending their own MPs. There is the legend—the kind of legend that exists to be questioned—that medieval borough members were worthy townsmen until the landed gentry 'invaded' their territories. The 'invasion', Sir John Neale himself admitted, reached back a long way.[19] Professor Brown, tentatively, puts it among those features of Tudor parliaments whose origins go back to the fourteenth century. Even for the thirteenth we are only 'baffled by lack of evidence'.[20] Roskell's analysis of the parliament of 1422 showed that one burgess in four failed to fulfil the residence qualification laid down in 1413—a statute presumably enacted because non-residence was a recognised problem. But he found no indication of 'a tendency to that wholesale invasion of the parliamentary boroughs which later fifteenth-century conditions were to accelerate'.[21] The 'invasion' must often have brought better prospects of influencing the government and its officers than the existing boroughs were likely to manage themselves. They too regularly presented petitions—usually on narrower grievances than those of the shires; and the counties often thought it worthwhile to support them.

'Borough member' is a misleading term. He might come from one of the few cities that were always likely to elect a merchant or rich alderman. He might, as a second best to the county seat, be allotted one of the manifestly bogus 'boroughs' in family control. But he was more likely to be returned by a market town or small county town that could, in earlier centuries or later, fluctuate between electing good local townsmen and obeying the orders of county gentry or aristocrats. The traders and minor lawyers could give way in one parliament to a resident or non-resident whose claim came from connection with a county family: they could still find the seats available again later. The cost of the whole process was often more important than any unbreakable allegiance. The creation of new boroughs to meet a demand for seats was an erratic affair that shows little sign of movement from an age of genuine urban representation to one of rotten boroughs run by the crown and magnates. Evidence about the number of borough seats in the fourteenth century suggests inconsistency: it appears to

[19] J. E. Neale, *Elizabethan House of Commons*, p. 148.
[20] McKisack, *Borough Representation*, pp. 14, 100; above, p. 118.
[21] Above, p. 163; Roskell, *Commons in 1422*, pp. 48–9.

have fluctuated between about 130 and 180. There were over 200 in 1478, 265 in 1500, 372 in 1600, 399 in 1640. But the newest boroughs were by no means always the smallest. Calne and Old Sarum sent members in 1295, Gatton by 1453, Much Wenlock under Edward IV. Towns that had to wait for their enfranchisement included Manchester, Halifax and Leeds, all momentarily recognised by the Instrument of Government in 1653.

The expansion continued to make territorial representation less and less rational. But out of it there emerged for the undeserved benefit of the Tudor and Stuart political nation a pattern of membership that survived for three centuries. Every parliament had its nominees of the crown. Opportunities for royal 'packing' grew, though not very much. They produced some blunders like the 'undertakers' of 1614; but they also helped to ensure the presence of men whose knowledge of the working of government was immensely helpful to parliament. Under Charles I there were 'normally not less than about thirty from the central courts and departments'.[22] Some were firmly the king's men; others, even in 1641 and after, put the functions of their office before political allegiances. Still more important to parliamentary authority was the amorphous body of crown servants in the shires and boroughs who had aspired as naturally to election as to office. It was as natural in earlier centuries too;[23] and the fact that many, probably most, MPs were involved in the governing that really mattered determined the whole character of parliament's survival.

The most startling accident of this haphazard 'constituency' development was that it produced, through all the changes, two groups in the house of commons identified and relied upon as representatives not only of places but also of occupations. The numbers of merchants and lawyers remained much the same from the early fifteenth century to the eighteenth. Roskell counted in 1422 'some forty burgesses . . . concerned in . . . commercial activity' and thirty-seven identifiable lawyers.[24] Neale reckoned for 1584, with remarkable symmetry, fifty-three practising lawyers and fifty-three 'merchants or borough officials not belonging to the gentry or professional classes'.[25] In 1640 there were about seventy lawyers and forty-five merchants. The notion that a separate assembly

[22] G. E. Aylmer, *The King's Servants* (London, 1961), p. 58.
[23] Above, pp. 74, 118–20.
[24] Roskell, *Commons in 1422*, p. 46.
[25] J. E. Neale, *Elizabethan House of Commons*, pp. 247, 304.

of merchants vaguely associated with parliament, might be used as a means to improve the levying of indirect taxes did not survive.[26] But the merchants were always a vital part of the links between parliament and government finance. Without their presence the opposition in 1640 would have been far less powerful.

Another striking characteristic of parliamentary membership was not at all accidental: there were bishops in the lords but no clergy in the commons. It is harmless fun to speculate on what might have happened if things had been different, and the commons had had the benefit of preaching ministers. Dr Denton has shown that the separation of convocation from parliament and the exclusion of clergy from the commons were not as unquestioned as has usually been supposed.[27] It was an awkward gap in the picture of a parliament representing the propertied community, or the whole community. But once the separation was accomplished it survived the Reformation, the Civil War, and the Restoration. 'The office of the ministry being of such great importance that it will take up the whole man,' said the witty draftsman of the Clerical Disabilities Act in 1641.

The most important heritage of parliament in the seventeenth century, however, was not its membership or its constitutional ideas but simply its methods of work. They remained, with the same quality of adaptable medievalism, even in the Rump, even under the Protectorate; and they gave parliament the confidence and stability without which it might on many occasions have collapsed in chaos. At every moment of the conflicts with the crown, the rules, conventions and assumptions evolved in earlier ages ensured that MPs knew how and within what limits political manoeuvres could normally be carried out and when there were innovations to be attempted. The process of creating a statute was, after long uncertainty, as clear as it would ever be.[28] King, lords and commons all knew how far it could be turned to their advantage. Roskell's work on the speakership reveals how the one office essential for the effective working of the house built up a position unshakable by the varying allegiances of its holders.[29] Voting was still regretted in a theoretically unanimous body; but if there had to be a division the speaker had no trouble in administering it.[30] The houses

[26] Above, pp. 42–3, 121.
[27] Above, pp. 99–100.
[28] Above, pp. 127–9.
[29] Roskell, *Speakers*, p. 125.
[30] Above, pp. 174–5.

knew how to communicate with the king and with the council—even if James sometimes broke the conventions. They knew how to communicate with each other. In the 1330s 'policy was sometimes decided in a small joint committee meeting in a separate room, often the chamberlain's chamber'. It is difficult to say how 'normal' a procedure this was at that time.[31]. In the 1640s the Painted Chamber was often used several times a day for the 'free conference' between peers and MPs where many of the most controversial policy decisions were settled. As Wallace Notestein was the first to emphasise, the development of the committee system had been the greatest procedural change. A commons committee to consider a particular bill was apparently still 'something of a novelty' in the Reformation Parliament.[32] By the 1620s the use of committees for almost every kind of business was driving members to complain of the burden and the chaos. It was also extending the work of parliament into all the processes of government. When the committee on the affairs of Trinity House included all the privy council, all the burgesses of the ports, the barons of the Cinque Ports, the knights of the maritime counties and 'all that have spoken', collaboration with the crown, representation of interests and expression of grievances seemed to be neatly combined.[33]

One function of parliament at least was unquestioned: the commons granted money to the king. As Dr Harriss has said elsewhere, 'the system of public finance remained . . . medieval in both its mechanism and its outlook'.[34] The notion of the 'grant' had the unhappy implication that parliament was outside the government. The king needed money, organised its collection, and spent it. The commons could question the need to criticise the previous spending, but ultimately they could not risk refusing completely. In the fourteenth and fifteenth centuries this was agreed, by parliaments that understood pretty well the amounts involved and the system by which they could be raised. Early Stuart parliaments refused to recognise that they lived in a different economic world. Edward Coke's response to Secretary Calvert's description of the vast expenses and small revenues of the crown was simply that the 'king's estate is not so desperate, his ordinary expenses and his receipts

[31] Above, pp. 38–9.
[32] E. B. Fryde, in Fryde and Miller, II, p. 18.
[33] *Journals of the House of Commons, I: 1547–1628* (London, 1603), p. 529 (27 February 1620/1).
[34] In Sharpe, *Faction and Parliament*, p. 75.

near equal'.[35] There was no lack of information from the crown. Bacon was alarmed that so much was revealed.[36] (A chancellor of the exchequer who worked out details of taxation in secret and then announced them to the house would probably have been impeached.) But the concern of MPs was still with the 'burden, not the necessity'. As much as in 1295, members who had been empowered to commit their constituents to pay had to be provided with good material for propaganda at home. The 'Romano-canonical doctrine of *necessitas*'[37] that had led a great council to refuse taxation to Henry III compelled Elizabeth, James and Charles, or their spokesmen and speech writers, to take great trouble in making out a case. But a good many opportunities were lost and earlier gains reversed. The commons had come near, in the fourteenth century, to establishing the principle of conditional grants. The details given by Dr Maddicott of how in the 1340s the grants 'and the conditions on which they had been made' were publicised in the counties suggests that there was nothing astonishing in popular resistance to taxation under Charles I. 'The wide audience . . . in county courts, boroughs, and market towns must have been well aware of the novel importance of parliamentary politics.'[38] Again, the sentence would read well in any account of the 1620s. A few decades later it is possible to say that 'the commons *often* made their grants of taxes on conditions' (my italics), appropriating them to the war, and to specific campaigns within it, paying them to specially appointed treasurers.[39] Taxation could be associated closely with complaints of the 'villanies of those around the king' and demands for new counsellors. Even the allegations against James I for his extravagant household and grants of office recalled those against Richard II.[40] But the commons' determination 'rose and fell', largely in response to the rise and fall of the king's expenditure on war. Essentially the aim was good government with no great need for parliamentary militancy.

Under James the system of subsidies meeting an emergency disintegrated. In 1621 and 1624 the commons granted sums hopelessly in-

[35] *Commons Debate, 1621*, ed. W. Notestein, F. H. Relf and H. Simpson (New Haven, 1935), pp. 13, 16; see also Russell, in *Origins of the Civil War*, ed. C. Russell, p. 103.
[36] Harriss, in *Faction and Parliament*, ed. Sharpe, p. 84.
[37] Above, pp. 41–2.
[38] Above, p. 82
[39] Above, p. 133.
[40] Above, p. 136.

adequate to pay for their own policy or that of the crown. The king and Buckingham failed to spend what they did get in the ways they had used to justify their requests. Because the subsidy no longer fulfilled its purpose the prospects of using it to influence policy diminished. A very few MPs came to realise the truth : the story of special needs was fraudulent, not just because the crown was more dishonest or incompetent than usual—though in some ways it was both—but because the medieval system no longer worked. For the commons to survive as a part of government they would have to pay a higher price than they had thought possible.

If there had been a sharp distinction between the king's own resources and the parliamentary subsidies for extraordinary occasions the problem might have been attacked more realistically. No one could suppose that the accidental assortment of lands, ancient revenues and later contrivances that made up the king's 'own treasure' could have any necessary relation to the expenses of government. Nearly all the means of increasing it were obnoxious to parliament, which could easily find itself denouncing the government both for the shortage of funds and for remedying it. The answer might have been inescapable—that direct taxation would have to provide not only for special but for regular needs. In particular it might have been recognised that the immediate use of taxes was increasingly to repay loans and make more of them possible. But between the king's own resources and the direct taxes there lay indirect taxation, where theories of parliament's role were more obscure.

There were, unfortunately, good arguments for treating taxation on trade as something completely different from taxation on the capital or income of individuals. Levies that fell, apparently, only on merchants were not the concern of the community and the commons as a whole. It was not easy to show in principle why the king, like anyone else, should not make bargains with groups or individuals for their mutual benefit. Dr Harriss has outlined the conflict under Edward III when a rather unsavoury scheme for using royal authority over the wool trade to acquire both a loan and the revenue to repay it produced bitter hostility in parliament.[41] It was a tempting but not a far-sighted solution to argue that the tax on wool should be permanent but that parliament should authorise it. (Dr Maddicott adds the point that the

[41] Above, pp. 42–3.

knights of the shire regarded it as very much the concern of the whole country and insisted that the terms and conditions must be reported to their counties.[42]) Eventually, there emerged the absurd convention that parliament retained control of customs duties by always voting them to a new king for life. The story of Mr Bate and his currants, the arguments about the 'new impositions' and the breakdown of the convention in 1625 make a wearisome story. Like the subsidies, the indirect taxes led to prolonged self-deception on both sides. The 'heritage' did not help.

Close analysis of parliamentary politics under James and Charles has shattered the illusion of the high road to civil war. The danger now is that it may be replaced by another illusion—that, if we allow for a few incidental changes such as the effects of inflation and the tactless notions of the Stuarts about monarchy, it had all happened before. But the Civil War had not. Nothing remotely like the rule of the Long Parliament could have been imagined in the crises of the fourteenth century. It could not have been imagined in the 1620s either; but it was then that the leaders who created the parliamentary regime of the 1640s developed their ideas, their skills and their enthusiasm. One great source of parliamentary power had no medieval precedent: whatever the sins of Plantagenet and Lancastrian kings, they were not in league with Satan. In the early seventeenth century the distinction between the pope and the devil could be left to theologians: to MPs there was now a sacred duty to protect the nation against evil. How far John Pym and his friends genuinely believed in the great conspiracy and how far they deliberately exploited it is an insoluble problem. Without the great fear the progress to destroying the monarchy would have been far more erratic.

There is a danger too in ignoring the extent to which the significance of parliamentary business had changed. The topics look much the same; the ways of petitioning, of legislating and of raising money, all without a parliament, were more familiar and usually effective. But parliament was now made up of men deeply involved in a state whose impact on the subject was vastly greater than it had been. They came to the work of government not as strangers but as people who administered the rule of the state in their 'countries' all the time. The pile of unfinished business in 1621 hinted at how a regular and unhurried parliament

[44] Above, pp. 81–2.

might have managed its relation with the communities. In the attacks on Buckingham there was forming dimly the idea of a general reform of the ways of the state that emerged in the Grand Remonstrance.

In April 1640 a new parliament was called. There was nothing dramatic or inevitable in the decision: it just seemed to Strafford and the council the least unhopeful of the choices available. MPs refused to be uncritically patriotic; and as so often before parliament was dissolved after a few weeks. The Scottish wars that had made twelve subsidies indispensable were resumed without them. So began the twenty years that blew to pieces the new ministerial absolutism and the ancient parliamentary monarchy. Parliament was victorious, and humiliated. Everything it had sought was achieved, and wrecked. The commons destroyed the monarchy, house of lords, the church, and in doing so submitted to outrages against their own cherished privileges that would have horrified their predecessors in every generation. A new electoral system, new definition of the powers of parliaments and new guarantees of their survival were introduced and casually discarded. Men devoted to the peaceful rule of the king and the law had fought and killed for parliament, and then lost interest in it. In 1661 hardly a trace of the upheaval remained. But if the two most eventful decades in English history had vanished like a dream, it was one of those that reveal suppressed truths about waking life. After the dissolution all the efforts of the organised opposition were concentrated on the new election they were sure would come soon. What they did is still one of the obscurer parts of the story; but the shires and the closely integrated boroughs made up a machine that could now be manipulated to an extent never tried before. In its first months the Long Parliament ended not only the Laudian regime but the constitutional doubts of centuries. As the petitions from county after county piled up on the table—suspiciously identical in wording—it looked as though the petitioning process was being applied to the fundamental troubles of the kingdom. It was not all stage-managed: Root-and-Branch radicalism demonstrated its support in county petitions too. The survival of parliaments was at last given the best guarantees ingenuity could devise. The preamble to the Triennial Act recalled that 'by the laws and statutes of this realm parliaments ought to be held once a year for the redress of grievances. . . .' So the forgotten law of 1330 was revived—for one occasion in three. The preambles to the acts abolishing the hated institutions were not mere formulae: they defined an attitude necessary for holding the support of the two houses. 'Whereas by the Great Charter many times confirmed in parliament . . .'; 'whereas in the parliament holden in the first year of the late Queen Elizabeth . . .'; 'whereas by Act of Parliament made in the first year of the reign of the late King Edward III . . .'. The statutes were in impeccably orthodox form. But when Charles at last was not available to give his assent, Simon D'Ewes, the most resourceful antiquarian lawyer of them all, produced a splendidly spurious precedent. 'An ordinance of the two houses had always been of great authority,' as proved by the rolls of parliament of 1373. Legislation by parliament alone was slipped smoothly into the system.

It had often seemed that the house of commons spent too much time on itself as an institution rather than on policies. But 'privilege', the one set of ancient powers that could be upheld independently of all other disputes, proved its value in January 1642. When Charles strode into the house to arrest the five members all the centuries of parliamentary life confronted him in the outraged cries of the members. This time it was the king who went away. The most important privilege of all was the house's control over its own membership. It now led to disaster. It was used between 1642 and 1644 to 'disable' two fifths of the members from sitting. It was used after great hesitation in 1645 to begin the process of letting new members occupy the seats. It was used to accept and to a small extent repair the atrocity of Pride's Purge. After that it was easy to claim that the high dignity of parliament had been brought into disrepute and its authority invalidated.

In the 1630s the king and council had shown that in peaceful times they could do without parliament. In the Civil War parliament had shown that it could do without the king. It had imposed taxation on a scale that made its own complaints in the 1620s look absurd. Half a dozen parliamentary committees had become departments of state exercising powers previously unheard of. Local government had been brought under strict central control. The commons' speaker had become virtually the head of state. In 1629 parliament had been overthrown as an opposing and petitioning body; by 1645 it was overwhelmingly successful as a government. But just as Charles I's success did not survive when a war broke out, parliament's succumbed to the perils of peace. Cromwell could not escape the conclusion that 'healing and settling' in a society still dominated by its landed families required a mixed monarchy. The Protectorate brought back the lords without a name and a king without a crown. But the idea that a parliament and nothing else could offer a prospect of popular participation in government proved indestructible. The nominated assembly of 1653 was the only attempt there has ever been to find an alternative to territorial representation. Its one hope of retaining power was, it decided, to proclaim itself a parliament. When Cromwell in his anger drove out the successive bodies that obstructed him his most damning accusation was 'You are no parliament.' More significant, the creators of new constitutions intended to take power out of the hands of the rich could think of no better ruling institution than a slightly reshaped parliament. In Gerrard Winstanley's comonwealth a parliament was the 'father of the land', and in the Putney Debates the magnificent vision of the equal rights of men arose from a dispute about details of the franchise. To many parliament already seemed indispensable in the political and constitutional processes of the realm. How this had come about is a field of historical study still deserving its time-hallowed place.

R. G. DAVIES

A Bibliography
of the Published Writings
# of John Smith Roskell,

1937–79

1937

The Knights of the Shire for the County Palatine of Lancaster, 1377–1460,
Chetham Society, new series, XCVI, pp. viii + 246.

1950

'Medieval speakers for the commons in parliament', *Bulletin of the Institute
of Historical Research*, XXIII, pp. 31–52.

1951

'An evaluation of the Grelle Charter' (with a translation of the text), in
*650th Anniversary of Thomas Grelle's Charter to the Burgesses of Man-
chester*. Manchester: Municipal Information Bureau.
'The medieval speakers', *Parliamentary Affairs*, IV, pp. 451–60.
'The social composition of the commons in a fifteenth century parliament',
Bulletin of the Institute of Historical Research, XXIV, pp. 152–72.

1953

'The evolution of the British monarchy. Powers—and limitations—in the
middle ages', *Manchester Guardian*, 30 May.
'The office and dignity of protector of England, with special reference to
its origins', *English Historical Review*, LXVIII, pp. 193–233.

1954

The Commons in the Parliament of 1422: English Society and Parliamentary

Representation under the Lancastrians. Studies presented to the International Commission for the History of Representative and Parliamentary Institutions, XIV. Manchester University Press, pp. xii + 266.

Review of H. G. Richardson and G. O. Sayles, *The Irish Parliament in the Middle Ages* (University of Pennsylvania Press: London, 1952), in *History*, new series, XXXIX, pp. 272–3.

1956

'John Bowes of Costock, speaker in the parliament of 1435', *Transactions of the Thoroton Society of Nottinghamshire*, LX, pp. 8–19.

'Sir Arnald Savage of Bobbing', *Archaeologia Cantiana*, LXX, pp. 68–83.

'Sir John Cheyne of Beckford', *Transactions of the Bristol and Gloucestershire Archaeological Society*, LXXV, pp. 43–72.

'The problem of the attendance of the lords in medieval parliaments', *Bulletin of the Institute of Historical Research*, XXIX, pp. 153–204.

'Three Wiltshire speakers' [Sir Thomas Hungerford (speaker in the parliament of January 1377), Sir Walter Hungerford, first baron Hungerford (speaker in April 1414), Sir Walter Beauchamp (speaker in March 1416)], *The Wiltshire Archaeological and Natural History Magazine*, LVI, pp. 272–358.

1957

'Roger Flore of Oakham', *Transactions of the Leicestershire Archaeological and Historical Society*, XXXIII, pp. 36–44.

'Sir Richard de Waldegrave of Bures St Mary', *Proceedings of the Suffolk Institute of Archaeology*, XXVII, part 3, pp. 154–75.

'Sir William Sturmy', *Transactions of the Devonshire Association for the Advancement of Science, Literature and Art*, LXXXIX, pp. 78–92.

'Two medieval Lincolnshire speakers: I. Sir John Bussy of Hougham', *Lincolnshire Architectural and Archaeological Society, Reports and Papers*, VII, part 1, pp. 27–45; 'II. Sir Henry de Retford', *ibid.*, VII, part 2 (1957–8), pp. 117–25.

'William Tresham of Sywell, speaker for the commons under Henry VI' *Northamptonshire Past and Present*, II, no. 4, pp. 189–203.

1958

'John Lord Wenlock of Someries', *The Publications of the Bedfordshire Historical Record Society*, XXXVIII, pp. 12–48.

'Sir James Strangeways of West Harlsey and Whorlton, speaker in the parliament of 1461', *The Yorkshire Archaeological Journal*, XXXIX, pp. 455–82.

'Sir John Popham, knight-banneret of Charford', *Proceedings of the Hampshire Field Club and Archaeological Society*, XXI, part 1, pp. 38–52.

'Sir Peter de la Mare, speaker for the commons in parliament in 1376 and 1377', *Nottingham Medieval Studies*, II, pp. 24–37.

1959

'Sir John Say of Broxbourne', *East Hertfordshire Archaeological Society Transactions*, XIV, part 1, pp. 20–41.

'Sir John Wood of Molesey', *The Surrey Archaeological Collections*, LVI, pp. 15–28.

'Sir Thomas Tresham, Knight', *Northamptonshire Past and Present*, II, no. 6, pp. 313–23.

'The parliamentary representation of Lincolnshire during the reigns of Richard II, Henry IV and Henry V', *Nottingham Medieval Studies*, III, pp. 53–77.

'William Allington of Horseheath, speaker in the parliament of 1429–30', *Proceedings of the Cambridge Antiquarian Society*, LII, pp. 30–42.

'William Allington of Bottisham, speaker in the parliaments of 1472–5 and 1478', *ibid.*, pp. 43–55.

'William Catesby, counsellor to Richard III', *Bulletin of the John Rylands Library*, XLII, pp. 145–74.

Review of J. G. Edwards, *The Commons in Medieval English Parliaments. The Creighton Lecture for 1957* (London, 1958), in *English Historical Review*, LXXIV, pp. 523–4.

1960

'William Burley of Broncroft, speaker for the commons in 1437 and 1445–6', *Transactions of the Shropshire Archaeological Society*, LVI, pp. 263–72.

'William Stourton of Stourton', *Proceedings of the Dorset Natural History and Archaeological Society*, LXXXII, pp. 155–66.

1961

'List of English and British parliaments and related assemblies', section for 1327–1509 in *Handbook of British Chronology*, ed. Sir F. Maurice Powicke and E. B. Fryde. London: the Royal Historical Society, 2nd edition.

'Sir William Oldhall, speaker in the parliament of 1450–1', *Nottingham Medieval Studies*, V, pp. 87–112.

'Two medieval Westmorland speakers: I. Sir James de Pickering of Killington', *Transactions of the Cumberland and Westmorland Antiquarian and Archaeological Society*, new series, LXI, pp. 79–103.

1962

'Sir Richard Vernon of Haddon, speaker in the parliament of Leicester, 1426', *Derbyshire Archaeological Journal*, LXXXII, pp. 43–53.

'Two medieval Westmorland speakers: II. Sir Richard Redmayne of Levens', *Transactions of the Cumberland and Westmorland Antiquarian and Archaeological Society*, new series, LXII, pp. 113–44.

1963

'Thomas Thorpe, speaker in the Reading parliament of 1453', *Nottingham Medieval Studies*, VII, pp. 79–105.
Review of S. B. Chrimes and A. L. Brown (editors), *Select Documents of English Constitutional History, 1307–1485* (London, 1961), in *English Historical Review*, LXXVIII, pp. 124–6.

1964

'Perspectives in English parliamentary history', *Bulletin of the John Rylands Library*, XLVI, pp. 448–75, reprinted in E. B. Fryde and E. Miller (editors), *Historical Studies of the English Parliament, II: 1399–1603* (Cambridge, 1970), pp. 296–323, with additional notes, p. 330.

1965

The Commons and their Speakers in English Parliaments, 1376–1523. Studies presented to the International Commission for the History of Representative and Parliamentary Institutions, XXVIII. Manchester University Press, pp. ix + 390.
'George Henry Tupling (1883–1962)', *Transactions of the Lancashire and Cheshire Antiquarian Society*, LXXII (for 1962), pp. 177–8.

1967

'A consideration of certain aspects of the English *Modus tenendi parliamentum*', *Bulletin of the John Rylands Library*, L, pp. 411–42.

1968

(*With W. H. C[haloner]*), 'Communication: a charter of 1467 relating to a burgage in the Marketsted, Manchester', *Transactions of the Lancashire and Cheshire Antiquarian Society*, LXXV–VI (for 1965–6), pp. 229–30.

1970

'On the retirement of Professor Albert Goodwin', *University of Manchester Gazette*, no. 49, pp. 6–7.

1971

(*With F. Taylor*), 'The authorship and purpose of the *Gesta Henrici Quinti*', *Bulletin of the John Rylands Library*, LIII (1970–1), pp. 428–64, LIV (1971–2), pp. 223–40.

1972

'In memory of E. F. Jacob', Chetham Society, third series, XX, p. iii.
Review of J. L. Kirby, *Henry IV of England* (London, 1970), in *English Historical Review*, LXXXVII, pp. 398–9.

1974

'On the retirement of Professor T. S. Willan', *University of Manchester Gazette*, no. 61, p. 9.
Review of K. B. McFarlane, *The Nobility of later Medieval England* (Oxford, 1973), in *English Historical Review*, LXXXIX, pp. 622–7.

1975

(*With F. Taylor*), *Gesta Henrici Quinti*, edited with a translation. Oxford University Press: Medieval Texts, pp. 1 + 206.

1978

'John Doreward of Bocking: speaker in 1399 and 1413', *Essex Archaeology and History*, VIII (for 1976), pp. 209–23.
Editor: Sir Goronwy Edwards, *The Second Century of the English Parliament*. The Ford Lectures for 1960–1, Oxford University Press.

1979

'Sir J. G. Edwards, 1891–1976', *Proceedings of the British Academy*, LXI (for 1978), pp. 359–96.

Index